D1430920

ALEKHINE'S
BEST GAMES OF CHESS

1938–1945

Chosen and Annotated by

C. H. O'D. ALEXANDER

Alekhine's Best Games of Chess 1938-1945

Edited by C. H. O'D. Alexander

First published in 1949 in England

This Printing in May, 2010
by Ishi Press in New York and Tokyo

with new translations and errata by Frank X. Mur
and a new introduction by Sam Sloan

ISBN 4-87187-827-9
978-4-87187-827-2

Ishi Press International
1664 Davidson Avenue, Suite 1B
Bronx NY 10453-7877

1-917-507-7226

Printed in the United States of America

Introduction plus Exhibits by Sam Sloan

Alekhine's Best Games of Chess 1938-1945

Edited by C. H. O'D. Alexander

Introduction by Sam Sloan

This book completes the trilogy starting with "*My Best Games of Chess 1908-1923*" by Alexander Alekhine ISBN 0923891498 and followed by "*My Best Games of Chess 1924-1937*" by Alexander Alekhine ISBN 4871878260.

This is a reprint of the original third book, with all of the games converted into Algebraic Figurine PGN Notation with diagrams in the back.

Alekhine died in 1946, so this third volume was edited by International Master and **British Chess Champion Conel Hugh O'Donel Alexander**, based in part on the notes left by Alekhine to some of the games.

Alexander Alexandrovich Alekhine (1892-1946) was not only one of the strongest and most original chess players who ever lived, but he was also the most controversial, second only to Bobby Fischer. Everything about his life and death was controversial and is still being written about even today, although he died in 1946.

Some of the controversies involving him are:

1. During World War II he played in numerous chess events in areas controlled by the Nazis. Articles were published under his name which he may or may not have written which expressed racist views.

2. During the war, while safely in Portugal, he applied for a

visa to go to Cuba which he said was to play a match with Capablanca, but after this visa was denied he returned to Nazi Germany, while the war was still raging.

3. After the war, he was invited and then dis-invited to the London Victory Tournament of 1946.

4. When he died in 1946, the official reason given for death was that he had chocked on a piece of meat. Some attributed this to heavy drinking. However, others say that he was murdered in retaliation for his pro-Nazi views.

In addition to these controversies, here are some controversies involving Alekhine from earlier periods of his life:

1. He defected from Russia.

2. He was married several times to wealthy women who were widows much older than himself.

3. He is said to have had an illegitimate daughter, Valentina, both in 1913 when Alekhine was just 21.

4. He defeated Capablanca in a match for the World Chess Championship in 1927 and then refused to give him a return match, but instead he played matches with lesser players, Bogoljubov and Euwe, whom he felt he could easily beat.

5. He surprisingly lost the 1935 match with Euwe for the World Chess Championship after having a large lead early in the match. His loss has been widely attributed to drinking.

6. He then came back and defeated Euwe in a return match, a match Alekhine had refused to give to Capablanca. It is said that he gave up drinking, enabling him to win.

These issues are still being debated to this day. One only needs to do a simple Internet search to find the most recent opinions rendered on all of this. The issues most widely debated today are:

1. His refusal to give Capablanca a rematch. In his defense, it is said that he merely insisted that Capablanca reach the same terms that he agreed to when he played the first match against Capablanca, especially in terms of prize money. As the Great Depression was on, it is said that the money was not available for a re-match as had been available for the first match in 1927. However, this was not the whole story, because while he was World Champion, he refused to play in any tournament in which Capablanca was also a player. Alekhine never played Capablanca again until Nottingham 1936 when he was no longer World Champion, having lost the title to Euwe.

2. Was Alekhine murdered and, if so, why? One report says that he was found dead on the street, then carried back to his room and propped up in a chair so as to make it look that he had died of natural causes.

3. Was Alekhine a Nazi? Did he write the 1941 articles in Pariser Zeitung attributed to him?

When World War II started in 1939, it happened by fortunate coincidence that the World Chess Olympiad was taking place in Buenos Aires Argentina. All of the great chess players of the world were assembled there and this saved the lives of many of them. Many of them stayed in Argentina until the war was over. The best known case of this was Grandmaster Najdorf, who represented Poland. He stayed in Argentina and changed his first name from a Jewish name to a Spanish name. His entire family back in Poland was exterminated. He alone survived.

Surprisingly, Alekhine, who was in Argentina when the War broke out, returned to France. He said that he needed to go back to defend the castle owned by his wife, who was one of the string of wealthy widows that Alekhine kept marrying. Alekhine moved about Europe during the war, playing in tournaments in Spain and in places now part of Eastern Europe.

It is difficult for us to understand how somebody could engage in a frivolous activity like a chess tournament when millions were dying on the battlefield or in the concentration camps. However, we need to remember that it was not obvious that Germany was going to lose the war. Germany seemed to be winning, at first. Had Germany won the war, there still would have been the same War Crimes Trials at the end of the war. The only difference would have been that instead of Germans standing trial, it would have been the Americans standing trial for fire bombing civilian populations in Dresden and Tokyo, not to mentioning dropping the A-bombs on Hiroshima and Nagasaki.

On the subject of the three articles by Alekhine in Pariser Zeitung, I feel that the issue is overblown. I have read the articles and while I agree that they are objectionable, I cannot understand why a big deal is made over them. The articles are entitled "Jewish and Aryan Chess". The author maintains that Jews play chess a certain way and that Aryans play chess in a different way. The author says that the Jewish grandmasters are not artists and that they are merely technicians, whereas the Aryan Grandmasters play chess as a high creative art.

On the other hand, the author does not call Aryans "The Master Race" nor does he ever say "Let's kill all the Jews" or anything like that.

I certainly disagree with the conclusions reached by the author.

He says that the Jewish grandmasters are not creative. They are merely tacticians.

I find it odd that he would say that, because the most creative and original players in the entire world history of chess were Steinitz, Reti and Nimzowitsch, and all three of them were Jewish.

I have my own theory about the articles, as follows:

1. I feel that Alekhine wrote the articles, although there might have been some editing by the magazine editors.

2. I believe that the views expressed in the articles were the views of Alekhine. I do not believe that he was in any way forced to write the articles. I also do not believe that he had to write the articles to save his own life, although they probably did not hurt his chances either. The articles did answer the question of whether Alekhine himself was Jewish. As Alekhine was a Russian who had defected and immigrated to France, nobody really knew for sure whether he was Jewish or not, especially since almost all of the leading grandmasters in Europe at that time were Jewish. Jews were being rounded up and sent to death camps, which provided a good enough reason for Alekhine to write the articles.

This last point is interesting and I have never seen anybody else mention it. In the articles, Alekhine provides names of Jewish and Aryan chess masters and compares their playing styles. He finds the Aryan players to be creative and artistic whereas the Jewish players were mere tacticians. Take a look at his list of Aryan players, such as Capablanca and Marshall. They were mostly in America, safe from the war.

I know of only one Jewish chess master who was executed by

the Nazis for being a Jew. That was Przepiorka, a Jewish player who had gone into a Prague cafe verboten to Jews. However, Przepiorka was a master, but not a famous grandmaster. Grandmaster Ossip Bernstein told a story about how he was lined up to be shot (by the Russians, not by the Nazis) but he saved his own life by winning a chess game against the Camp Commander, thereby proving that he was the famous grandmaster by the same name.

A grandmaster strength chess player who lost his life during this period was Petrov, who was reportedly executed by Stalin because he was Latvian. A player who was clearly in danger of being executed was Keres of Estonia. His life is believed to have been saved because he was a stronger and more famous chess master than Petrov. Was there some sort of Darwinian process here? Only the strong chess players survived. The slightly weaker chess players went to the death camps.

As to Alekhine's motivations for writing the articles, I do not believe that he was ordered to write them. The articles were not very good. They were barely publishable. The editors probably had a shortage of material and put them in to fill up space. The only thing that made them worth reading was that they were written by the World Chess Champion.

The articles discussed a subject of great interest only to Alekhine himself. His main rivals for the World Chess Championship were predominantly Jewish. Therefore, he had to study their playing styles and prepare to meet them across the board. After Alekhine died, a tournament for the World Chess Championship to replace him was organized. Six players were invited. Four of them were Jewish. These were Botvinnik, Reshevsky, Fine and Smyslov. (Although not a religious man, the mother of Smyslov was Jewish.) When Fine declined, the leading candidate to replace him was Najdorf, who was also

Jewish. The only non-Jews who got into the tournament were Keres and Euwe. (Euwe finished last.)

After that, there was a match for the World Chess Championship between Botvinnik vs. Bronstein. Both of them were Jewish. The next world champions, Smyslov and Tal, were also Jewish. Spassky has recently taken to saying that there is "no truth" to the statement that his mother was Jewish, although he had never said this before during the last 50 years when the statement that he was Jewish was often published.

On this subject, there is a curious fact that nobody seems to have noticed: Of the top ten rated chess players in the World today on the official FIDE rating list, NONE OF THEM ARE JEWISH. What is going on here? Are the Jews getting weaker? Actually, one reason for this is the recent emergence of new chess playing countries. India got its first grandmaster relatively recently and now the World Chess Champion is from India. Many of the top grandmasters are now Chinese, whereas chess was not even played in China until relatively recently.

Kasparov in a speech recently lamented that in the World Chess Championship match just concluded in which Topalov of Bulgaria lost to Anand to India, that was the first match for the World Chess Championship in which neither player was Russian since Capablanca defeated Lasker in 1921. Kasparov says that this proves that Russian chess is going down hill. However, better explanation is that now the top players all use computers to analyze. Before computers, in order to become a top grandmaster, one had to live in one of the major chess centers such as Moscow, Leningrad or New York. Nowadays, however, any bright kid with a computer and an Internet connection anywhere in the world can become a grandmaster, if he has the talent and applies himself.

In a published interview, Grandmaster Boris Gelfand lamented that US Champion Hikaru Nakamura has became one of the world's leading chess players by playing tens of thousands of one-minute chess games on the Internet Chess Club, without even bothering to learn the fundamentals of chess theory and by playing ridiculous openings. What is this world coming to?

The main point here is that Alekhine had to face all these Jews across the chess board, as they were his main opponents. He never says that the Jews are inferior. He merely states that they are not creative, and that they are defensive, not attacking players. All of this "positional maneuvering" is just an excuse for waiting for the opponent to blunder. He says that Lasker, for example, plays weak moves and just waits for his opponent to make a mistake. "What if the opponent fails to make this mistake?", wonders Alekhine. Alekhine has a big problem with explaining Grandmaster Spielmann, who was one of the most ferocious attacking players of all time and was also Jewish.

If the truth were known, almost everybody in the world has racist ideas and beliefs. Anthropological studies of remote jungle tribes have been done and invariably the tribe being studied believes that they are racially superior to the tribe across the river or in another part of the jungle. Here in New York City, people who live in the West Side of Manhattan believe that they are better than those who live on the East Side of Manhattan, whereas those who live on the East Side of Manhattan believe that they are better than those living on the West Side of Manhattan. In all the years that I have lived in New York City, I have constantly been hearing these East Side vs. West Side arguments, and race is not even an issue.

(I live in The Bronx now. We are better than all of them, as proven by the fact that we have the best baseball team!)

One disturbing thing about the conclusion that Alekhine wrote the articles is that nowhere in the articles entitled "Jewish and Aryan Chess" does Alekhine ever cite a specific move, a specific game or a specific position. Since Alekhine had studied every game ever played by any of his leading rivals, he should have been able to cite without difficulty examples to prove his thesis.

Here is an experiment to prove this. Ask any rated chess master what happened in Game 11 of the First Fischer-Spassky Match. Without looking in a book and without setting up a chess board, the chess master will be able to tell you the name of the opening, the result of the game, at least the first few moves of the opening and the reason why the game ended the way that it did. Watch two chess masters discuss a well-known game played years earlier. They will be able to talk to each other about what happened on the 11th move or the 14th move or whatever, without ever setting up the board.

Chess Masters have in their memory thousands of chess games and positions. This is what makes them masters and why it takes years to become one.

It would therefore seem that Alekhine should have been able to cite some games proving his points. He should have been able to say that in such-and-such game in San Sebastian 1911 Grandmaster this-or-that played such-and-such move because he was a Jew, whereas had he been an Aryan he would have played this other (better) move.

Since Alekhine never does this, this weakens the theory that he wrote the articles.

Alekhine does complain that after the Lasker-Steinitz Match for the World Chess Championship, both players claimed that they were the best two players in the world because of their superior strategy. Alekhine says that their strategy was not superior. It was their tactics that were superior, according to Alekhine. He does not dispute the fact that they were the two best players in the world, even though both of them were Jewish.

If you will look at the list of the rivals Alekhine had to face across the board, you will see the names of Rubinstein, Reti, Nimzowitsch, Bernstein, Lasker, Reshevsky, Fine, Spielmann, Flohr and the list goes on. About as many non-Jews got into the top levels of chess in those days as Jews got into Harvard University back then. (If your knowledge of history is weak, you will know that a quota system was imposed whereby Jews were not allowed to enter Harvard University, with few exceptions, and Jews were absolutely forbidden to join the New York Stock Exchange back then.)

The final controversy involving Alekhine was his dis-invitation to the London Victory Tournament of 1946. He was first invited and then un-invited because of objections by Euwe and by the Americans, primarily the US Champion, Arnold Denker. Subsequently, Denker said that he regretted that, since Alekhine had been his friend and one does not turn his back on a friend, especially when the friend is down-and-out as Alekhine was in 1946.

It was noteworthy that the one grandmaster who spoke in favor of Alekhine and said that he should be allowed to play was Tartakower, who was Jewish.

Alekhine died a few weeks later.

Sam Sloan
New York NY
May 23, 2010

Alekhine Controversy - Articles written by the World Chess Champion in 1941

One of the greatest controversies in chess history concerns the authorship by World Chess Champion Alexander Alekhine of a series of three articles published in France while under occupation by Nazi Germany in 1941 during World War II entitled **"Jewish and Aryan Chess"**. Because of these articles, Alekhine was branded as a Nazi and was ostracized from the world chess community after the conclusion of the war. He was not allowed to play in the London Victory Tournament in 1946. He died in a squalid hotel room in Portugal shortly thereafter in 1946, when a piece of meat got stuck in his throat.

One of the questions is whether Alekhine actually wrote the articles. His "defenders" tried to contend that he did not. However, from the articles themselves, it seems reasonably clear that Alekhine did write the articles. Certainly the author evinces knowledge and familiarity of the playing styles of the great chess players of the period between the two world wars, and there were few people living in Nazi Germany in 1941 who knew this subject as well as Alekhine did.

The more serious question is whether Alekhine deserved to receive the international opprobrium which he has suffered ever since the appearance of these articles. To this day, it is said that Alekhine was a Nazi and wrote articles for the Nazis. But, what do these articles really say? Do they say anything so terrible as to deserve the universal condemnation which Alekhine has received ever since?

Here are the articles, in three parts. Let the reader judge for himself.

Sam Sloan

Jewish and Aryan Chess

Is it too much to hope that, with the death of Lasker, the second and in all probability last Jewish chess champion of the world, Aryan chess (perverted hitherto through Jewish defensive ideas) will find its way to becoming world chess? I cannot be too optimistic, for Lasker has left many disciples and many followers who might endanger World Chess yet.

Lasker's great faults as the leading chess master (I am neither willing or qualified to speak of him as man or "philosopher") were manifold. After vanquishing the 30-years-older Steinitz by his tactical skill, it was rather amusing, by the way, to observe how these two skilful tacticians tried to convince the chess world that they were great strategists or discoverers of new ideas! - he did not think for a moment of giving the chess world a creative idea of his own. Instead, he contented himself with publishing in book form a series of lectures he had delivered in Liverpool under the title "Common Sense in Chess."

Lasker Plagiarizes the Great Morphy

In these lectures, in this book, Lasker plagiarized the great Morphy and his ideas about the "fight for the center" and about "attack in and for itself." For the idea of attack as something optimistic, something creative, was entirely unfamiliar to Lasker the chess master and in this regard he was the natural successor to Steinitz, the greatest "grotesque" the history of chess had to endure.

What is Jewish Chess, the Jewish chess idea in its real essence? It is not hard to answer this question:-

Introduction plus Exhibits by Sam Sloan

1. Material profit at all costs;

2. Opportunism - an opportunism pushed to the highest point with the aim of eliminating even the shadow of a potential danger and which consequently reveals an idea (if one can apply the word "idea" to this) namely "defense, in and for itself." As far as future possibilities are concerned, Jewish chess has dug its own grave in developing this "idea" which, in any form of combat whatever cannot mean anything else, finally than suicide. For by merely defending one's self, one may occasionally (and how often?) avoid defeat - but how does one win? There is a possible answer: by a mistake on one's opponent's part. What if the opponent fails to make this mistake? All that the defender-at-all-costs can then do is whine in complaint of this absence of errors.

It is not easy to explain how the defense idea succeeded in gaining so many adherents. As far as Europe is concerned, there came, between the matches La Bourdonnais and Macdonald fought with remarkable enthusiasm and spirit, and the appearances of Anderssen and Morphy, a very characteristic period of "chess dawn" - culminating probably in the match between Staunton and Saint-Amant. Staunton won this match, his victory justifiably entitling this Englishman to claim a place in the chess history of the nineteenth century. As I write this, I have before me a book of his, namely that about the first international world tournament, played in 1851, in which the German chess genius Adolf Anderssen took first prize. His congress was really the victory of our aggressive fighting chess over the English-Jewish conception (in the first round of the tournament, Anderssen crushed the Polish Jew Kieseritzky); but the "theoretician" Staunton describes the congress in his book, for his English readers, as a mere matter of coincidences. According to his words, he was in ill-health because he had been overburdened with the toil of organizing

13

the congress, etc., etc., etc., in other words, the usual and all-too-well-known rubbish of excuses! Staunton's defeat at the hands of Anderssen was in reality much, much more than a decision between two chess masters; its significance lay in the fact that it spelled the defeat of the English-Jewish idea of defense at the hands of the German-European idea of aggression.

Europe's Chess Drama

Soon after Anderssen's victory, the great drama of European chess developed: the genius was confronted by another and greater genius, emerging from New Orleans. That did no harm in itself, for Morphy's chess was real chess in the truest sense of the word. It became harmful only because, first, Morphy lost his mental balance immediately after his dazzling successes and was thus lost to the cause of chess, and, second, Anderssen failed to recover from the defeat he had suffered at Morphy's hands and consequently yielded the chess scepter without greater ambitions, to Steinitz the Jew.

To cast light on the question of who Steinitz really was, and why he deserved to play a leading role in our chess, it is necessary (strange as it seems) to delve into the problems of professionalism in chess. For in any art - and chess is, notwithstanding its element of conflict, a creative art - there are two kinds of professionals: Those who do not hesitate to sacrifice, in devoting themselves passionately to the urge of their inclination, all other hopes and possibilities of life and living. These "victims of their art" one cannot blame for trying to make a livelihood from their life's work, for they create for their fellow-men aesthetic and spiritual delights enough. Entirely different is that other type of professional chess player which I do not hesitate to call the "Eastern Jewish" type. Steinitz the Jew was born in Prague; one might call him the first of his species and quickly, much too quickly, he had a following.

Are the Jews, as a race, gifted for chess? After a chess experience of thirty years, I should answer this question as follows: Yes, the Jews are extremely well endowed with the ability to exploit the ideas of chess and the practical potentialities entailed; but, as yet, no real chess artist of Jewish origin has yet existed. I could mention (and only give outstanding names) the following representatives of Aryan chess:- Philidor, Labourdonnais, Anderssen, Morphy, Tchigorin, Pillsbury, Marshall, Capablanca, Bogoljubov, Euwe, Eliskases, Keres. As to the "Jewish harvest" for the same historical period, one cannot but call it poor and meager. Apart from Steinitz and Lasker, various groups might profitably be examined in historical sequence. In the decadence period of Lasker's hegemony (1900-1921) two of his closest Jewish competitors, Janowski and Rubinstein, are somewhat noteworthy.

"Brilliancy" Games Against Weaker Opponents

The typical representative of this group is probably the Polish Jew Janowski, who lived in Paris. He succeeded in finding there a rich man, namely the Dutch "artist" Leo Nardus, also a Jew, and did not loosen his hold on this man for 25 years. Somebody once showed this Nardus a few of Morphy's games with brilliant sacrifices; from that moment forth, his idol was Morphy, and he asked his protege Janowski to play "beautiful games" at all costs. Janowski in response created "brilliancy" games willy-nilly, but it soon became apparent that he could do this only against his weaker opponents. In combat with real masters, his style was just as matter-of-fact, dry and materialistic as that of 99% of his fellow racials. He was never a serious opponent for Lasker, who vanquished him almost playfully in several matches. We might comment here that one of the most typical features of Lasker's "talent" was to avoid the most dangerous opponents and face them only when they were no longer a real danger to him as a result of age, illness or decline of their fitness. It is easy to quote instances of these tactics, e.g., how he avoided matches with Pillsbury, Maroczy and Tarrasch, taking up the latter's challenge only in 1908 when he could no longer be considered a serious competitor for the title. Then there was the "short match" against Schlechter (Vienna 1910); the drawn result of this match was intended, of course, to serve as "decoy-bird" for the chess public to arrange a much larger - and appropriately remunerated - return match.

Brought Up in Hatred Against the "Goyyim"

Lasker's second Jewish competitor was the Lodz master, Akiba Rubinstein. Brought up as a strict orthodox, in Talmudic hatred of the "Goyyim," he was obsessed, from the commencement of his career, by the idea of making some sort of "mission" out of his inclination for chess. Consequently he set out, as a young man, to study the theory of chess with the same eagerness as he devoted, as a boy, to the Talmud, and this at a time of decadence in chess, when the "Viennese" school (founded by the Jew Max Weiss and subsequently developed by the Jews Kaufmann and Fahndrich), which saw the secret of success not in victory but in avoidance of defeat, was in complete occupation of chess's world stage.

No wonder Rubinstein, who, throughout this period, was always better primed in the openings than his opponents, was able to celebrate, from his first debut in international chess, impressive victories. His outstanding success, I suppose, was his tie for first place with Lasker in St. Petersburg in 1909, a memorable tournament which I attended as a youth of sixteen. From this peak achievement commenced his decline, at first slow, afterward more and more apparent. It is true he continued to study indefatigably, and a few isolated successes resulted; but one noted that this study was actually too much for his brains, which were talented for chess but otherwise very mediocre. And so it happened that, when I came to Berlin after four years' experience of the Soviets, I found there a Rubinstein who was only half a grand-master and a quarter of a human being. Blacker and blacker the shades closed round his brains, partly from megalomania, partly from persecution mania.

The following small anecdote illustrates this well. Towards the end of the same year (1921) a small tournament was arranged through Bogoljubov's efforts in Triberg, with Rubinstein participating. I was tournament director and asked Rubinstein after one of his games "Why did you play this move in the opening? It is so obviously inferior to that by which I beat Bogoljubov a few months ago and which we examined so convincingly, together with you."

He Wanted to Avoid His Opponent's Influence

"Yes," replied Rubinstein, "but it is a strange move!" In other words, he could not appreciate anybody else's ideas; his chess only, HIS chess only, was utilized by him in that period. In spite of a few partial successes, the persecution mania became stronger and stronger. In the last two or three years of his chess career, he used to run away - literally! - from the chess board as soon as he had made his move; used to sit somewhere in a corner of the tournament room and not return to the board until it was his turn to move again. This, as he himself explained, was "in order to escape the vicious influence of his adversary's Ego." Rubinstein is somewhere in Belgium now, dead to chess for ever.

The Riga Jew Niemtsovitch belongs to the Capablanca rather

than to the Lasker period. His instinctive, anti-Aryan conception of chess was curiously - subconsciously and against his own inclinations - affected by the Slav-Russian aggressive conception (Tchigorin!). I say "subconsciously," for how he did hate us Russians, us Slavs! I shall never forget a little conversation we had after the New York tournament of 1927. I surpassed him in this tournament, and the Jugo Slav master Professor Vidmar had repeatedly beaten him in their encounters. Furious though he was, he dared not attack us directly but one evening, whilst talking about the Soviets, he turned to me and said "Who says 'Slav' says 'Slave'" whereupon I replied "But who says 'Jew' need say no more!"

In some circles, he was considered a deep thinker, mainly after the publication of two books entitled My System and Praxis of My System. I am firmly convinced that his whole "system" (notwithstanding the fact that it is not even original) is based on wrong premises. Not only does he make the mistake of striving for a synthetic end from an analytical beginning but, continuing to err, he bases his analysis solely on his own practical experience and afterwards hands out the results of his analysis as the ultimate synthetic truth. Undoubtedly, there are a few true and correct elements in Niemtsovitch's doctrines; but whatever is correct is not his own but was created by others, old masters as well as contemporaries, and he plagiarized it, consciously or unconsciously. Correct were:

1. The idea of battle for the center, a Morphy conception; this had previously been illustrated by Tchigorin's best achievements as well as the games of Pillsbury and Charousek.

2. and 3. The truths of M. de la Palisse, namely that it is of advantage to occupy the seventh rank and, finally that it is better to be able to take advantage of two weaknesses in the opponent's camp than only one. And such was the

ingenuousness of the English and New York chess public (not the American chess public for New York, the city of Jews is, thank heaven, not identical with America) that they granted him fame as a chess writer.

These were truths. On the other hand, there were many inaccuracies which were a direct consequence of his attitude toward chess, for whatever was half-way to being original had a cadaverous smell denying all that is creative. Examples: (1) "maneuvering" is nothing more than the Steinitz-Lasker idea of waiting until one's opponent blunders; (2) "over-protection" (a premature protection of supposedly weak points) is again a purely Jewish idea contradicting the whole spirit of struggle, i.e., being afraid of battle. Doubt in one's own spiritual powers - truly, this is a sad picture of intellectual self-humiliation! This is the poor literary bequest Niemtsovitch left when he died, to only a few successors and fewer friends - apart from some fellow-racialists.

To the Bratislava master, Richard Reti, the chess world owes, without a doubt, gratitude for having proved the Niemtsovitch idea of "over-protection" to be an absurdity. For he applied the theory of concentrating on an opponent's weaknesses from the very beginning, no matter how that opponent built up his game.

It is becoming more and more apparent that the purely negative Jewish conception of chess (Steinitz-Lasker-Rubinstein-Niemtsovitch) prevented for half a century, the logical development of our art of battle.

Jewish and Aryan Chess [II]

Reti was applauded by the plurality of Anglo-Jewish intellectuals for his work *Modern Ideas in Chess*, just as

19

Niemtsovitch had been for *My System*, and these people were particularly impressed by the absurd cry Reti invented, namely "We, the young masters" (he was then 34) "are not interested in rules but in exceptions." If this sentence makes sense at all, it means "We (or rather, I) know the rules governing the game of chess much too well. To carry on with further research in this field will be, in future, the task of the more feeble-minded of the chess community. But, I, the grandmaster, will devote myself exclusively to the more delicate filigree of brilliant exceptions, with my own clear elucidations."

This cheap bluff, this shameless half-attempt at self-boosting, was swallowed without a struggle by a chess world already doped by Jewish journalists, the exulting cries of the Jews and their friends "Long Live Reti and the hyper-modern, neo-romantic chess!" finding an echo far and wide.

Reti died young, at 40. Even earlier, his "double bluff" idea had suffered a quiet and inglorious death. Contemporary representatives of Jewish chess chose to imitate older examples (Steinitz, Rubinstein) rather than him. Hence Salo Flohr of Prague, is, in a chess sense, a product partly of Steinitz's timid defensive ideas and partly of Rubinstein's religious belief in a comprehensive study of openings and end-games. A difference being that, unlike Rubinstein, he is bodily and mentally sound and, therefore, likely to be able to hold his own for some time to come.

Reuben Fine, a New Yorker of Eastern Jewish extraction, is certainly more intelligent than Flohr. Brought up in a communistic school at the expense of a Jewish community, he has been influenced chessically, if not politically, by the ideas of modern Russia. This is why he is more aggressive than the other Jewish masters, in his attitude and his manners, as well as in his chess. His main idea towards chess is, however, just the same, the purely traditional laying-in-wait; nothing ventured! He tries to attain his goal in a comparatively new way; not by merely waiting or pure defense, but by delving ever more exhaustively into the ramifications of the openings. In order to improve his chances in practical chess, he undertook, for instance, to modernize the old English treatise by Griffith and White; for this purpose, he had to study thousands upon thousands of opening variations and he succeeded, by his superior knowledge of modern theory, in attaining a partial success in the AVRO tournament of 1938; the surprise was general, but I do not think there will be a repetition of this success.

Poor Chess America!

There are two more Jewish chess masters to mention: Reshevsky and Bovinnik. The Eastern Jewish child prodigy (there have been so many wonder children of this race in all branches of the arts - why not have a Jewish chess child prodigy once in a while, too?) - Samuel Reshevsky was systematically exploited, from his fifth year onward, by his likewise Jewish chess managers. Of course, there was money enough at that time (1919-1922) for all kinds of appetite, in democracies intoxicated by war profits. No wonder that Reshevsky, having become Americanized and even U. S. Champion by the age of 30 owns a fortune that would enable him to play his future career as an amateur. What a surprise it caused when it became apparent that the adult Reshevsky, when he returned to Europe, represented the worst type of chess professional and was employing every sort of chess trick that would suit his purpose! If, as has been told, Reshevsky is really the image of present-day Chess America, all one can explain is "Poor Chess America!"

The Soviet chess master Botvinnik owes, in my opinion, even

more than his American co-religionist than to the influence of the younger Russian school. Instinctively inclined to "safety first," he has slowly become a master who knows how to use the weapons of aggression. How this occurred, is a curious and typical story: Not the idea of attack and , if necessary, sacrifice, but - however, paradoxical this might seem - the idea of procuring, by attacking possibilities, even greater security for himself, is responsible for this change. Only by subtle knowledge, by intensely careful study of (a) new potentialities in the openings and (b) the attacking and sacrificial technique of the old masters, Botvinnik has succeeded in rounding off his original style and impressing it with the marks of a certain many-sidedness. That he is strong, very strong now, there can be no doubt. Otherwise, he would hardly have been able, considering the high development of chess in present-day Russia, to attain to the championship of his country five or six times in succession, in such convincing fashion. With this apparent superiority, one might yet compare the succession of impressive victories scored by Germany's master Erich Eliskases in Germany and abroad, during the last few years. All the same, most of Botvinnik's games make a dry and soulless impression. This is easily explained: There is no art in which the most perfect copy could arouse the same feelings as the original and, as far as attack is concerned, Botvinnik's chess is just no more than an excellent copy of the old masters. In spite of these shortcomings, I should say that one can consider Botvinnik to be an exception, compared with all the others we have mentioned.

Jewish and Aryan Chess [III]

Hailed as a kind of child-prodigy in his hometown (he won the championship of Cuba at the age of twelve), admired as a fiery attacking player with real Morphy insight at the outset of his

22

career, Capablanca would have become not only the god of the Latin chess world - as he actually was for long - but the idol of the whole world chess community, had he not been sent, as a young man, to **Columbia University** in New York and there assimilated, in Jewry's capital, the professional methods of the chess-Yankees. Repressing his tactical endowments, he forced himself, even as an eighteen-year-old, to regard chess not as an end in itself, but as a means of livelihood and to pursue the Jewish principle of "safety-first" to the limit. So great were his natural gifts, that for a certain time he was able to set himself up as a master of defense; and so shrewd was he that he sought to justify the negative principle of defensive chess, through pseudo-strategical conceptions, in numerous writings. Continual transitory brilliant exceptions, fiery "blitzes", occurred, even in his world championship matches - subconscious reactions of his repressed temperament. Nowadays these are becoming more and more rare.

So it came about that these two, the Jew Botvinnik and the Latin Capablanca, each finally took intellectually the same turning (or, rather, wrong turning). Their existence is undoubtedly necessary for our art, and for the combating of defensive thought in chess, for they are the exceptions which prove the rule. Exceptions? Yes, real exceptions. Unfortunately, there exist false exceptions, too, chess artists who utilize the Aryan spirit of attack in their attempt to gratify their professional lust for gold. The typical representatives of this tendency are undoubtedly the Viennese Jew Rudolf Spielmann, now settled in Stockholm, and the Leipziger Jack Mieses, now living in London. Spielmann, who undoubtedly has combinative gifts, came to the conclusion, early in his chess career, that these would gain him most money from the great Public, if he could succeed in making his name as a "brilliant sacrificial player." In the same way as Fine and Botvinnik studied the openings and the laws of attacking play, Spielmann

23

applied himself to the much simpler problem of the ultimate technique of sacrificial play. One must admit that he achieved some success in his aim, in the course of a lengthy experience. In 1935 he even went so far as to publish a booklet under the corrupting title: "Correct Sacrifices." (The English version, The Art of Sacrifice.-Ed.) In this, every possible variety of sacrifice in chess is analyzed, up to the only kind which marks the true artist, the intuitive sacrifice. Just as far removed from the realm of truly sacrificial thought is the chess master and journalist J. Mieses, who used to swamp a large part of the German press of years ago with "brilliancies" of just this realm. He contributed a convincing demonstration, for example, to the chess magazine Chess, which is run by the Jew Baruch Wood in Birmingham; as the best performance of his career, he put forward his prizewinning game against von Bardeleben at Barmen in 1905.

Hitherto, I have said much about the Jewish defensive idea, but little of Aryan attacking concepts. Let us elaborate these. As an introduction, it is necessary to mention an important, because totally exploded attitude towards chess. About 1830 and 1840, there came upon chess, as sequel to the meteoric splendor of Mahe de la Bourdonnais, a marked quietness. As strongest player in the world was regarded - possibly with justice - the Englishman Howard Staunton. His chess, which unfortunately had a certain influence on his colleagues, was so monotonous, boring and poor in ideas, that nobody can wonder at the annihilating judgment passed by the genial Edgar Allan Poe in his "***Murders in the Rue Morgue***." Early on in the story Poe writes (of no inner necessity) -

"To calculate is not in itself to analyze. A chessplayer, for example, does the one without effort at the other. It follows that the game of chess, in its effects upon mental character, is greatly misunderstood. I am not now writing a treatise, but I

24

will take occasion to assert that the higher powers of the reflective intellect are more decidedly and more usefully tasked by the un-ostentatious game of droughts than by all the elaborate frivolity of chess. In this latter, where the pieces have different and bizarre motions, with various and variable values, what is only complex is mistaken (a not unusual error) for what is profound. The attention is here called powerfully into play. If it flag for an instant, an oversight is committed, resulting in injury or defeat in nine cases out of ten it is the more concentrative rather than the more acute player who conquers."

Now on the positive side.

"In draughts, where the moves are unique and have but little variation, the probabilities of inadvertence are diminished." And further: "Men of the highest order of intellect have been known to take an apparently unaccountable delight in whist, while eschewing chess as frivolous. Beyond doubt, there is nothing of a similar nature so greatly tasking the faculty of analysis as whist. The best chessplayer in Christendom may be little more than the best player of chess; but proficiency in whist implies capacity for success in all those more important undertakings where mind struggles with mind."

Enough! These quotations adequately prove that the ingenious poet of the "The Raven," the charming author of "Eureka" and the "Colloquy of Monos and Una" has in this case either been altogether stupidly misled or, for some unknown reason, knowingly deceived his readers. Chess can be compared with no other board game, because of a basic distinction which stamps it as an art; not that this implies any disparagement of other board games, each of which has its rightful place. This distinction lies in the fact that chess alone, in contrast to all these other games, has an aim other than mere capture or gain of territory, namely the conception of mate. Admittedly one must strive for gain of material or space to begin with. But as soon as mate, the idea of encircling the principal enemy piece, enters the scene, no sacrifice of time, space or material is too great to achieve it. This is why chess is necessary, this is why it is so attractive; because it calls forth in us - often only subconsciously, maybe - humanity's striving after an ideal; the joy of dedicating one's self for an idea. And this is why chess awakes in us aesthetic feeling, this is why conception of the beautiful is awakened in chess too; because its inner spirit corresponds in every way to the virtue of self-sacrifice in us.

Of what other game can this be even remotely maintained? No, **Edgar Allan Poe** could not, with all his genius, provide half as much justification for the existence of any other game! Even more disputable is his comparison of chess with whist; for this reason, that in that card game, the human mind has to work wholly otherwise than in chess. Chess is a fight of the moment, and of the future - as soon as a move has occurred, the players are no longer concerned with what has gone before. In Bridge, on the other hand (to restrict ourselves to this most modern of card-games), anybody who aspires to become a good player must bear in mind not only the make-up of each trick, but also the cards which have previously been played. As for alleged "analysis" this becomes, as a result of the presence of too many imponderables, a practical impossibility. So the American's attack loses all point, except only as a sign of his times.

Introduction plus Exhibits by Sam Sloan

So concludes the final part of the Chess translations (1941) of the version of articles which appeared in the Deutsche Schachzeitung. This incomplete version omitted the last 20 paragraphs from the original articles as well as one on Schlecheter, wherein the latter Alekhine apparently erroneously refers to Schlechter as a Jew.

According to Moran:

Highlights of the remaining 20 paragraphs (devoted to "Aryan" chess masters from Morphy to Eliskases) include Dr. Euwe's "Jewish connection" and - in the penultimate paragraph - this clarification:

For all that I would like to emphasize forcefully that my chess fights do not bear a personal character - against no individual Jew himself - but are directed against the collective Jewish chess ideas. [Ken Whyld]

'Again in the 1937 return match with Euwe the collective chess Jewry was aroused. Most of the Jewish masters mentioned in this review attended as press reporters, trainer and seconds for Euwe. At the beginning of the second match I could no longer let myself be deceived: that is, I had to fight not Euwe, but the combined chess Jewry, and in the event my decisive victory (10:4) was a triumph against the Jewish conspiracy.'

Note: In this return match, Euwe was seconded by Reuben Fine (who developed appendicitis soon after the start and had to withdraw) and Alekhine by Eliskases. In the first match, Alekhine had the services of Landau (a Jew) and Euwe had Maroczy.

Alekhine's defense began soon after the liberation of Paris (therefore not post-war as has been alleged).

27

Introduction plus Exhibits by Sam Sloan

Both the BCM and Chess reported that News Review (23 November 1944) reported an interview with Alekhine wherein he claims that whilst in occupied France "he had to write two chess articles for the Pariser Zeitung before the Germans granted him his exit visa...Articles which Alekhine claims were purely scientific were rewritten by the Germans, published and made to treat chess from a racial standpoint."

After being 'disinvited' from the London Victory tournament in 1946 Alekhine wrote an open letter to the organizer W. Hatton-Ward:

Dear Mr. Hatton-Ward,

I have received your letter on my return from the Canaries on November 28th. Before I knew the contents of this letter it was manifestly impossible for me to undertake anything, for I had no idea what reasons had induced you to cancel the invitation. Now I can and must do it, and this not solely on account of the tournament which you are organizing - whatever purely chess interest it might have had for me - but especially because of these very reasons.

First of all you inform me that certain circles have formulated objections based on my alleged sympathies during the war. Now anybody not swayed by prejudice must realize what must have been my real sentiments towards people who took from me all that makes life worth living; people who have wrecked my home, pillaged my wife's castle (and evidently all I possessed) and finally even stole my name!

Having devoted my life to chess I have never taken part in anything not directly connected with my profession. Unfortunately, all my life - especially after I had won the World's Championship - people have ascribed to me a political

28

aspect which is entirely preposterous. For nearly twenty years I have been nicknamed "White Russian" which was particularly painful to me, for this made impossible any contact with my country of origin which I have never ceased to love and admire.

Finally in 1938/9, I had hoped, over negotiations and correspondence with the U.S.S.R. champion, M. Botvinnik, to have put an end to this absurd legend, for in fact a match between him and myself in the U.S.S.R. was practically fixed. Then - came the war - and after its termination here I am, being vested with the degrading epithet "Pro-Nazi", accused of collaboration, etc., etc.

In any event, far from bearing any ill-will towards you, I am grateful to you for having provoked this accusation - for the false position in which I have been placed during the last two years was in the long run morally intolerable.

Dr. Euwe's protest I find far from surprising - the reverse rather would have surprised me. For, among the mass of monstrosities published by the Pariser Zeitung, insults were featured against members of the organizing committee of the 1937 match; the Netherlands Federation has even addressed a protest on this subject with Mr. Post. At that time I was quite unable to do the one thing which would have clarified the situation - to declare that the articles had not been written by me.

Dr. Euwe was so convinced of my "influence" with the Nazis the he wrote me two letters in which he asked me to take steps in order to ease the fate of poor Mr. Landau and of my friend Dr. Oskam. The fact is that, in Germany and in occupied territory, we were under constant supervision and the threat of the concentration camp on the part of the Gestapo. Dr. Euwe's reaction on my being invited is therefore quite natural; but, in common with so many, he is wholly mistaken.

The principal reason which has induced you to dispense with my participation is the "ultimatum" as you call it, of the U.S.A. Chess Federation. This is a serious matter, for these gentlemen have evidently taken their decision, giving reasons which in their opinion justified this step. I cannot at the moment know these reasons accurately, but I am entitled to suppose that it is a question of an accusation of collaborating with the Nazis. The term collaborator is generally used against those who, officially or otherwise, have acted according to the views of the Vichy Government. But I have never had anything to do with this Government nor with their representatives. I have played chess in Germany and occupied countries because this was our only means of livelihood, but also the price I paid for my wife's liberty. Reviewing in my mind the situation in which I found myself four years ago, I can only state that to-day I should have acted in the same way. In normal times my wife has certainly the means and necessary experience to look after herself, but not in time of war and in the hands of the Nazis. I repeat, if the allegation of "collaboration" rests on my forced sojourn in Germany, I have nothing to add - my conscience is undisturbed.

It is another matter if facts are alleged against me which are non-existent, notably the articles which appeared in the Pariser Zeitung. Here I must object strongly. During three years, until the liberation of Paris, I had to keep silent. But at the first opportunity I have, in interviews, tried to place the facts in their true perspective. In these articles, which appeared in 1941 during my stay in Portugal, and which [be]came known to [me] in Germany as reproduced in [the] Deutsche Schachzeitung, there is nothing that was written by me.

The matter which I had provided related to the necessary

reconstruction of the International Chess Federation [FIDE] and to a critical appreciation, written long before 1939 of the theories of Steinitz and Lasker.

I was astonished, on receipt of letters from Messrs Helms and Sturgis at the reaction which these purely technical articles had produced in America and replied in this sense to Mr Helms.

It is only when I obtained knowledge of the perfectly stupid balderdash which emanated from a mind imbued with Nazi ideas, that I understood what was on foot. At that time I was a prisoner of the Nazis and our only chance was to keep silent before the whole world. These years have destroyed my health and my nerves, and I am astonished that I can still play good chess.

My devotion to my art, the esteem which I have always shown for the talent of my colleagues, in short my whole pre-war professional life should have led people to think that the vapourings of the Pariser Zeitung were a fake. I particularly regret not to be able to come to London in order to re-affirm this fact in person.

Please excuse the length of this letter (of which I am sending copies to the British and U.S.A. Federations).

I remain, Yours sincerely,
Signed A. Alekhine Madrid, December 6th, 1945

In his book Legado, published posthumously, Alekine wrote:

"Once more I insist on repeating that which I have published on several occasions: that is, that the articles which were stupid and untrue from a chess point of view and which were printed signed with my name in a Paris newspaper in 1941 are a

31

falsification. It is not the first time that unscrupulous journalists have abused my name in order to publish inanities of that kind, but in the present case what was published in Pariser Zeitung is what has caused me the most grief, not only because of its content but also precisely because it [is] impossible for me to rectify it...Colleagues know my sentiments and they realize perfectly well how great is the esteem in which I hold their art and that I have too elevated a concept of chess to become entangled in the absurd statements poured out by the above-mentioned Parisian newspaper."

From Francisco Lupi's The Broken King, a memoir of Alekhine (Chess World, October 1, 1946):
Grand Tribunal

When I left for England, Alekhine had not yet received any important letter by which he could accurately judge what the chess world thought about him. So, before I left I promised I would sound in London the opinions of the distinguished players in the tournament, his former colleagues from many countries. Actually, 24 hours before the end of the contests, the masters Euwe and Denker convoked an assembly to judge Alekhine's case. Among those present, besides Denker and Euwe, were Sir George Thomas, Dr. Ossip Bernstein, Dr.Tartakover, List, Friedmann, Medina, Abrahams, and Herman Steiner. The meeting was somewhat lively and it can easily be understood that some of the Jews present showed hard feelings. I must say, however, that the attitude of Denker and Euwe was very calm and dignified. They seemed to realize the responsibility of trying a man for his professional life while he was many miles away in Lisbon. In the end, the question was referred to the International Chess Federation, while Alekhine was asked to present himself to his own French chess authorities to defend himself from the accusations made against him. When I got back to Lisbon I found Alekhine very willing to fall in with this advice. He immediately applied for a French visa. He was dead before it arrived.

Friendship with Nuremberg Criminal

In those last weeks, grief, sickness, and poverty entirely crushed him. In desperation some of us decided to appeal again to his wife. "Since his arrival here a month ago, " we wrote, " your husband has been in an impossible situation - sick, with no material resources and living virtually on charity in an Estoril boardinghouse." Days went by, and nothing new happened. Alekhine spent his time in bed, or pacing his room like a lion in a cage.

One afternoon I asked him how it was that he received so many privileges from the Germans and in German-occupied countries. He revealed that this arose from an old acquaintance with the notorious Dr. [Hans] Frank, the Nuremberg war criminal, who was a chess enthusiast and had one of the most complete chess libraries Alekhine had ever seen. "And was Dr. Frank kind to you?" "Yes, in the beginning he showed great generosity toward me. But later he began to show signs of suspicion, especially after he knew about a comment I had made on the execution of Przepiorka, a Jewish player who had gone into a Prague cafe verboten to Jews." And Alekhine added nervously: "Maybe some of my colleagues do not understand that I had to act discreetly if I wanted to stay alive." Fifteen days before his death, I was called on the telephone and heard Dr. Alekhine ask me sadly, whether I wanted to work with him on "Comments on the Best Games of the Hastings Tournament." adding: "I am completely out of money and I have to make some to buy my cigarettes."

The Cable from Moscow

I went to Estoril and tried to cheer him up a little. We began work immediately. And when we were almost at the end of Tartakover's games, deep into the task, we heard a knock at the door. I can see him now, rising, and with uncertain steps walking to the door to receive this telegram from Mr. Derbyshire in Nottingham:

"Moscow offer substantial sum (1) for chess championship of world to be played in England between you and Botvinnik suggest you appoint someone in England represent you and arrange all details wire reply."

This was the cause of Alekhine's second cardiac stroke. It was hard for him to overcome the shock, and he could not believe that he would soon be back in the great chess world. He answered Mr. Derbyshire immediately, accepting the match provided that Botvinnik would agree to the conditions of 1939. Poor Alekhine! He would have accepted any conditions. Some days later Michael Botvinnik himself sent a letter through the British Embassy in Lisbon. The text was in Russian, with an English version attached:

"World's Championship. "Mr. A. Alekhine! "I regret that the war prevented the organization of our match in 1939, But I herewith again challenge you to a match for the world's chess championship. "If you agree, a person authorized by myself and the Moscow Chess Club will conduct negotiations with you or your representative on the question of conditions, date and the place where the match should be held, preferably through the British Chess Federation. "I await your answer, in which I also ask you to state your ideas about the date and place of the match. I beg you to send a telegraphic reply, with subsequent postal confirmation, to the Moscow Chess Club."

February 4th, 1946. "(Sgd.) Michael Botvinnik."

Secret Weapons

A few days after this letter arrived, when Alex had already asked Mr. du Mont in London, the editor of the British Chess Magazine, to be his intermediary, something happened which will seem out of place mentioned here - Churchill's sensational speech at Fulton. (2) As soon as Dr. Alekhine read Reuters' report of the speech in the Portuguese papers he telephoned me in alarm, asking me to take the first train to Estoril, because he urgently wanted to speak to me. When I arrived he was slumped in an armchair, utterly demoralized. He said: "See how unhappy I am! The world has got no sense and is moving towards another war. I am sure my match with Botvinnik will never be possible." I tried to reassure him. We got to work again over the games of the Hastings Tournament, and once, while we stopped to have a cup of coffee, I asked him what was the opening plan he had for his play with Botvinnik. He whispered, forgetful at once of his usual preoccupations, that the world would be startled by the ideas he had in mind. And he said, with a child-like look in his eyes, that he was going to play Botvinnik a little trick. "I intend to play open games, trying all the time to get him into the Ruy Lopez." I answered: "But Botvinnik will never get into the Lopez.(3) You know very well that the Russian masters have a deep knowledge of the French game. So..." He replied that he had been studying some variations of the Panov atack. When I asked him to show me some of them he made a gesture as if to say: "Whoever displayed his secret weapons?"

Night Club Flicker

This was the old Alekhine. But 24 hours later, at about one in the morning of Friday, March 22, as I climbed the stairs of my apartment in Lisbon, I saw, leaning against the door, somebody whom a few steps closer I recognized as my friend. When I was near him, his hands grasped nervously the sleeves of my coat, and he said, in a voice I shall never forget: "Lupi, the loneliness is killing me! I must live. I must feel life about me. I have already worn down the floorboards of my room. Take me to some night club." This was the last time he felt the dynamic life force within him. While the band played melancholy tangos it made me ill to watch the shadow of him who was once the greatest chess player of all time. As we sat, he again talked of the match with Botvinnik. "Could it, would it, ever take place?" It was late when we parted, and this was the last time I was to see him alive. The autopsy said of him that he suffered from **Arteriosclerosis**, chronic gastritis and duodenitis, that his heart weighed 350 grammes, that the perimeter of his skull was 540 millimeters, and so on...

"Old Dr. Alex"

All I know is that on Sunday morning about 10:30 I was awakened and asked to hurry to Estoril, because something had happened to "old Dr. Alex." I entered his room together with the Portuguese authorities. There he was, sitting in his chair, in so calm an attitude that one would have thought he was asleep. There was only a little foam at the corner of his mouth.(4) The medical verdict as to the cause of death - that a piece of meat had caught in his throat - had no meaning for me. To me he looked like the King of the chessmen, toppled over after the most dramatic game, the one played on the board of Life.

"'Tis all a Chequerboard of Nights and Days " Where Destiny with Men for Pieces Play; " Hither and thither moves and mates and slays " And one by one back in the Closet lays." (5) Checkmate! That is in the original Persian shah mat - the King is dead.

THE END

Introduction plus Exhibits by Sam Sloan

Notes by translator Frank X. Mur:

The reader ought to know that I translated *Agony of a Chess Genius* but not Lupi's *"The Broken King"*, which may well have been written in English before being sent to Purdy's *Chess World.*

1) $10,000: winner and loser to split 2/3 to 1/3 according to J. du Mont, 3/5 to 2/5 according to B. H. Wood.

2) Winston Churchill called war with Russia inevitable ("Iron Curtain" speech, Fulton, Missouri, March 5, 1946.)

3) Lupi was unaware that in the 1941 USSR Absolute Championship, Botvinnik beat Smyslov twice as Black: in a French Defense and a Ruy Lopez. Alekhine wisely included the Lopez in his arsenal to meet 1..e5.

4) He died in the company of his dearest friends: a peg-in traveling set lay open beside him - C.J.S. Purdy

5) From the Rubaiyat of Omar Khayyam

Errata by Frank X. Mur

Frank X. Mur was the translator into English of the authoritative work: *A. Alekhine, Agony of a Chess Genius* by Pablo Moran. This is the the authoritative work on the controversial final three years of the life of the World Chess Champion. The book is soon to be reprinted.

Mr. Mur, who resides in Oakland, California and who I know through Arden Van Upp has been kind enough to take some time to point out some errors in C. H. O'D. Alexander's *Alekhine's Best Games of Chess, 1938-1945*

===

C. H. O'D. Alexander's *Alekhine's Best Games of Chess, 1938-1945* (1950), page 9 (Tournaments 1945), – see Alexander's own page 9 – omits the World Champion's Cracow 1942 rank: Prize 1, P[layed] 10, W[ins] 6 (see Game 27 v. Junge), D[raws] 3, L[osses] 1. Games 4A (against Naharro, Madrid 1941, not Navarro, Madrid 1940) and 38-42 correspond to Games 65, 90, 101 (Notes by Max Walter), 120, 121, and 126 in *A. Alekhine: Agony of a Chess Genius* by Pablo Moran (McFarland, 1989). Alexander/Moran 41/121 may well have been an exhibition game, the Almeria Tournament game probably being Moran's 141 (Notes by B.H. Wood). See Moran's Chapter 7 for the publication history of Alekhine's anti-semitic, 1941 *Pariser Zeitung* diatribe, and that book's Appendices C through E for supplementary material. See also "Alekhine: Nazi Articles" (1986) by Ken Whyld. The last word, however, belongs to Irving Chernev who, during the course of a 1976 telephone conversation regarding Alekhine's wartime propaganda, asked me, "What does all that have to do with his games?"

The issue of Alekhine's two Martinez Moreno games (121 and 141) arose because someone once pointed out – if memory serves, in a 1990's issue of *Chess* – that Alekhine was supposedly White in his Tournament game against M.M. Other than these corrections, I can't think of anything essential to add by way of Preliminary Note, except of course my name at the end. My great grandfather, Mauricio Mur, hailed from Olot, Gerona province, which hosted at least one major tournament in recent years.

Salud,

Frank X. Mur

Alekhine Genealogy

In 1913, at the age of 21, Alekhine fathered an illegitimate daughter, Valentina (born on December 15, 1913) with a Russian baroness (Anna von Sewergin). Alekhine and the baroness married in 1920 to legitimize the daughter's birth (Moran and Hooper & Whyld). Alekhine married Anna von Sewergin (some Internet genealogy sources say Aleksandra Bataeva), a Russian baroness several years older than he (Moran). She was an artist from St. Petersburg and widow of a Russian landowner killed in World War I. This was his first wife. They married in Moscow to legitimize their seven-year-old daughter, Valentina (Hooper and Whyld). There is no record of a divorce. In early 1921, Alekhine's first wife, Anna von Sewergin, and daughter, Valentina, left for Austria. Valentina died in the mid 1980s in Vienna.

On March 15, 1921, Alekhine married a second time to Anneliese Ruegg, who was 13 years older than he. She was 41 and he was 28. He may have not divorced his first wife at the time. Anneliese was already expecting a baby, and wanted to have the birth back home in Switzerland.

On April 29, 1921, Alekhine was given permission to leave Russia for a visit to the West with his wife. Alekhine never returned to Russia. The couple traveled to Riga, Latvia, and Berlin, where he only had 200 marks in his pocket. Alekhine wanted to go to France and from there, tour the world playing chess. But the entry visa into France was refused by the French Consulate. Alekhine finally obtained a visa on the understanding he would not undertake any communist propaganda.

In June 1921, Annaliese Ruegg returned to Switzerland, where she gave birth to a son, Alexander Aleksandrovich Aljechin, in January 1922.

In December 1922, Alekhine took 4th-6th at the Austrian Chess Association Congress, held in Vienna. The event was won by Rubinstein, followed by Tartakower and Wolf. This was the last meeting between Alekhine and his first wife, Anna von Sewergin, who was living in Austria with their daughter, Valentina. They never met again.

Alekhine Genealogy

In 1924, Alekhine divorced his second wife, Anneliese Ruegg. Her social commitments and refusal to accompany Alekhine to chess tournaments led to marital problems.

In 1924, at a Paris ball, Alekhine met Nadezhda Semyenovna Fabritskaya (Fabrickaja) Vasiliev (Vasileva or Wasilief), widow of the Russian General V. Vasiliev. She was born on March 19, 1884 in Odessa. Her daughter, Gvendolina, was almost as old as Alekhine. In 1925, he married his third wife, Nadezhda Semyenovna Fabritskaya Vasiliev. They lived at 211 rue de la Croix-Nivert in Paris. Kotov claims that Alekhine divorced his second wife, Anneliese, to marry Nadezhda.

In 1933, Alekhine met Grace Freeman Wishart (sometimes given as Wishard, Wishaar, Wislar, or Wishar) at a minor chess tournament which she had won in Tokyo. Her prize was one of Alekhine's books (Deux cents parties d'echecs – 200 games of Chess). She asked him to sign the book and their relationship developed from that moment.

Grace, born in New Jersey on October 26, 1876, was a widow of the English Captain Archibold Freeman, her third (possibly fourth) husband who died in the early 1930s. She had been previously married to a British tea planter in Ceylon and a French Morocco Governor (Moran). Grace retained her British citizenship to the end of her life. She owned a chateau called Saint-Aubin-le-Chef, located a few miles southeast of Dieppe in Normandy. She also owned an art studio in Paris. Soon, Grace was living with Alekhine, even though Alekhine was still married to his third wife, Nadezhda. In March, 1934, he divorced his third wife, Nadezhda in Amsterdam.

On March 26, 1934 Alekhine married for the 4th time to Grace Wishart at Villefranche-sur-Mer in the French Riviera. The marriage certificate spells her maiden name as Wishaar.

On May 2, 1934, Alekhine's second wife, Annaliese Ruegg died in Luasanne, Switzerland. Alekhine put his son, Alex, in a boarding school in Zurich, Switzerland under the guardianship of the Swiss master Erwin Voellmy (1886-1951). Alekhine saw very little of his son.

Alekhine Genealogy

In June 1935, Grace Alekhine played in the French Women's Championship, but was not among the top four finishers. In 1935 Alekhine wanted to establish his residence in Mallorca, but his wife, Grace, disliked the idea. In January 1937, Alekhine won the 17th Hastings tournament for 1936-37. He won 15 sterling pounds for his effort, His wife, Grace, won 3rd prize in the Third Class tournament at Hastings, winning 1 pound. In April 1938, Alekhine won at Margate. His wife, Grace, competed in Section A of the Second Class Tournament.

In September 1939, he won a tournament at Montevideo. Alekhine could have remained in Argentina or he could have gone to the United States with his American-born wife, but decided to return to France to join the French Army.

Alekhine played a lot of bridge in South America, but was not a strong bridge player. His wife, Grace, once said to him after he played a bad hand, "If you go on like this, you'll lose us our chateau in France." (Golombek)

In January, 1940, Alexander and Grace (and two cats) sailed from Buenos Aires to Estoril, Portugal, where they stayed a few days before going to France.

From Marseilles, he wanted to leave for Portugal where he hoped to sail for South America so as to play a return match with Capablanca. But he was not yet 48 years old, and the French law prohibited all men under 48 from leaving France (CHESS, May 1946). He tried to obtain a passport both at Marseilles and at Nice, but could not do so, Alekhine then returned to Paris to see his wife, Grace.

Alekhine then went to Spain. His wife had insisted on staying in Paris to protect their chateau at Saint Aubin-le-Cauf. She was an American citizen and could move throughout France a little bit more freely.

At this time, news reached Alekhine that his wife and chateau in France was in the hands of the Germans. To protect his wife and their French assets, including his six cats, he agreed to cooperate with the Nazis. He wrote six articles critical of Jewish chess players and participated in Nazi chess tournaments in Munich, Salzburg, Warsaw, and Prague. The Nazis looted his French chateau at Saint Aubin-le-Cauf, near Dieppe. Mrs. Alekhine later sold the castle under American Embassy protection. (Chess magazine) The Germans refused Mrs. Alekhine an exit visa.

In 1941, Ehrardt Post, General Secretary of the Grossdeutscher Schachbund (GSB), the Great German Chess Federation, wrote Alekhine that although he would not be allowed to return to France, if he consented to play in a chess tournament in Munich, his wife would be permitted to join him there. At the time, she was 62 years old and in failing health, Alekhine agreed to the terms.

On March 18-23, 1941, six anti-Semitic articles appeared under Alekhine's name and published in the Pariser Zeitung (Paris Journal). He argued that there was a "Jewish" way of playing chess (cowardly and for money), and an "Aryan" way of playing chess (aggressive and brave). A part of these articles were published in the April, May, and June 1941 issues of the German chess magazine Deutsche Schachzeitung (DSZ). His first article on Jewish and Aryan chess appeared on March 21, 1941 in Deutsche Zeitung in den Niederlander (German News in the Netherlands). Alekhine's anti-Semitic articles were published in France, Holland, and Germany. It is possible that the articles were falsified by Austrian master and chess journalist Theodor Gerbec (Herbertz), who was a chess editor of Pariser Zeitung, co-editor of Deutsche Schachzeitung, and a fascist. He died in 1945.

In April, 1941, Alekhine tried to go to America by traveling to Lisbon and applying for an American visa. But because the anti-Semitism from his articles showed in his published articles, the visa was not approved. In an interview quoted in a Madrid paper on September 3, 1941, Alekhine said he was proud of his articles that were published in the Pariser Zeitung. Alekhine gave two exhibitions and several interviews during this period. In 1941-1942 he participated in Nazi chess tournaments in Munich, Salzburg, Warsaw, and Prague. Alekhine was residing in Poland and Czechoslovakia during this time. In September 1941, he tied for 2nd-3rd at Munich. The event was won by Stoltz. The event was attended by leaders from the Nazi Party, the State Government, and the Wehrmacht. The reception was attended by Josef Goebbels and Dr. Hans Frank (1900-1946). In 1943,

The Gestapo gave Alekhine an exit visa, but would not permit his wife to accompany him. She had to return to Paris.

When asked if he knew about the controversy aroused by his articles against the Jews, Alekhine replied, "I swear I did not write a word of that." (Moran).

In 1944, his older sister died in the USSR. In 1944, Grace Alekhine won the women's chess championship of Paris. In August 1945, he won at Sabadell, near Barcelona, Spain (6 wins, 3 draws). During this time, his wife had written, telling Alexander that she wanted no more to do with him. (Moran)

In September 1945, the British Chess Federation sent Alekhine an invitation to tournaments in London and Hastings. Alekhine accepted the invitations by cable from Madrid. In October 1945, the United States Chess Federation (USCF) protested the invitation of Alekhine to the victory tournament in London. The USCF refused to take part in any projects or tournaments involving Alekhine. Protesters included Reuben Fine and Arnold Denker. In November 1945, a telegram arrived, signed by Mr. W. Hatton-Ward of the Sunday Chronicle, the paper that was organizing the victory tournament in London that, due to a protest from the United States Chess Federation, the invitations to tournaments in England had been canceled. Shortly after, Alekhine had a heart attack.

In December 1945, he said that none of the anti-Jewish articles were written by him. In January 1946 a Victory Tournament was to be held in London. World Champion Alekhine was first invited by the British. The there were objections from the Dutch and the U.S. Chess Federation because of his articles of anti-Jewish content published under the signature of Alekhine. Some of the masters (USA) had threatened to withdraw from the tournament if Alekhine was invited. Alekhine was not invited to the event, which was won by Herman Steiner.

Alekhine decided to return to France and to defend himself before the French Chess Federation. He applied for a visa, but Spain's borders were closed and the visa never reached him.

Alekhine Genealogy

In early March, 1946, he received a telegram from Mr. Derbyshire, the President of the British Chess Federation, transmitting a challenge to a match by the Russian champion, Mikhail Botvinnik (dated February 4, 1946). The Moscow Chess Club was offering $10,000 for the match. The match would take place in England subject to the British Chess Federation's (BCF) approval. Alekhine would receive $6,600 to play in the challenge match.

On March 23, 1946, the BCF unanimously agreed to sponsor the match in England between Alekhine and Botvinnik. On the evening of March 23 or early March 24, 1946 (a chambermaid found his body at 10:30 am on March 24) Alekhine died in his shabby hotel room (the Park Hotel) in Estoril, Portugal (just outside Lisbon) at the age of 53. He was dressed in an overcoat to keep warm and slumped back in a ratty armchair with a peg chess set on the table and his dinner dishes in front of him. Kasparov says he died on March 24. Other sources say he died on March 23.

Some say he died of a heart attack (Hooper and Whyld). Others say he choked on a piece of meat. An autopsy took place at the Department of Legal Medicine of the Medical School of the University of Lisbon on March 27, 1946. Dr. Antonio J. Ferreira wrote the official death certificate, and said that the autopsy revealed the cause of death as asphyxia due to a piece of meat which lodged itself in the larynx. Years later, Dr. Ferreira claimed that Alekhine was shot. Brace and Kotov state that when Alekhine died, he did not have enough money even to buy cigarettes. Alekhine's son later hinted that Alekhine might have been murdered by Soviets (Kasparov).

One conspiracy theory is that the French Resistance created a super secret 'Death Squad' after World War II to deal with some of the people who had collaborated too willingly with the German Nazis. Dr. Antonio Ferreira later supposedly told friends that Alekhine's body was found on the street, in front of his hotel room. He had been shot and Portuguese government pressure forced him to complete the death certificate that now exists. An overcoat was put over him to hid the bullet wound.

Some medical doctors have commented on Alekhine's death. Some point out that patients who become unconscious from a heart attack always fall to the floor and never remain sitting peacefully in chairs. If someone were choking to death, the gag reflex would kick in. Even an unconscious person would gag and cough, usually throwing out whatever is blocked in their airway and not die immediately. A conscious person would gag and struggle, moving around, knocking pieces over. A person choking to death would not end up in a calmly sitting position.

On April 10, 1946, Grace Alekhine wrote a letter to the CHESS editor that said her husband never accepted a salary nor the title of 'Sachberator fur Ostfragen. She writes that Alekhine was offered a very advantageous position provided he became a Nazi, but he refused to to so. She said that he had no influence with any of the Nazi party leaders and never mixed politically.

Grace Wishart Alekhine died in 1956. After she died, the Aryan and Jewish Chess notes in Alekhine's handwriting were allegedly found in her effects by Brian Reilly (1901-1991), then the Editor of the British Chess Magazine. However, Reilly denied ever having seen the handwritten notes (Winter).

In 1956, the 10th anniversary of his death, the USSR and French Chess Federation agreed to transfer his remains to the Cimetiere du Montparnasse (division 8) in Paris. The Soviets were anxious to have him buried in Moscow, but his widow refused and wanted him buried in Paris. FIDE provided the tombstone. It is in the shape of a chess board made out of red granite and there is a bust of him made out of Carrara marble at the head of his tomb.

The ceremony in Paris was attended by Alekhine's son, Alexander, who came from Switzerland, the Soviet ambassador to France, the FIDE president and vice president, Bronstein, Geller, Keres, Petrosian, Smyslov, Spassky, Ossip Bernstein, and several French players and journalists.

Grace is buried next to Alexander. The headstone gives her maiden name as Wishar.

CONTENTS

LIST OF GAMES

	Against	Opening	Moves	Played at		Colour
1	BALPARDA	Q. Pawn, Queen's Indian Defence	39	Montevideo	1938	Black
2	Böök	Queen's Gambit Accepted	25	Margate	,,	White
3	GOLOMBEK	Q. Pawn, Nimzowitsch Defence	31	,,	,,	White
4	BRUCE	Caro Kann	12	Plymouth	,,	White
[4A	NAVARRO	Caro Kann	13	Madrid	1940	White]
5	EUWE	Queen's Gambit Declined	41	AVRO	1938	White
6	FLOHR	Ruy Lopez	41	,,	,,	White
7	CAPABLANCA	French Defence	35	,,	,,	White
8	KAUSZ	Dutch Defence	29	Caracas	1939	Black
9	ELISKASES	Caro Kann	47	Buenos Aires	,,	White
10	ZVETCOFF	Sicilian	58	,,	,,	White
11	CZERNIAK	English	51	,,	,,	Black
12	ENEVOLDSEN	Q. Pawn, Nimzowitsch Defence	38	,,	,,	Black
13	GOLOMBEK	Sicilian	35	Montevideo	,,	White
14	SILVA ROCHA	Queen's Gambit Declined	47	Rio de Janeiro 1939		White
15	ROHACEK	Ruy Lopez	33	Munich	1941	White
16	LEEPIN	English	21	,,	,,	Black
17	KIENINGER	Ruy Lopez	44	,,	,,	Black
18	KERES	King's Gambit	52	Salzburg	1942	Black
19	BOGOLJUBOW	Queen's Pawn	53	,,	,,	Black
20	KERES	Ruy Lopez	57	,,	,,	White
21	SCHMIDT	Ruy Lopez	33	,,	,,	White
22	JUNGE	Catalan	52	Munich	,,	Black
23	KERES	Q. Pawn, Queen's Indian Defence	33	,,	,,	White
24	BARCZA	Ruy Lopez	29	,,	,,	White
25	RICHTER	Caro Kann	46	,,	,,	White
26	RABAR	Catalan	27	,,	,,	White
27	JUNGE	Ruy Lopez	28	Cracow	,,	White
28	PODGORNY	Sicilian	28	Prague	,,	White
29	SUCHA	French	30	,,	,,	White

7

	Against	Opening	Moves	Played at		Colour
30	FLORIAN	Philidor	44	Prague	1942	Black
31	PACHMAN	Q. Pawn, Nimzowitsch Defence	28	,,	,,	White
32	JUNGE	Catalan	29	,,	,,	White
33	BOGOLJUBOW	Catalan	32	Warsaw	1943	White
34	SAEMISCH	Ruy Lopez	27	Prague	,,	Black
35	BARTOSEK	French	34	,,	,,	White
36	SCHIDMT	Ruy Lopez	65	Salzburg	,,	White
37	FOLTYS	Q. Pawn, Nimzowitsch Defence	46	,,	,,	Black
38	MEDINA	Giuoco Piano	41	Gijon	1944	Black
39	PÉREZ	Ruy Lopez	35	Madrid	1945	White
40	LOPEZ JULIO	French	30	Almeria	,,	White
41	MARTINEZ	Q. Pawn, Queen's Indian Defence	27	,,	,,	Black
42	FUENTES	Evans Gambit Declined	28	Melilla	,,	White

TOURNAMENTS 1938–45

Year	Place				Prize	P	W	D	L
1938	Montevideo	..	..	..	1	17	9	8	–
	Margate	..	..	..	..	1	9	6	2	1
	Plymouth	..	..	..	..	1 & 2 =	7	5	2	–
	AVRO	..	..	..	..	4, 5 & 6 =	14	3	8	3
1939	Caracas	..	..	..	..	1	10	10	–	–
	Buenos Aires [Team Tournament]			–	10	5	5	–
	Montevideo	..	..	..	1	7	7	–	–
1941	Munich	..	..	..	..	2 & 3 =				
	Cracow	..	..	..	..	1 =	11	6	5	–
1942	Salzburg	..	..	..	..	1	10	7	1	2
	Munich	..	..	..	..	1	11	7	3	1
	Prague	..	..	..	..	1 =	11	6	5	–
1943	Prague	..	..	..	..	1	18	16	2	–
	Salzburg	..	..	..	..	1 =	10	5	5	–
1944	Gijon	..	..	..	..	1	8	7	1	–
1945	Madrid	..	..	..	..	1	9	8	1	–
	Gijon	..	..	..	..	3	9	6	1	2
	Sabadell	..	..	..	..	1	9	6	3	–
	Almeria	..	..	..	..	1 =	8	4	3	1
	Melilla	..	..	..	..	1	7	6	1	–
	Navidad	..	..	..	..	2	5	3	1	1

MATCHES

							P	W	D	L
Dr Rey Ardid	..	..	..	..	..	..	4	1	3	–
F. Lupi	..	..	..	..	..		4	2	1	1

INTRODUCTION

THIS volume is the third of a trilogy; the first volume (1908–1923) showed Alekhine's rise to a position in the chess world second only to that of Capablanca—the second (1924–1937) covered the period when his powers reached their greatest height, the victory over Capablanca in 1927 and his overwhelming triumphs at San Remo (1930), Bled (1931) and Berne (1932). This volume (1938–1945) deals with his final years; although his play in this period has not quite the same sureness as it had ten years earlier, it retains the unmistakable stamp of his genius. Except for "AVRO" and Munich 1941 he won every tournament of any importance in which he played in this period, and his score against Paul Keres (3 wins, 3 draws, 0 losses) is alone sufficient to show the strength of his play.

Many of the games given in this book were played during the war in occupied Europe, in tournaments sponsored by Nazi Germany. The average strength of Alekhine's opponents was unquestionably lower than in the great pre-war tournaments, which meant that, if the high standard of play of the games in the previous volumes was to be maintained, the number given in this book had to be very much less. I am conscious, too, that I cannot hope in my annotations to reach the superlative standard set by Alekhine in his own notes. Nevertheless, I believe it is right that Alekhine's own two books should be rounded off by this collection of his last games.

Alekhine was one of the greatest players—possibly the greatest—the world has ever seen—and his games have an intrinsic worth which is independent of the circumstances in which they were played or the manner in which they have been annotated. There should be a complete record of his career with all his best games from every period: these games are the product of the life of a man of genius and, as such, have an unassailable right to be preserved for chess and chess players.

In this introduction I do not propose to give a biographical account of Alekhine's life and career, a task already admirably carried out by Mr. du Mont in the second volume of this series. I should, however, like briefly to say something of Alekhine as a chess player. There is a great danger, in any appraisal of this kind, of giving a totally misleading and one-sided impression by attaching some label such as "brilliant," which makes the reader think the player in question is never happy except when he is making sacrifices. All great players can play every type of position

11

outstandingly well, and the differences in their play are largely a matter of taste and temperament rather than of ability.   However, when one has said this, it remains a fact that each of the greatest players is distinguished to some extent by some special quality in which he is pre-eminent.   With Lasker it was his "fighting spirit," his ability to win so-called lost games; with Capablanca it was "lucidity," the clarity of thought and perfect feeling for the game, which made everything look so simple and made it seem impossible that he could ever lose.   In Alekhine's play "imagination" is the key word; the ability to perform the apparently impossible, to conjure up diabolical complications in the most harmless looking position.   Again and again in playing through an Alekhine game one suddenly meets a move which simply takes one's breath away—when it is actually played we ordinary mortals receive it in stunned surprise, and heaven knows how far ahead Alekhine has seen it.   Capablanca at his best one thinks of as "unbeatable," Alekhine at his best as "irresistible"— and when the irresistible force met the immovable object, the object moved!   [To avoid a breach with my friend Harry Golombek I hasten to add that it did not move very much.]

We can illustrate this imaginative power of Alekhine's by some positions from the games in this book; many more examples could of course be found in his earlier games.   In Game No. 5 (v. Euwe), in a perfectly ordinary humdrum position in the Queen's Gambit, he suddenly plays 9. P—K Kt 4!—a move most players would never even consider—and Black finds himself quite unexpectedly in serious difficulties, fails to find the best line, and four moves later has a lost game.   In Game No. 22 (v. Junge), after White's 14th move, Alekhine as Black has apparently an indifferent position: White has Pawns on K 4 and Q 4 and a generally well centralised game—Alekhine's only compensation lies in his two Bishops, posted on Q Kt 5 and Q B 3.   He plays 14. ....B—K 1! and 15. ....B—B 1!—not as defensive moves but inaugurating an attack on the White Queen's side; five moves later White has a lost position. Against Richter (Game No. 25) there is an even more striking example of "reculer pour mieux sauter."   Richter as Black has, after 17 moves, apparently reached a highly satisfactory position with several awkward threats, the worst being a double attack on the White Q P.   Alekhine plays 18. Q (Q 3)—B 1! a most improbable move and after 18. ....R × P; 19. Q—Kt 5! and Black cannot avoid a disadvantage however he plays. Finally, the most striking example of all, Game No. 33 (v. Bogoljubow). After Black's 21st move both players have 2 R's, B, Kt and 7 P's; Black appears to be a little cramped but nothing seriously wrong—a dull game apparently, which might drag on for twenty or thirty moves more and end in a draw if Black defends carefully.   Alekhine plays 22. Kt (B 3)—Q 2!! threatening Kt—Q B 4 followed by Kt × Kt P mate and the game is over— an astonishing conception.   All these examples are distinguished by the freshness and originality of the ideas—the lines of play would not be analysed and rejected by the ordinary strong player, they simply would not occur to him at all.

Whether or not Alekhine at his best was better than Capablanca, Lasker or Morphy at their respective bests no one knows or can ever know, and it does not matter; what does matter, and is undeniable, is that Alekhine was one of the very greatest players who has ever lived, and that his games have a beauty and fascination entirely of their own. If the games in this book succeed in awaking in readers the same feelings of admiration and delight which they have given me I shall have attained my object in collecting and annotating them.

C. H. O'D. A.

1

MONTEVIDEO 1938

White: J. BALPARDA (Uruguay)

Queen's Pawn, Queen's Indian Defence

1. P—Q 4	Kt—K B 3
2. Kt—K B 3	P—Q Kt 3

One of the best lines of play against White's rather quiet second move. It is less good immediately against 2 P—Q B 4 because of the danger of an early P—Q 5 by White.

3. P—K Kt 3	B—Kt 2
4. B—Kt 2	P—B 4
5. P—B 3 ?	

Timid and bad. White needs B 3 for his Kt and this move quite unnecessarily deprives him of the square and puts him on the defensive. Over-caution against a strong player is one of the worst and most fatal faults; it is far better to be over-bold against a better player and too cautious against a worse if one cannot avoid these extremes entirely. The correct line is 5. Castles, P × P; 6. Kt × P, B × B; 7. K × B with an equal game.

5.	P—K 3
6. Castles	B—K 2
7. P—Kt 3	

A clumsy move. White would do best to admit his previous error and play 7. P—B 4 followed by Kt—B 3.

7.	Castles
8. B—Kt 2	P × P
9. P × P	

B

After this the Q B is locked out of the game for a long time. It would be better to play 9. Kt × P, B × B; 10. K × B, P—Q 4; 11. Kt—Q 2 followed by P—Q B 4.

9.	P—Q Kt 4 !

A powerful move, initiating a strong Queen's side attack.

10. Q Kt—Q 2	Q—Kt 3
11. P—K 3	P—Q R 4
12. P—Q R 3	

Black threatened P—R 5 followed by P—R 6 or P × P according to circumstances.

12.	Kt—B 3
13. Kt—K 5	P—Q 3
14. Kt × Kt	B × Kt
15. B × B	Q × B
16. R—B 1	Q—Kt 2
17. Q—B 3	P—Q 4
18. R—B 2	B—Q 3 !

Preventing an entry on Q B 7 by the White Rooks, allowing Q—K 2 with the threat on the Q R P and preparing for an assault later on against the King's side—a lot to accomplish in moving a Bishop from K 2 to Q 3 !

19. K R—B 1	Q—K 2
20. Q—K 2	K R—Kt 1
21. Kt—Kt 1	

If 21. P—Q R 4, P × P; 22. P × P, Q—Q 2; 23. R—R 1, R—Kt 5; and wins the Q R P.

21.	P—R 4 !

Having driven White's minor pieces out of play on the Q side, Black turns his attention to the K side—a beautiful example of play over the whole board. The power

15

to see the board as a whole is one of the hall-marks of a great master.

22. R—B 6

A meaningless foray. 22. P—B 3 allowing the Queen to come across to the defence would be much more to the point.

22. ......   P—K R 5
23. P—K Kt 4

If 23. P × P, P—Kt 3; followed by ....K—Kt 2 and ....R—R 1 with a very powerful attack.

23. ......   Kt—K 5
24. P—B 3   Kt—Kt 4
25. K—Kt 2   P—Kt 5

The attack on the Q R P having served its purpose, Black winds up operations on the Q side by depriving White of the square Q B 3; also by moving the Kt P he frees his K R for action in the centre.

26. P—R 4   P—K 4 !

Position after Black's 26th move

Having advanced on both flanks, Black now comes on in the centre. Neither here nor on the next move does White dare to exchange pawns, *e.g.* 27. P × P, B × P; 28. B × B, Q × B; 29. Kt—Q 2, R—K 1; 30. Kt—B 1, P—Q 5; 31. R—K 1, P—R 6 ch; 32. K—B 2 (32. K—Kt 1

or R 1; Q—Q 4 winning the K B P), P × P ch; 33. Q × P, Q—Kt 7 ch; 34. R—K 2, R × Q; 35. R × Q, R × P ch; 36. K—Kt 1, R—K 1; 37. R—B 1, R—K 5; and wins.

27. Kt—Q 2   R—K 1
28. Q—Kt 5

Black threatened 28. ....P × P; 29. B × P, Kt—K 3; with the double menace of Kt × B and Kt—B 5 ch. However a better way of unpinning the Queen would be Q—B 2, keeping it in the defence.

28. ......   P—K 5 !
29. P—B 4

If 29. P × P, P—R 6 ch; 30. K—Kt 1, Kt × P; 31. Kt—B 3, Kt—B 7 !; and wins.

29. ......   P—R 6 ch.
30. K—Kt 3

If 30. K—R 1, B × P !; 31. P × B, P—K 6; and wins, *e.g.* 32. Q—Q 3, P × Kt; 33. Q × P, Q—K 5 ch; 34. K—Kt 1, Kt—B 6 ch., winning the Queen, or 32. P × Kt, P × Kt; 33. R moves, Q—K 5 ch. The constant threat of B × P prevents White from moving his K from Kt 3 and Black is therefore able at his leisure to play P—Kt 3, K—Kt 2, R—R 1 and Kt moves—whereupon the threat of Q—R 5 mate will force a King move and the sacrifice on White's B 4 will take effect.

30. ......   Q R—Q 1
31. R—B 1   P—Kt 3
32. Q—Kt 6   K—Kt 2
33. B—B 1   Kt—K 3

Beautifully timed. As long as the Black Knight was on Kt 4, the threat of Kt—B 6 followed by Q—R 5 ch tied the White Knight to Q 2—and hence prevented the King from retiring to B 2. Now the Kt is released, but White dare not play 34. Kt—Kt 1 because of 34. ....R—K R 1; 35. K—B 2, Q—R 5 ch winning the Kt P. He must first play 34. R—Kt 1 whereupon R—R 1 forces the King to retreat before the Kt on Q 2 can move and Black's sacrifice on B 4 can then be played !

34. R—Kt 1	R—K R 1
35. K—B 2	Kt × B P !
36. K—K 1	

36. P × Kt, P—K 6 ch ; 37. K—K 2 (37. K—B 1, P × Kt ; 38. B × P, K R—K 1 ; 39. Q—Kt 5, Q—K 5 and wins), P × Kt ch ; 38. K × P, B × P ch ; 39. K—Q 1, B × P winning easily.

36.	Kt—Q 6 ch
37. K—Q 1	B × P
38. R—B 1	B—Q 3
39. Resigns	

The Black K R P will cost a Rook.

2

MARGATE 1938

Black: E. E. Böök

Queen's Gambit Accepted

1. P—Q 4	P—Q 4
2. P—Q B 4	P × P

The Queen's Gambit Accepted leads to a game in which Black gives up the centre and attempts to compensate for this by an early Queen's-Side Pawn advance. In preparing and making this advance, he is liable to fall behind in development and unless therefore he plays the opening with great accuracy he may easily succumb to a White attack breaking through in the centre.

3. Kt—K B 3	Kt—K B 3
4. P—K 3	P—K 3
5. B × P	P—B 4
6. Castles	Kt—B 3

This natural move is not the best. The correct line is 6. ....P—Q R 3; 7. Q—K 2; P—Q Kt 4; 8. B—Kt 3, B—Kt 2; 9. R—Q 1, Q Kt—Q 2; 10.

P—Q R 4, P—Kt 5; 11 Q Kt—Q 2, Q—B 2; with an equal game. On Q 2 the Knight supports the Q B P and leaves the Q B an open diagonal besides giving temporary protection to the Q after R—Q 1. On B 3 it is misplaced as the course of this game shows.

7. Q—K 2	P—Q R 3
8. Kt—B 3	P—Q Kt 4

This is now too dangerous. 8. ....B—K 2; 9. R—Q 1, Q—B 2; should be played, but after 10. P × P, B × P; 11. P—Q R 3 White's superior development gives him rather the better game.

9. B—Kt 3	P—Kt 5

There is no good move here. If 9. ....B—K 2; 10. P × P, B × P; 11. P—K 4 !, Kt Q 2 (best); 12. P—K 5, with advantage to White. If 9. ....B—Kt 2; 10. R—Q 1, Q—Kt 3; 11. P—Q 5 !, P × P 12. B × P, P—Kt 5; 13. B × P ch ! (Stahlberg–Böök, Kemeri 1927) winning easily, e.g. 13. ....K × B; 14 Q—B 4 ch, K—K 1; 15. Q—K 6 ch, B—K 2; 16. Kt—K 5, R—K B 1; 17. Kt—B 4 and 18. Kt—Q 6 ch.

If 9. ....P × P; 10. R—Q 1 !, Q—Kt 3; 11. P × P, Kt—Q R 4; 12 B—B 2, B—K 2; 13. Kt—K 5, Castles; 14. B—Kt 5, R—R 2; 15. R—Q 3 (Ichim v. Troyanovsky, 1940) with a strong attack. If 9. ....P—B 5; 10. B—B 2, B—K 2; 11. P—Q R 4 with advantage.

The text-move is as good a chance as any.

10. P—Q 5 !	Kt—Q R 4

If 10. ....P × P; 11. Kt × P !, Kt × Kt; 12. R—Q 1, Q—B 2 (12. ....B—K 3 ?; 13. P—K 4, Q Kt—K 2; 14. P × Kt, B moves; 15. P—Q 6) 13. B × Kt followed by P—K 4 with a beautiful position. If 10. ....P × Kt; 11. P × Kt, P × P; 12. B × P and White again has much the better of the position.

11. B—R 4 ch	B—Q 2
12. P × P	P × P
13. R—Q 1	

Beginning a remarkable sacrificial attack. It is possible that Black might theoretically have avoided loss but Spielmann's remark to Böök after the game is the best comment on this, "How can you play like that ? Such sacrifices are always correct in over-the-board play!" Moreover, even an Alekhine will not normally analyse exhaustively such a sacrifice—he will examine as many variations as he can in the limited time available, and for the rest trust, that if his general judgment of the position is correct, he will be able to find a reply to an unexpected counter-stroke.

13.	P × Kt
14. R × B !	Kt × R
15. Kt—K 5	R—R 2
16. P × P !	

Played with extraordinary coolness! A Rook behind, White calmly stops to recapture a Pawn. 16. Q—R 5 ch would not have been good because of 16. ....P—Kt 3; 17. Kt × P, P × Kt; 18. Q × R, K—B 2; and Black should win.

Position after White's 16th move

| 16. ...... | K—K 2 |

Here, if anywhere, was Black's chance to save the game. The natural move 16. ....P—Kt 3; will not do as shown by Böök in the following analysis: 16. ....P—Kt 3; 17. Q—Q 3 !, K—K 2 (17. ....B—Kt 2; 18. Kt × Kt, R × Kt; 19. B—R 3); 18 P—K 4 !, Kt—B 3 (18. ....Kt × Kt ? ?; 19. B—Kt 5 ch); 19 Q—B 3, B—Kt 2; 20. B—K Kt 5, R—B 1; 21. R—Q 1, Q—B 2; 22. Kt—Q 7, Q × Kt; 23. R × Q ch, R × R; 24. B × R, K × B; 25. Q—Q 3 ch, K—B 1; 26. Q × P ch, Kt—Kt 2; 27. Q—B 6 ch, K—Kt 1; 28. B—B 4 ch, K—R 2; 29. B—B 7 followed by mate. Black's only chance lies in an immediate return of almost all the sacrificed material which he can offer in two ways. A. 16. Q—Kt 1; 17. Kt × Kt, R × Kt; 18. Q × P, Q—B 2; 19. Q × P ch (best), K—Q 1; 20. P—K 4 !, threatening B—B 4 and B—Kt 5 ch and it is difficult to find anything good for Black, e.g. 20. ....B—K 2 ?; 21. B—B 4 !, Q—Kt 2; 22. B × R, Q × B; 23. Q—Kt 6 ch, etc., or 20. ....Kt—Kt 2; 21. B—Kt 5 ch, K—Q 1 (21. ....B—K 2; 22. B × B ch, R × B; 23. R—Q 1 ch); 22. R—Q 1, B—Q 3; 23. P—K 5, or 20. ....Q—Q 3; 21. B—Kt 5 ch, B—K 2 (21. ....K—B 2; 22. B—B 4! or 21. ....K—B 1; 22. Q—K 8 ch, K—B 2; 23. B—B 4 !); 22. B × B ch, Q × B; 23. Q—Kt 6 ch, R—B 2; 24. Q—Kt 8 ch, R—B 1; 25. R—Q 1 ch. B. 16. ....B—K 2 !; this simple move threatening to Castle is the best chance. 17. Q—R 5 ch, P—Kt 3; 18. Kt × P, P × Kt; 19. Q × R ch, B—B 1 !; and now I can find nothing decisive for White. With two Pawns for the piece and a pair of Bishops and with Black still tied up, I think, however, that even in this variation White's practical chances are extremely good.

| 17. P—K 4 ! | Kt—K B 3 |
| 18. B—K Kt 5 | Q—B 2 |

19. B—B 4   Q—Kt 3

If 19. . . . . Q—Kt 2; 20. Q—K 3 !,
K—Q 1; (20. . . . . Kt × P; 21. B—
Kt 5 ch, Kt × B; 22. Q × Kt ch,
K—Q 3; 23. R—Q 1 ch, K—B 2;
24. Q—Q 8 mate); 21. Q—Q 3 ch,
K—B 1; 22. R—Kt 1, Q × P; 23.
Kt—B 7 ! and mate follows.

20. R—Q 1   P—Kt 3

White threatened B—K Kt 5 followed by Q—R 5. There is nothing
to be done.

21. B—K Kt 5   B—Kt 2
22. Kt—Q 7   R × Kt
23. R × R ch   K—B 1
24. B × Kt   B × B
25. P—K 5   Resigns

If 25. . . . . B moves; 26. Q—B 3
ch and mate follows—if 25. . . . . else;
26. Q—B 3 and the game is over.
An outstandingly brilliant game.

3

MARGATE 1938

Black: H. GOLOMBEK

Queen's Pawn, Nimzowitsch Defence

1. P—Q 4   Kt—K B 3
2. P—Q B 4   P—K 3
3. Kt—Q B 3   B—Kt 5

See Game No. 12 for a general
discussion of this defence.

4. P—K Kt 3

A slow and not particularly
effective method of proceeding
against the Nimzowitch Defence.
The chief point of the K fianchetto

is to put pressure on Black's Q 4 and
Q Kt 2. The Nimzowitsch Defence,
by pinning the Kt on Q B 3, automatically reduces this pressure to
some extent, and the K fianchetto is
not therefore a very suitable line of
play. If White wants to adopt this
formation he does better to play the
Catalan (see note to move 6).

4. . . . . . .   P—Q 4
5. B—Kt 2   Castles
6. Kt—B 3

Compare this position with a
corresponding position in the Catalan
after the following moves: 1. Kt—
K B 3, P—Q 4; 2. P—B 4, P—K 3;
3. P—K Kt 3, Kt—K B 3; 4. B—
Kt 2, B—K 2; 5 Castles, Castles;
6. P—Q 4, Q Kt—Q 2; 7. Kt—B 3.
White has exactly the same piece
position except that he has castled:
Black, however, has his B on K 2
instead of Kt 5 and his Q Kt on Q 2,
i.e. his whole position is more
cramped and defensive.

6. . . . . . .   P—B 4

Black plays the whole of the opening energetically and well: it is the
fact that his Bishop relieves the
pressure on his Q 4 that enables him
to challenge White so vigorously in
the centre.

7. B P × P   Kt × P
8. B—Q 2   Kt—Q B 3
9. P—Q R 3   Kt × Kt
10. P × Kt   B—R 4
11. Castles

If 11. P × P ?, Q—Q 4 !; with a
fine game.

11. . . . . . .   P × P

Now, however, White was threat-
ening 12. P × P, Q—Q 4; 13. Kt—
Q 4, Q × P; 14. Kt × Kt, P × Kt;
15. Q—R 4, B—Q 2; 16. B—K 3,
Q—B 4; 17. P—Kt 4 and ultimately
White wins a piece.

12. P × P	B × B
13. Q × B	Q—K 2
14. Q—Kt 2	

Position after White's 14th move

14. . . . . . .   R—Q 1 ?

Up to here Black has played extremely well, but this apparently harmless move causes a rapid deterioration in his game. The formation Black wants is B on Q 2, R's on Q Kt 1 and Q B 1 after which he has if anything a shade the better of the game, his long-term prospects being better than White's. He should therefore play 14. . . . . R— Kt 1 !; 15. K R—Q B 1, B—Q 2 ; etc. The text-move loses a vital tempo and White seizes the chance to prevent Black from executing the manœuvre satisfactorily. An instructive position and an object lesson of the danger of "routine" play.

15. K R—Q B 1 !   Q—Q 3

Now if 15. . . . . R—Kt 1 ?; 16. R × Kt ! and if 15. . . . . B—Q 2 ?; 16. Q × P.

16. P—K 3	R—Kt 1
17. Kt—Kt 5	B—Q 2
18. Q—B 2 !	

Black has played R—Kt 1 and B—Q 2, but to do so he has had to play his Queen away from K 2 (where it is needed) to Q 3 (where it is merely a nuisance) and White is able to exploit this tactically.

18. . . . . . .   P—B 4 ?

18. . . . . P—K Kt 3 ; is necessary, but after 18. . . . . P—K Kt 3 ; 19. Kt—K 4, Q—K 2 ; 20. Kt—B 5 White has the advantage on both sides of the board—on the Queen's side because of the immediate pressure and on the King's side because of the weakness on the Black squares.

19. P—Q 5 !

Position after White's 19th move

A beautiful and unexpected reply.

19. . . . . . .   Kt—K 2

Not 19. . . . . P × P; 20. B × P ch !, Q × B;   21. R—Q 1, Q any; 22. Q—R 2 ch, and wins. This "lightning from a clear sky" is characteristically Alekhine.

20. P × P	B × P
21. R—Q 1	Q—K 4
22. B × P	P—K R 3

Of course not 22. ....R × R ch;
23. R × R, R × B ? ?   24. R—Q 8
mate.

23. Kt × B	Q × Kt
24. Q—B 7	R × R ch
25. R × R	R—K 1
26. B—B 3	P—R 3
27. R—Q 6	Q—K 4
28. Q—B 4 ch	K—R 2
29. R × P	R—Q B 1

29. .... Kt—Kt 1; would prolong
the game without, however, giving
Black the faintest chance of saving
it.

30. Q—B 7	R—B 8 ch
31. K—Kt 2	Resigns

White threatens 32. R × P ch,
K × R; 32. Q—R 5 mate. If 31.
.... K—R 1; 32. R—K 6, Q—R 8;
33. R × Kt, R—Kt 8 ch; 34. K—
R 3, Q—B 8 ch; 35. K—R 4,
P—Kt 4 ch; 36. K—R 5, Q—R 6 ch;
37. K—Kt 6 and if 31. .... Kt—
Kt 1; 32. Q—Kt 6 ch, K—R 1;
33. R—R 8, R—B 2 (to stop
Q—B 7); 34. R—K 8, Q—B 3;
35. Q × Q, P × Q; 36. B—Q 5,
R—Kt 2; 37. R × Kt ch, and in
either case White wins very easily.

4

PLYMOUTH 1938

Black: R. M. BRUCE

Caro Kann

This "miniature" and the game
against Navarro given in the notes
illustrate an interesting opening
trap in the Caro Kann and show
in pointed fashion the dangers of
transposition.

1. P—K 4	P—Q B 3
2. Kt—Q B 3	

White's idea is to delay P—Q 4
and to transpose into a variation of
the Caro in which he can make use
of his spare move. Black falls into
the trap, continuing mechanically as
if White had played P—Q 4 instead
of using the transposition to play a
line not otherwise available to him.

2.	P—Q 4
3. Kt—B 3	P × P

3. ....B—Kt 5; 4. P—K R 3,
B × Kt; 5. Q × B, P—K 3; is also
satisfactory for Black who has a
solid position and has disposed of his
Q Bishop, usually a problem piece
in the irregular defences. One of
the great advantages of the Caro
Kann is that it is much less difficult
to develop the Q B than in either
French or Sicilian. 3. .... P—Q 5;
is playable, but after 4. Kt—K 2,
P—Q B 4; 5. P—Q 3 White has a
slight advantage—he will be able to
play P—K Kt 3 (if 5. ....B—Kt 5;
6 Kt—B 4 and 7 P—K R 3 or even
6. P—K R 3 at once—Black's Pawns
being on Black squares, he does not
want to exchange his Q B), B—Kt 2,
Castles, Kt—K 1 and P—K B 4
with an excellent game.

4. Kt × P	B—B 4 ?

A very instructive mistake. If
the White Pawn is on Q 4 and K Kt
on Kt 1 this is correct, the "book"
being 5. Kt—Kt 3, B—Kt 3;
6. P—K R 4, P—K R 3; 7. Kt—B 3,
Kt—Q 2; 8. B—Q 3, B × B; 9.
Q × B, P—K 3; with a very slight
positional advantage to White. In
the actual game there is the vital
difference that Black cannot play
Kt—Q 2 in time to prevent White's
Kt—K 5. Black should play 4.
....B—Kt 5 ! (a move that is not
available in the normal variation);
5. Kt—Kt 3, Kt B 3; 6. B—K 2,
P—K 3; 7. Kt—K 5, B × B;
8. Q × B, Q—Q 4; followed by
P—B 4 and Kt—B 3 with equality.
4. .... Kt—B 3; is also good.

5. Kt—Kt 3   B—Kt 3 ?

Rushing blindly on to his doom. 5. ....B—Kt 5 was relatively best admitting his error on the previous move.

6. P—K R 4   P—K R 3
7. Kt—K 5 !

Now the effect of the transposition of moves becomes only too clear to Black.

7. ......   B—R 2

Here Alekhine/Navarro (Madrid, 1940) continued 7. ....Kt—Q 2; 8. Kt × B, P × Kt; 9. P—Q 4 (preventing Kt—K 4), P—K 4; 10. Q— Kt 4, Q—B 3; 11. B—K 3 ! (if 11. B—K Kt 5, Q—B 2 !; —the text holds B—Kt 5 as a threat, e.g. 11. ....Castles ?; 12. B—K Kt 5 ! winning the exchange), Kt—K 2 ? (fatal, but Black's position is hopelessly compromised whatever he does) ; 12. Kt—K 4!; Resigns. The Black Queen is lost.

Final Position in the game v. Navarro

8. Q—R 5   P—K Kt 3
9. B—B 4 !

Gaining an important tempo.

9. ......   P—K 3
10. Q—K 2   Kt—B 3 ?

Disastrous, but after 10. ....Q— B 2; 11. P—Q 4. Black has a lost game.

11. Kt × K B P !

Position after White's 11th move

11. ......   K × Kt
12. Q × P ch   Resigns

12. ....K—Kt 2; 13. Q—B 7 mate.

5

AVRO 1938

Black: Dr M. EUWE

Queen's Gambit Declined (Slav Defence)

1. P—Q 4   P—Q 4
2. P—Q B 4   P—Q B 3
3. Kt—K B 3   Kt—B 3
4. P × P   P × P

Like a good many symmetrical variations, this is less innocuous than it appears at first sight. In all symmetrical openings the danger for Black lies in the fact that he cannot indefinitely continue to imitate White (*cf.* his 7th move in this game) and is liable to find himself confronted with a position in which White makes a strong aggressive move and Black is forced to make a very humble reply, with consequent disadvantage: examples of this can be found not only in the Slav but in the 4 Knights', Petroff's Defence and the English opening. 4. .... Q × P; is of course not good here because of 5. Kt—B 3 and 4. .... Kt × P; is met by 5. P—K 4.

5. Kt—B 3	Kt—B 3
6. B—B 4	B—B 4
7. P—K 3	

7. Q—Kt 3 is ineffectual because of 7. .... Kt—Q R 4; 8. Q—R 4 ch, B—Q 2.

| 7. ...... | P—Q R 3 |

Not 7. .... P—K 3; since then 8. Q—Kt 3 ! is very strong, 8. .... Kt—Q R 4; 9. Q—R 4 ch, 8. .... Q—B 1; 9. Kt—Q Kt 5, and 8. .... Q—Q 2; 9. Kt—K 5, all giving White a winning game. However a good alternative to the text is 7. .... Q—Kt 3; 8. B—Q 3, B × B (8. .... Q × Kt P; 9. Castles, B × B; 10. Q × B gives White an overwhelming position for the sacrificed pawn); 9. Q × B, P—K 3; 10. Castles, B—K 2; and White has little, if any, advantage. The move played leads to complications in which it is difficult for Black to hold the position.

| 8. Kt—K 5 ! | R—B 1 |
| 9. P—K Kt 4 ! | |

A characteristic move transforming the game.

| 9. ...... | B—Q 2 ! |

Position after White's 9th move

A very difficult decision, but this unpleasant move is certainly the best. If 9. .... B—Kt 3; 10 P—K R 4 !, P—R 3 (10. .... Kt × Kt; 11. P × Kt, Kt—K 5; 12. Q—R 4 ch !, Q—Q 2; 13. Q × Q ch, K × Q; 14. Kt × P, R—B 4; 15. R—Q 1 and wins); 11. Kt × B, P × Kt; 12. B—Q 3 with a won game. Or 9. .... Kt × Kt; 10. P × B, Kt—B 5 (10. .... Kt—B 3; 11. B—R 3 ! and Black is hopelessly tied up) ; 11. Q—R 4 ch, Q—Q 2; 12. Q × Q ch, K × Q; 13. Kt—R 4 !, K—K 1 (14. B × Kt was threatened); and White has two Bishops with much the better game.

10. B—Kt 2

Not 10. P—Kt 5, Kt—K 5; 11. Kt × Q P ?, Q—R 4 ch !

| 10. ...... | P—K 3 |
| 11. Castles | |

11. P—Kt 5, Kt—K 5; 12. Kt × Kt, P × Kt; 13. B × P, Kt × Kt; 14. P × Kt, B—Kt 5 ch; 15. K—B 1, B—Kt 4 ch; 16. K—Kt 2, Q—K 2; would give Black compensation for the sacrificed Pawn.

| 11. ...... | P—K R 3 |

Now, however, this is necessary, or White will win a Pawn with impunity.

| 12. B—Kt 3 | P—K R 4 ? |

He should play 12. . . . .B—K 2;
and if 13. P—B 4, Kt × Kt; 14.
B P × Kt; Kt—R 2; and Black's
game is far from lost, since although
White has an advantage in space
and some attacking chances, he has
also weaknesses in his Pawn structure. For this reason 13. Kt × B,
Q × Kt; 14. P—B 4 might be a
shade better, but Black can then
play Kt—Q R 4—B 5 with counter-
chances on the Queen's wing.

| 13. Kt × B | Kt × Kt ? |

And after this move the game is
probably lost. 13. . . . .Q × Kt;
14. P—Kt 5, Kt—Kt 1 ; is necessary,
when Black's position, although
most unpleasant, might still be
defensible.

14. P × P	Kt—B 3
15. B—B 3	B—Kt 5
16. R—B 1	K—B 1

If 16. . . . .Castles ; 17. K—R 1
followed by R—Kt 1 gives White a
winning attack. The White Pawn
on R 5 is very dangerous should
Black castle since it prevents
P—K Kt 3 and White constantly
threatens P—R 6.

17. P—Q R 3	B × Kt
18. R × B	Kt—K 2
19. Q—Kt 3	R × R
20. P × R	

Although Black has succeeded in
reducing the material—the classical
method of diminishing the force of
an attack—White retains too many
advantages for the game to be
saved.

| 20. . . . . . . | Q—Q 2 |

If 20. . . . .P—Q Kt 4; 21. P—
Q R 4 and the Black Q R P will fall.

| 21. Q—Kt 6 | Kt—B 1 |

Otherwise 22. R—Kt 1 wins.

| 22. Q—B 5 ch | K—Kt 1 |
| 23. R—Kt 1 | P—Q Kt 4 |

White threatened 24. P—B 4

24. P—R 6

This Pawn, which has played a
major part throughout, makes a
final and decisive advance.

Position after White's 24th move

| 24. . . . . . . | P × P |

If 24. . . . .R × P; 25 P—Q R 4,
Kt—R 2; 26 Q—Kt 6, P × P;
27. Q × R P and White wins.

| 25. B—K 5 | K—Kt 2 |
| 26. P—Q R 4 | P × P |

This would not have been playable with the Black Rook on R 3
and K on Kt 1 because of R—Kt 8.

| 27. P—B 4 ! | Kt—K 2 |

27. . . . .P × P ?; 28. B × Kt ch,
K × B; 29. Q—K 5 ch and wins the
Rook.

| 28. P × P | Kt × P |

If 28. . . . .P × P; 29. R—Kt 6.

29. K—R 1 !

Not 29. B × Kt, P × B; 30. R—
Kt 6, Q—Kt 5 ch and White must
submit to perpetual check or release
the pin on the Knight. The text-
move, however, threatens this line
by forestalling Q—Kt 5 ch.

29.	R—Q B 1
30. R—Kt 1 ch	K—R 2
31. Q—R 3	R—K Kt 1

Forced to meet the threat of
22. Q—Q 3 ch, K—R 1; 33. B × Kt,
Q × B ch; 34. P—K 4. If 31. ....
Kt—K 1 ? 32. Q—B 8 followed by
mate. Now, however, Black loses a
piece.

32. P—K 4	R × R ch
33. K × R	Q—Kt 4
34. P × Kt	Q—Kt 8 ch
35. K—Kt 2	Q—Kt 3 ch
36. K—B 1	Q—Q Kt 8 ch
37. K—Kt 2	Q—Kt 3 ch
38. B—Kt 3	Kt × P
39. B × Kt	P × B
40. Q × P	P—K R 4
41. P—R 4	Resigns

The ending is of course quite hopeless. An original and forceful game.

6

AVRO 1938

Black: S. Flohr

Ruy Lopez

1. P—K 4	P—K 4

A sensation! Flohr almost invariably plays irregular defences
against P—K 4.

2. Kt—K B 3	Kt—Q B 3
3. B—Kt 5	P—Q R 3
4. B—R 4	Kt—B 3
5. Castles	B—K 2

The close form of the Morphy
defence, in which White's long-term
strategy is a King's side attack and
Black counters with an advance on
the Queen's wing.

6. R—K 1	P—Q Kt 4
7. B—Kt 3	P—Q 3
8. P—B 3	Kt—Q R 4
9. B—B 2	P—B 4
10. P—Q 4	Q—B 2
11. Q Kt—Q 2	

Here 11. P—K R 3 to prevent
B—Kt 5 is more usual. White
plays to get his Knight to K 3
(controlling B 5 and Q 5) as quickly
as possible—the drawback of the
line is that, since it allows Black to
put pressure on Q 4 by 12. .... B—
Kt 5, White is unable to keep the
centre fluid as long as in the normal
line.

11.	Castles
12. Kt—B 1	B—Kt 5
13. P × K P	

Against Fine (Margate 1936–37),
Alekhine here played 13. Kt—K 3,
B × Kt; 14. Q × B, BP × P; 15. Kt—
B 5 and in *My Best Games*, 1924–37
says that this Pawn sacrifice is
not quite sufficient but that he
should have played 15. P × P,
Kt—B 3; 16. P—Q 5, Kt—Q 5;
17. Q—Q 1, Kt × B; 18 Kt × Kt,
P—Q R 4; 19. B—Q 2, which he
says "Would have been in White's
favour." It seems to me that
Black is at little, if any, disadvantage
in this line and it was probably in
anticipation of this variation that
Flohr allowed the Lopez to be
played. If 13. P—Q 5, a position
similar to that in the 11. P—K R 3
variations arises, but better for
Black since after 11. P—K R 3 he
has to play Kt—B 3 to force
P—Q 5 after which he returns to
Q R 4, thus losing time.

13.	P × P
14. Kt—K 3	B—K 3
15. Q—K 2	K R—K 1

The idea of this move is that after an eventual Kt—Q 5 by White and an exchange on that square the Rook shall be ready to protect the K P. It would, however, be better to proceed at once with the Queen's side counter-attack by 15. ....P—B 5. If then 16. Kt—Kt 5, Kt—Kt 2; 17. Kt × B, P × Kt; 18. B—Q 2, Kt—B 4; with an equal game. Or if here 17 Kt—Q 5, B × Kt!; 18. P × B, B—Q 3 with a satisfactory game for Black.

| 16. Kt—Kt 5 | P—B 5 |
| 17. P—Q Kt 4 | P × P *e.p.* |

If 17. .... Kt—B 3; 18 Kt—Q 5, Kt × Kt; 19. P × Kt, B × Kt; 20. P × B, B × B; 21. P × P ch, Q × P; 22. Q R × B with the better game, White having a Bishop against a Knight and a strong square on K 4. If 17. .... Kt—Kt 2; 18. Kt × B, P × Kt; and White has a slight advantage because of his two Bishops and better Pawn formation —note that Black cannot now (in contrast to the variation in the previous note) get his Knight to Q B 4. This would, however, be better than the text as it would leave Black with fewer weaknesses. The point of P—Q Kt 4 is that whether Black exchanges or not, the pressure on White's Queen's side is completely eliminated.

18. Kt × B	P × Kt
19. P × P	P—Kt 5
20. P × P !	

Not the obvious 20. P—Q B 4 in reply to which Black can play Kt—Kt 2—B 4 blockading the passed Pawn with a good game.

| 20. ...... | B × P |
| 21. B—Q 2 | B × B |

If 21. .... Kt—B 3; 22. B × B, Kt × B; 23. Kt—B 4! Kt × B; 24. Q × Kt followed by Q—B 3 and R—R 5. The trouble with Black's

game is that he has two weak spots to watch, at K 4 and R 3, whereas White has only his Q Kt P to worry about. It would be much less serious for Black if he had not played 17. ....P × P *e.p.*; as he would then only have had the weakness on the K file and White would not have Q B 4 for his Knight.

22. Q × B	Kt—B 3
23. Q—B 3	Q—Kt 3
24. B—Q 3	Kt—Q 5
25. P—Q Kt 4	K R—B 1
26. Kt—B 4	Q R—Kt 1

If 26. ....Q moves; 27. R—R 5 and the K P will fall without compensation.

27. R—R 5	Q × P
28. Q × Q	R × Q
29. Kt × P	Kt—Kt 6

Position after Black's 29th move

It seems as if Black has extricated himself rather neatly—if the Rook retreats then 30. .... Kt—B 4; and White can only win the Q R P at the cost of his K P.

30. R × P ! !

A shattering surprise: it is amazing that White can safely allow the Kt—B 4 fork.

30. ......   Kt—B 4
31. R—Q B 1   R (5)—Kt 1
32. B—B 4 !   K—R 1

Not 32. ....Kt × R ?; 33. B ×
P ch, K—B 1; 34. R × R ch, R × R;
35. B × R with an easily won
end-game. However 32. ....K—
B 1; would be better than the text
and after 33. R—R 7 (I can see
nothing better), Kt(B 3) × P; Black
has good drawing chances although
White has a clearly superior position.

33. Kt—B 7 ch   K—Kt 1
34. Kt—Q 6   R—B 2

If 34. ....R—Q 1; 35. R—B 6,
retaining the Pawn with a winning
end-game.

35. R (6)—R 1   K—B 1
36. P—K 5   Kt—Kt 5
37. R—K 1   P—Kt 4

Hastening the end, but Black is
lost whatever he does.

38. R—R 3 !   Kt—K R 3
39. R—B 3 ch   K—Kt 2

If 39. ....K—K 2; 40. R—R 3
wins a second Pawn.

40. R—K Kt 3   P—Kt 5
41. P—R 3   K—R 1

Here the game was adjourned and
Black resigned without resuming—
after 42. P × P he has no chance of
saving the game.

7

AVRO 1938

Black: J. R. CAPABLANCA

French Defence

1. P—K 4   P—K 3
2. P—Q 4   P—Q 4
3. Kt—Q 2

This move—a favourite of Keres'
and, in his later years, of Alekhine's—preserves the option of
protecting the centre by P—Q B 3
and avoids the pin 3. ....B—Kt 5.
Its drawback, however, is that since
it puts less immediate pressure on
the Black centre than 3. Kt—Q B 3
it allows Black to counter safely
with the energetic 3. ....P—Q B 4 !
[See Game No. 35, v. Bartosek.]

3. ......   Kt—K B 3

This, although quite playable, is
rather less good than P—Q B 4,
since it leads to a type of game in
which it is valuable to White to
have P—Q B 3 available. Capablanca, however, having just lost to
Keres with 3. ....P—Q B 4; did
not care to try the move again.

4. P—K 5   K Kt—Q 2
5. B—Q 3   P—Q B 4
6. P—Q B 3   Kt—Q B 3

And this leads to a definite inferiority for Black. The best line
is 6. ....P—Q Kt 3; after which
White will not be able in the long
run to avoid the exchange of his K B
for Black's Q B. This exchange
greatly eases Black's position and
reduces White's attacking chances
as it leaves the latter somewhat
weak on the white squares.

7. Kt—K 2   Q—Kt 3
8. Kt—B 3

It is interesting to compare this
position with the somewhat similar
one that arises in Spielmann's
favourite variation 1. P—K 4,
P—K 3; 2. P—Q 4, P—Q 4; 3. Kt—
Q B 3, Kt—K B 3; 4. P—K 5, K Kt
—Q 2; 5. Q Kt—K 2, P—Q B 4;
6. P—Q B 3, Kt—Q B 3; 7. P—
K B 4, Q—Kt 3; 8. Kt—B 3. The
difference in the positions is that in
the present game the B stands on
Q 3 instead of K B 1 and the K B P
on B 2 instead of B 4. Both these
differences are favourable: the

developmeut of the B on Q 3 is obviously a great advantage and the preservation of K B 4 for the Kt and an open diagonal for the Q B also strengthens White's game.

8. ......   P × P
9. P × P   B—Kt 5 ch
10. K—B 1 !

In a closed position such as this loss of the privilege of castling is comparatively unimportant: it is much more important to prevent Black from easing his position by exchanges.

10. ......   B—K 2
11. P—Q R 3   Kt—B 1

Black should play 11. ....P—Q R 4; to stop 12. P—Q Kt 4. Note that if 11. ....Castles; 12. Kt—B 4 followed by P—K R 4 and Kt—Kt 5 would give White a winning attack. The effect of the Pawn on K 5 is virtually to prohibit King's side castling.

12. P—Q Kt 4 !

Further restricting Black.

12. ......   B—Q 2
13. B—K 3   Kt—Q 1
14. Kt—B 3   P—Q R 4
15. Kt—R 4   Q—R 2
16. P—Kt 5   P—Kt 3
17. P—Kt 3   P—B 4

Black now embarks on an attempt to free himself which merely hastens his defeat. However, if he does absolutely nothing (the alternative plan !), he will almost certainly succumb to an attack in the long run: White can prepare for P—K B 5 at his leisure and Black will not have room to post his pieces properly for the defence.

18. K—Kt 2   Kt—B 2
19. Q—Q 2   P—R 3
20. P—R 4   Kt—R 2
21. P—R 5!

K Kt 6 is a far more valuable square for White than Kt 4 or Kt 5 is for Black.

21. ......   Kt (B 2)—Kt 4
22. Kt—R 4   Kt—K 5
23. Q—Kt 2   K—B 2

Not 23. ....B × Kt ?; 24. P × B ! and the Kt on K 5 (which has gone to such trouble to get there) is trapped !

23. P—B 3   Kt (5)—Kt 4
25. P—Kt 4 !

A very fine move, resulting in the re-incarceration of Black's K R just as it was about to emerge.

25. ......   P × P
26. B—Kt 6 ch   K—Kt 1
27. P—B 4 !   Kt—B 6

If 27. ....Kt—K 5; 28. B × Kt, P × B; 29. Kt—Kt 6. If 27. .... Kt—B 2; 28. B—Q 3, Kt—B 1; 29. Q—K 2 followed by Q × P and R (either)—K Kt 1. Finally if 27. ....Kt—R 6; 28. B × Kt ch, R × B (28. .... K × B; 29. Q—B 2 ch); 29. Kt—Kt 6 followed by Q—K 2 and Q × P. In every case White wins easily.

28. B × Kt ch   R × B

Or 28. ....K × B; 29. Q—B 2 ch, K—Kt 1; 30. Kt—Kt 6 and wins.

29. Kt—Kt 6   13. B—Q 1
30. Q R—Q B 1   B—K 1

Position after Black's 30th move

31. K—Kt 3 !

Winning the Knight in an original manner.

31.	......	Q—K B 2
32.	K × P	Kt—R 5
33.	Kt × Kt	Q × R P ch
34.	K—Kt 3	Q—B 2
35.	Kt—K B 3	

Here Black exceeded the time limit, but his position was of course quite hopeless in any case. This fine game was the last between the two great rivals and was Alekhine's only tournament victory against Capablanca. Black lost the game because his weak opening play allowed White to obtain an unbreakable grip on the centre: in variations in the French where White has Pawns on K 5 and Q 4 the result turns on whether or not Black can destroy the White centre —in this game he was not able even to threaten it seriously.

8

CARACAS 1939

White: KAUSZ

Dutch Defence

1. P—Q 4   P—K B 4

This enterprising defence was always a favourite of Alekhine's. It aims at using the Pawn on K B 4 to control the centre and as a spearhead of a later King's side attack. White's best line of play is an immediate King's fianchetto which (a) prevents the satisfactory development of Black's Q B, (b) sets up the strongest King's side defensive position, (c) prepares for central advance by P—K 4 which is the best way of meeting Black's projected flank attack. In this game we see what happens when White plays weakly, mistiming his moves, and allows Black to attain his objectives without difficulty.

2. Kt—K B 3

2. P—K Kt 3 is better and in many variations this Knight is better on R 3, whence it can effectively go to B 4.

2. ......   Kt—K B 3
3. P—B 4

Again committing himself prematurely ; 3. P—K Kt 3 ! should be played.

3. ......   P—K 3
4. Kt—B 3   B—Kt 5

Now we see the result of White's routine play: Black is able to occupy K 5, to fianchetto his Q B and to place his K B aggressively on Kt 5—all because White played moves which, though usually good in the Queen's Pawn, have no revelance to the needs of this position.

5. B—Q 2   Castles
6. Q—B 2

Vainly attempting to force Black to give up his K B as a price for occupying K 5; an immediate P—K Kt 3 would be a little better.

6. ......   P—Q Kt 3
7. P—K Kt 3   B—Kt 2
8. B—Kt 2   Kt—K 5
9. Castles K R

Better 9. Kt × Kt, B × Kt; 10. Q—Q 1, Kt—B 3; Castles.

9. ......   Kt × B
10. Kt × Kt   B × B
11. K × B   Kt—B 3

Now Black has a clear superiority in position, with good attacking chances on the K side and the better minor piece position.

12. P—K 3   P—K 4 !
13. Kt—Q 5 ?

Presumably overlooking the force of Black's reply. Best is 13. P × P, Kt × P; 14. Kt—Q 5, B—Q 3; Black has still much the better of affairs, since he can play Q—K 1— R 4 (as in the game) with a strong King's side attack, but White's position is defensible.

13. ......   P × P
14. P—K 4

14. Kt × B, Kt × Kt; 15. Q—Kt 3, P × P; loses a Pawn without compensation. This being so, White is right to try and "mix it"—at worst the result will be a quick death instead of a slow one.

Position after White's 14th move

14. ......   P—B 5 !

Finely played. After the obvious 14. ....B × Kt; 15. Q × B, P × P; 16. Q R—K 1, R—K 1; 17. Q—B 4 Black's win will be a good deal more difficult than it is after the text-move.

15. Kt—K B 3   B—Q 3
16. Q—Q 2   Q—K 1

A typical move in the Dutch: in most openings in which P—K B 4 is played (by either side) Q—K 1— Kt 3 or R 4 is a very strong attacking manœuvre.

17. Q R—K 1   Q—R 4
18. Kt—R 4

18. Kt × Q P, dangerous though it looks, would give White much better practical chances. Best is then 18. .... Kt × Kt ! (18. .... P—B 6 ch; only leads to equality, White having a defence in every variation); 19. Q × Kt, P—B 3 !; 20. P—K 5 ! (20. Kt × BP ?, B × Kt; 21. P × B, Q—Kt 5 ch; 22. K—R 1, Q—B 6 ch; 23. K—Kt 1, R × P and wins or 20. Kt—B 3 ?, P—B 6 ch; 21. K—R 1, Q—R 6; 22. R—Kt 1, R—B 3 !; and wins), P × P ! (again P—B 6 ch is not so good as it looks); 21. B P × P, R × R; 22. R × R, B—B 4; 23. Kt—B 4, B × Q; 24. Kt × Q, B × K P and Black has a winning ending. It is remarkable that there is no stronger line for Black, but in every case White just seems to survive, e.g. 18. .... P—B 6 ch; 19. K—R 1, Q—R 6; 20. R—K Kt 1, Kt—K 4; 21. Kt— B 4, R × Kt (21. ....Q—R 3; 22. Kt—B 5); 22. P × R, Kt—Kt 5; 23. R × Kt, Q × R; 24. R—K Kt 1, Q × P; 25. Q × Q, B × Q; 26. Kt × P, and if in this variation 20. .... B—Kt 5 ! ?; 21. Kt × B, Kt—K 4; 22. Kt—Q 3!, Kt—Kt 5; 23. Kt × P, R × Kt; 24. R—Kt 2.

18. ......   P—B 6 ch
19. K—R 1   Q R—K 1
20. Kt—B 5   Q—Kt 5 !

The point of this move is that White dare not protect the K P by 21. Q—B 2 or Q 3 because of 21. ....Q—R 6; 22. R—K Kt 1,

R × Kt!;   23.   P × R,   R × R   and wins. The White Queen is tied to the protection of the Rook.

Position after Black's 20th move

21. P—Kt 4

If 21. Kt × B, P × Kt; followed by ....R—K 4—R 4 winning quickly. Or 21. Kt—B 4, B × Kt; 22. Q × B, Q—R 6 !; followed by .... P—Kt 3; winning a piece. Or 21. Kt × Q P, Kt × Kt; 22. Q × Kt, R—K 4; and White is helpless against the threat of Q—R 6 and R—R 4.

21. ......   R × P
22. R × R

If 22. Kt × B, R—K 7 !;   23. R × R, P × R; 24. R—K Kt 1, R × P;   25. Kt—B 4, Q—B 6 ch; 26. Kt—Kt 2, P × Kt winning in a few moves.

22. ......   Q × R
23. Kt × B   Q—K 7 !
24. Q—B 1

24. Q × Q, P × Q;   25. R—K 1, P—Q 6; 26. Kt—K 4, Kt—Q 5; 27. Kt—B 4, R × Kt; 28. P × R, Kt—B 6; 29. R—Q Kt 1, P = Q; 30. R × Q, Kt × R; 31. K—Kt 1, Kt—B 6 ch; 32. K—B 1, Kt × P ch; leaves White hopelessly lost.

c

24. ......   P × Kt
25. Kt—B 4   R × Kt !

The game is of course easily won for Black—all that remains is to admire the speed and efficiency with which it is finished.

26. P × R   Kt × P
27. K—Kt 1   Kt—Q 6
28. Q—Q 1   Kt × P (B 7)
29. Resigns

For if 29. Q × Q, Kt—R 6 ch !; 30. K—R 1, P × Q; 31. R—K 1, P—Q 6 and wins.

9

BUENOS AIRES 1939

Black : E. ELISKASES

Caro Kann

This rather quiet game is difficult to annotate in detail and a general description may be helpful. White gains a slight initiative out of the opening which allows him to post his pieces more aggressively than Black. An injudicious Pawn move (16. ....P—K R 3 ?) weakens Black's King's side and, despite the reduced material, enables White to obtain a permanent grip on the position. Alekhine gradually increases the pressure and finally Eliskases (32. .....R—Kt 4 ?) makes an error leading to a lost Rook endgame—at this stage, however, the game was probably gone anyway.

1. P—K 4   P—Q B 3
2. P—Q 4   P—Q 4
3. P × P

It is harder to build up an attack against the Caro Kann than against any other defence; the associated proposition, that if White is content to draw it is easier for him to do so than against most defences, also holds good. Such being the nature of the defence, it is an excellent line to play against Alekhine, and it is interesting to see that neither in this game nor in that against Richter (Game No. 25) does he succeed in building up an attacking position from the opening. The line played here (the Panov attack) can lead to great complications, but only if Black is prepared to allow these: he can always—as here and in the Richter game—avoid them if he likes and maintain an equal, or very nearly equal position.

3.	P × P
4. P—Q B 4	Kt—K B 3
5. Kt—Q B 3	P—K 3

The most solid line of play avoiding the uncertain complications arising from 5. . . . . Kt—B 3; 6. B— Kt 5.

| 6. Kt—B 3 | B—K 2 |
| 7. P × P | |

Deciding to content himself with a minimal positional advantage—a surprisingly modest line for Alekhine to adopt. The strongest line is 7. B—Kt 5, Castles; 8. R—B 1 ! as in Botvinnik-Konstantinopolsky [see Game No. 25 v. Richter, for further comment on this].

| 7. . . . . . . | Kt × P |

If 7. . . . . P × P; 8. B—Kt 5 ch, B—Q 2; 9. B × B ch, Kt × B; 10. Castles, Castles; 11. B—B 4 with a similar position to that in the game, but one giving White slightly more chances since each side has an additional piece, usually an advantage to the player with the freer game.

| 8. B—Kt 5 ch | B—Q 2 |
| 9. B × B ch | Kt × B |

If 9. . . . . Q × B; 10. Kt—K 5, Kt × Kt; 11. P × Kt (not 11. Q—B 3 ! ?, Q × P !; 12. Q × P ch, K—Q 1; with advantage to Black), Q—Kt 4; 12. P—Q B 4, Q—R 4 ch; 13. B—Q 2, B—Kt 5; 14. R—Q Kt 1 and White has rather the better game, his superior development and advantage in space more than compensating him for the weaknesses in his Pawn position.

10. Kt × Kt	P × Kt
11. Q—Kt 3	Kt—Kt 3
12. Castles	Castles
13. B—B 4	B—Q 3
14. B × B	Q × B

Position after Black's 14th move

Most players would feel inclined to abandon this position as a draw. White, however, has two advantages—pressure on the Q P and Q Kt P, and a better placed Knight, and he exploits these with great skill.

15. K R—K 1

Black threatened 15. . . . . Kt—B 5 (if 16. Q × P ?, K R—Kt 1; winning the Queen); and White could not reply 16. Kt—K 5 because of 16. . . . . Kt—Q 7; winning the exchange. After 15. K R—K 1, however, he can meet 15. ....Kt—B 5; with 16. Kt—K 5, and if then 16. Kt × Kt; 17. R × Kt winning a Pawn.

| 15. ...... | Q R—B 1 |
| 16. Q R—B 1 | P—K R 3 ? |

Both players need to make a hole for the King, but this is not the right way to do it since now after 17. Kt—K 5 Black will not dare to turn the Knight out by P—B 3. 16. ....P—Kt 3; was much better.

17. Kt—K 5	R—B 2
18. P—Kt 3	K R—B 1
19. R × R	R × R
20. Q—Kt 5	Kt—Q 2

Or 20. ....R—K 2; 21. Q—R 5, P—B 3; 22. Kt—Kt 6, R × R ch; 23. Q × R and in spite of the very reduced material White still has good winning chances because of Black's weakness on the white squares.

21. Kt × Kt	R × Kt
22. R—K 8 ch	K—R 2
23. P—K R 4 !	

Position after White's 23rd move

| 23. ...... | P—R 3 |

If 23. ....P—K R 4 (to prevent P—R 5 once and for all); 24. Q—K 2, Q—K Kt 3; 25. R—K 5, Q—Kt 8 ch; 26. K—R 2, P—K Kt 3; 27. R × P ch, P × R; 28. Q × P ch, K—K 2; 29. Q—Kt 4 ch and White should win though the Q and P ending is not easy. Or 24. .... P—K Kt 3; 25. R—R 8, P—R 3; 26. Q—K 8 and wins. Naturally, if 23. ....R—K 2; 24. R × R, Q × Q; 25. Q × Q P.

24. Q—K 2	R—Q 1
25. R—K 7	R—Q 2
26. R—K 5	P—K Kt 3

Black cannot release White's grip on his position, e.g. 26. ....Q—K Kt 3; 27. P—R 5, Q—Kt 8 ch; 28. K—Kt 2, Q × R P; 29. Q—B 2 ch, P—Kt 3; 30. Q—B 8, Q—R 5; 31. P × P ch, P × P (31. ....K × P; 32. Q—Kt 8 ch, K—B 3; 33. P—K Kt 4, Q × P; 34. Q—R 8 ch, K—Kt 3; 35. R—Kt 5 ch ! and wins); 32. R—K 8, R—KB 2 !; 33. R—R 8 ch, K—Kt 2; 34. Q—Kt 8 ch, K—B 3; 35. R × P, Q—B 7; 36. Q—Q 8 ch, K—K 3; 37. Q—K 8 ch, etc.

| 27. P—R 5 | Q—K B 3 |
| 28. Q—Q 3 | R—Q 3 |

This turns out badly, but Black has no satisfactory move: White threatens to tie him up completely by 29. Q—Kt 3, Q—Q 3; 30. R—K 8. The idea of the text-move is to meet R—K 8 with R—K 3.

| 29. Q—Kt 3 ! | R—Kt 3 |
| 30. P × P ch | Q × P |

If 30. ....P × P; 31. Q × P followed by Q—Q 7 ch.

| 31. Q × P | R × P |
| 32. R—B 5 | R—Kt 4 ? |

Position after Black's 32nd move

Fatal. The best chance was 32. ....K—Kt 1; but after 33. R—B 4 White's passed Pawn should win as the Black Queen is permanently tied to the defensive.

33.	R × P ch !	K—Kt 1
34.	R—B 6 ch	R × Q
35.	R × Q ch	K—R 2
36.	R—Kt 6	R × P
37.	R × P ch	K—Kt 1
38.	R—Kt 6	R—Q R 5
39.	R × K R P	R × P

This type of ending is always an easy win for the player with the two Pawns.

40.	K—Kt 2	P—R 4
41.	R—R 6	P—R 5
42.	R—R 7	P—R 6
43.	P—Kt 4	R—R 8
44.	K—Kt 3	R—Kt 8 ch
45.	K—B 4	R—Q R 8
46.	P—Kt 5	K—B 1
47.	K—B 5	Resigns

There is nothing to be done, *e.g.* 47. ....P—R 7 (threat R—K B 8); 48. P—B 4, K—K 1; 49. P—Kt 6, K—B 1; 50. K—B 6. A model of how to exploit a small positional advantage.

10

BUENOS AIRES 1939

Black: A. ZVETCOFF

Sicilian

1.	P—K 4	P—Q B 4
2.	Kt—K B 3	P—Q 3
3.	P—B 3	

A favourite line of Alekhine's and rather better than its reputation. It is, however, preferable to play it a move earlier as in Alekhine–Podgorny [Game No. 28]. Readers who are tired of well-worn paths might well try the variation, which has the advantage of giving rise to a type of game somewhat different from the normal Sicilian: it resembles more the Danish 1. P—K 4, P—-K 4; 2. P—Q 4, P × P; 3. P—Q B 3, P—Q 4; but is rather better for White.

3.	......	Kt—K B 3

This would have been inferior against 2. P—Q B 3 since then 3. P—K 5 would have driven the Knight away with gain of time: this is the reason why it is better to play 2. P—Q B 3 rather than 3. P—B 3.

4.	P—K 5	P × P
5.	Kt × P	Kt—B 3 !

Well played. Black's advantage in development and open lines is full compensation for his weakened Pawn position. Moreover White's Q P is a mark for attack.

6.	Kt × Kt	P × Kt
7.	B—B 4	B—B 4
8.	P—Q 3	P—K 3
9.	Q—B 3	Q—Q 2
10.	P—K R 3	

Sooner or later this will be necessary to prevent B or Kt—Kt 5.

10. ....   B—K 2

If 10. ....B—Q 3; 11. Kt—Q 2
followed by Kt—K 4.

11. Kt—Q 2

Better to play first 11. Castles in
order to meet 11. ....R—Q 1; with
12. R—Q 1.

11.	R—Q 1
12. Castles	B × P
13. B × B	Q × B
14. Q × P ch	Q—Q 2 ?

This allows White to exchange
Queens on his own terms. Better
14. ....R—Q 2; 15. Kt—B 3
(otherwise Black can castle in
peace and will keep the Queens on
with excellent middle-game chances),
Q—Q 4; 16. Q × Q, P × Q; with
equality. Black is too anxious to
avoid complications . . .

15. Q—R 6 ?

. . . and White is too anxious to
produce them! He should simply
exchange Queens with the better
end-game.

15.	Castles
16. Kt—B 4	Q—B 2
17. Q—R 5	Q × Q ?

Allowing White to rectify his
previous error. He should play
17. ....Q—Kt 2; 18. B—K 3,
Kt—Q 4!; 19. B × P, Kt—B 5;
20. Kt—K 3 (best), B × B; 21.
Q × B, Q × P (threatening 21. ....
Q × B P; 22. Q × Q, Kt—K 7 ch;);
and Black has at least an equal
game. Now, after an indifferently
played middle-game, there is a most
instructive ending in which White
exploits in truly masterly style the
weakness of the Black Queen's side
Pawns.

| 18. Kt × Q | R—Q 3 |
| 19. B—K 3 | R—R 3 |

20. Kt—Kt 3   R—B 1

If 20. ....P—B 5; 21. Kt—Q 2,
R—B 1; 22. P—Q Kt 3, Kt—Q 4;
23. B—Q 4, B—B 3; 24. Kt × P,
Kt × P; 25. B × Kt, B × B; 26.
Q R—B 1 with advantage to White;
or, here, if 22. ....P × P; 23.
P × P, R × R; 24. R × R, R × P;
25. R × P, B—B 1; again with
advantage to White. This would,
however, have been a better chance
than the text. White now prevents
P—B 5 and then gradually squeezes
the life out of Black. In my view
it is generally better in endings of
this type for the player with the
inferior game to precipitate a crisis
rather than to try to hang on by
purely defensive manœuvres.

21. P—Q B 4!

Not only preventing P—B 5 but
taking away Q 4 from the Black
Knight.

| 21. ...... | K—B 1 |
| 22. K R—Q 1 | R—Q 3 |

Further reducing the material—
the correct policy for the player on
the defensive. The remaining R, B
and Kt are, however, just enough for
White to exercise decisive pressure
on the Queen's wing.

23. R × R	B × R
24. R—Q 1	K—K 2
25. Kt—R 5	B—K 4

He must play this or R—B 2 to
meet the threat of Kt—Kt 7:
White's reply is the same in either
case.

26. R—Q 3!   R—B 2

If 26. .... B × P; 27. R—Kt 3,
B—K 4; 28. R—Kt 7 ch winning
the Q R P since if 28. ....R—B 2;
29. Kt—B 6 ch and wins a piece.

It is the difference between White's active and Black's passive Rook that decides the game.

27.	R—Kt 3	Kt—Q 2
28.	P—B 4	B—Q 3

If 28. . . . . B—Q 5; 29. B × B, P × B; 30. R—Q 3 and wins a Pawn and if 28. . . . . B—B 3; the Bishop cannot take part in the defence of the Queen's side. Notice the excellent timing of White's moves ; if 27. P—B 4 ?, B × Kt P ; and if White delays until Black has played Kt—Kt 3, then . . . . B—Q 5 will be possible.

29.	K—B 2	Kt—Kt 3
30.	K—B 3	K—Q 2
31.	R—Q 3	K—K 2

White threatened 32. P—Q Kt 4, K—K 2 (32. . . . . P × P ?; 33. P—B 5); 33. R × B, K × R; 34. P × P ch, R × P; 35. Kt—Kt 7 ch and wins—or 32. . . . . Kt—R 5; 33. P × P, Kt × P; 34. B × Kt, R × B; 35. Kt—Kt 7, R—B 3, 36. P—B 5 and wins.

32. P—K Kt 4

Here an alternative way to win is 32. P—Q Kt 4, Kt—Q 2 (33. R × B is the threat); 33. P—Kt 5, Kt—Kt 1 (otherwise 34. Kt—B 6 ch wins); 34. P—Q R 4 followed by Kt—Kt 3 and P—R 5—R 6, Kt—R 5—Kt 7. Alekhine, however, prefers to build up the position further while preserving all his options—undoubtedly the surest policy when one's opponent is helpless.

32.	. . . . . .	P—B 3
33.	P—K R 4	Kt—R 5
34.	R—Kt 3	Kt—Kt 3
35.	R—Kt 5	K—Q 2
36.	P—R 5	K—K 2
37.	P—R 3	

Position after White's 37th move

Having set up the best possible Pawn formation on the K side, White now returns to the Q side for the decisive attack. He will protect his Q B P with the K, thus freeing the Knight on R 5 which then goes to Q Kt 5.

37.	. . . . . .	K—Q 2
38.	K—K 4	K—K 2
39.	K—Q 3	K—Q 2
40.	Kt—Kt 3	Kt—R 5
41.	Kt—Q 2	K—B 3
42.	P—Kt 3	Kt—Kt 3
43.	Kt—K 4	Kt—Q 2
44.	R—R 5	B—K 2
45.	Kt—B 3	R—Kt 2
46.	Kt—Kt 5	

The Knight arrives—and the necessity for defending the second weak Pawn (Q R P) leads to an intensification of the attack on the Q B P, with fatal results for Black.

46.	. . . . . .	K—Kt 3
47.	P—Kt 4	P—Q R 3
48.	Kt—B 3	K—B 2

Otherwise Kt—R 4 ch will win the Q B P.

49.	R × P	P × P
50.	Kt—Kt 5 ch	K—Q 1
51.	P × P	B × P
52.	R × P	B—B 4
53.	B—Q 2	Kt—B 1

White threatened 54. B—R 5 ch, B—Kt 3 (54. .... Kt—Kt 3; 55. R—B 6, B—Kt 8; 56. P—B 5); 55. R × B !, R × R (55. .... Kt × R ; 56. P—B 5); 56. K—Q 4, K moves; 57. B × R with an easily won ending. If 53. .... R—Kt 1 ; 54. B—R 5 ch, K—B 1 ; 55. R—B 6 ch, K—Kt 2; 56. R—B 7 ch, K—R 3 ; 57. R × Kt, K × B; 58. R × P.

54. R—B 6	Kt—Q 2
55. K—K 4	K—K 2
56. K—Q 5	B—Kt 8
57. B—Kt 4 ch	K—Q 1
58. K—K 6 !	Resigns

Black must give up a piece to avoid mate in 2 by 59. B—K 7 ch and 60. Kt mates. A beautiful end-game.

Final Position

11

BUENOS AIRES 1939

White: M. Czerniak

English

1. P—Q B 4	Kt—K B 3
2. Kt—Q B 3	P—K 4
3. P—K Kt 3	P—Q 4

4. P × P	Kt × P
5. B—Kt 2	Kt—Kt 3
6. Kt—B 3	

The opening is a Sicilian (Dragon variation) with colours reversed. White, however, can take advantage of his move in hand to turn the game into a different channel from that of the normal Dragon by 6. Kt —K R 3 ! followed by Castles and P—B 4 (a line developed and played with much success by H. Golombek). By this method the Black centre and Queen's side is kept under severe pressure and it is difficult for him to equalise. The text-move, however, allows Black immediate equality.

6.	Kt—B 3
7. Castles	B—K 2
8. P—Q 3	Castles
9. B—K 3	P—B 4

An energetic move, forcing White to proceed with his Queen's side plans rather faster than he would like. 9. P—Q R 4, P—Q R 4; 10. B—K 3 would have been better for White since he would then always have had the threat of B × Kt leaving Black with the inferior Pawn position. Now, however, he does not wish to capture on Kt 3 because of R P retakes. Consequently he has to take hurried steps to protect Q B 5 and his minor pieces become awkwardly placed.

10. Kt—Q R 4	P—B 5
11. B—B 5	B—Kt 5
12. R—B 1	B—Q 3

Otherwise White will play 13. B × B, Q × B; 14. Kt—B 5.

13. R—K 1

This is not a very satisfactory move, yet it seems to be necessary. White wants to occupy his strong point on K 4 with the K Kt, but he cannot play 13. Kt—Q 2 ? because of 13. .... Kt × Kt; 14. Q × Kt, B × P.

13. Kt × Kt, R P × Kt; is obviously unsatisfactory so he is driven to play the text-move.

13. ......   Q—K 2
14. Kt—Q 2   K—R 1 ! ?

Position after Black's 14th move

Threatening 15. .... Kt × Kt; 16. B × B, P × B; 17. Q × Kt, Kt—Q 5; with an excellent game for Black. If 14. .... Kt × Kt; 15. Q × Kt !, B × B; 16. Q—B 4 ch and White retains some Queen's side pressure. The text-move does, however, allow White an opportunity of winning a Pawn which he should have taken since it is very doubtful whether Black gets adequate compensation.

15. Kt—K 4 ?

Cowardly. He should play 15. B × B, P × B (15. .... Q × B; 16. Kt—B 5, B—B 1; 17. Kt (2)—K 4, Q—K 2; gives White an excellent game); 16. Kt × Kt, P × Kt; 17. B × Kt, P × B; 18. R × P, R × P; 19. R × Kt P, P—Q 4 (threat 20. .... Q—B 4); 20. Q—Kt 3 and White has the advantage.

15. ......   B × B
16. Q Kt × B   Kt—Q 5 !

Threatening 17. .... P—B 6; 18.

P × P, B × P; 19. Q—Q 2, B × B; 20. K × B, Kt—B 6; winning.

17. Kt—Kt 3

17. P—B 3, B—B 1; 18. P—K 3 !, P × K P; 19. R × P, Kt—Q 4; 20. R—K 1, P—B 3 !; 21. Kt—Kt 3 is a better line for White, giving him counter play in the centre.

17. ......   P—B 3

If 17. .... Kt × P ch; 18. R × Kt, P—B 6 ?; 19. R—K 1 ! or 17. .... B × P; 18. R × B, P—B 6; 19. Kt × Kt ! or 17. .... Kt × Kt; 18. Q × Kt, P—B 6; 19. P × P, B × P; 20. B × B, R × B; 21. R—K3 with equality or, finally, 17. .... P—B 6; 18. Kt × Kt !, P × B; 19. Kt—B 3.

18. Kt × Kt   P × Kt
19. Q—Q 2   Kt—Q 4
20. R—B 4

The attack beginning with this move merely leads to White's pieces being misplaced. It is difficult to find anything really satisfactory for him. 20. Kt—B 5 (to tie the Queen or induce the weakening move P—Q Kt 3) followed by passive defence is all I can see, but Black will probably win ultimately on the King's side.

20. ......   Q—K 4
21. P—Kt 4   Q R—Q 1
22. Q—Kt 2   Kt—Kt 3
23. R—B 5   R—Q 4
24. Q—R 3   Kt—Q 2 !
25. R × R

This gives up control of the important K 4 square which results in an immediate intensification of Black's attack. Alekhine suggests as an adequate defence 25. R (5)—B 1 and against 25. .... P—Q R 4 !; gives 26. Kt—B 5—but this is met by 26. .... P × P; 27. Kt × Kt, P × Q; 28. Kt × Q, R × Kt and

Black will win. Since any other reply to 25. ....P—Q R 4; leaves Black with a clear advantage on the Queen's side 25. R (5)—B 1 will not do and White's attack of the last 5 moves has been refuted.

25. ....   P × R
26. Kt—B 5   P—B 6 !

Position after Black's 26th move

The beginning of the end. The unprotected position of the R on K 1 (a direct consequence of White's ill-advised Queen's side adventure—other consequences will soon appear) allows Black to make this advance and break up the White position.

27. P—R 3

The best chance would be 27. Kt × Kt, B × Kt; 28. B—B 1 !, P—K R 4; 29. Q—B 1, R—K 1; 30. P—K 3, P—R 5; though Black, with the threat of R—K 3—R 3, should still win.

27. ......   P × B
28. P × B   Kt—B 3

Threatening 29. ....Kt × P.

29. P—Q Kt 5

Parrying the threat, which would now be met with 30. Kt—Q 7 winning.

29. ......   Q—K 2

Now, however, owing to the unfortunate position of White's Q the Kt is lost (the second consequence of White's attack !).

30. Q—Kt 4

If 30. Q—B 1, R—B 1 ; and wins.

30. ......   Kt—Q 2
31. Q × P

If 31. Kt—R 6, Q—B 3 ! and the Kt is lost.

31. ......   Kt × Kt
32. Q × P   R—Q 1
33. Q—B 3   R × P

Much stronger than 33. .... Kt × P ?; 34. R—Q 1, Kt—K 4; 35. R × R ch, Q × R ; 36. Q × Q Kt P with counter chances.

34. P × R   Q × R ch
35. K × P   Q—K 2
36. P—Q 4   Kt—K 5
37. Q—K 3   Q—K 1
38. P—B 3   Kt—B 3
39. Q—K 5   K—Kt 1
40. P—Kt 5   Q × Q
41. P × Q   Kt—Q 4
42. P—B 4   Kt—B 6
43. K—B 3   Kt × R P
44. P—B 5   Kt—B 6
45. P—Q Kt 6 P—Q R 4
46. K—K 3   Kt—Q 4 ch
47. K—Q 4   Kt × P
48. P—K 6   P—R 5
49. P—B 6   P × P

Of course not 49. ....P—R 6 ? ?; 50. P—K 7, K—B 2; 51. P × P winning.

50. P × P   P—R 6
51. Resigns

51. K—B 3 is forced, whereupon 51. ....Kt—B 5; followed by the advance of the Q Kt P wins at once.

12

BUENOS AIRES 1939

White: G. ENEVOLDSEN (Denmark)

Queen's Pawn, Nimzowitsch Defence

1. P—Q 4	Kt—K B 3
2. P—Q B 4	P—K 3
3. Kt—Q B 3	B—Kt 5

One of the most popular defences to the Queen's Pawn. By pinning the Knight, Black puts pressure on the centre while not yet committing himself to the advance of any particular Pawn—according to White's reply he can play either (1) P—Q 4 or (2) P—Q B 4 or (3) P—Q 3 and P—K 4. It is always a great advantage in the opening to be able to preserve one's options in this way, and this is one of the chief merits of the defence. Its main drawback is that in most variations Black has to give up his K B (always much the better of his two Bishops in Q P openings) for White's Q Kt and White remains with the advantage of two Bishops.

There are three main lines of play which White can adopt in reply. (1) Q—B 2 as played in the present game and in Games 31 and 37. Against this Black should play as Alekhine does here. (2) P—Q R 3 (Saemisch's line) dealing with the troublesome Bishop at once. Black's best line then is to try to exploit the weakness of the doubled Q B P by blocking the centre with P—Q 3, P—K 4 and P—Q B 4—having set up this formation he must at all costs avoid any exchanges of Pawns which would liquidate White's doubled Pawns and give the latter an overwhelming centre. If Black can satisfactorily fix the position he can later attack White's weakened Pawns. (3) P—K 3 (Rubinstein's and Botvinnik's line)

in which White plays quietly in the early stages and attempts later to get a steam roller Pawn advance by B—Q 3, K Kt—K 2, Castles, Q—B 2, Q R—K 1, Kt—Kt 3, P—K B 4, P—K 4, and so on. (Botvinnik-Capablanca is a classic example of this variation.) It is difficult for Black to maintain equality in this line, his best being an immediate P—Q Kt 3 followed by B—Kt 2 and P—Q 4; in this way he can maintain sufficient pressure on the centre to hold the position.

4. Q—B 2	Kt—B 3

The Milner-Barry variation, the most energetic line against 4. Q—B 2 or 4. Q—Kt 3, Black playing for an early P—K 4.

5. Kt—B 3	P—Q 3
6. B—Q 2	P—K 4
7. P—Q 5	

A positional error. White must play to remain with two Bishops in an *open* position: closing the position with P—Q 5 nearly always leads to Black getting an equal or superior game. 7. P × P, P × P; is also incorrect since, although the position is then kept open, Black can retain his two Bishops by B—K 2 or K B 1 later on. Correct is 7. P—Q R 3 !, B × Kt (7.....P × P; 8. P × B, P × Kt; 9. B × P, Q—K 2; 10. P—Kt 5, Kt—Q 1; 11. P—K 3, Kt—K 5; 12. B—Q 4, B—B 4; 13. B—Q 3 with advantage to White); 8. B × B, and White's Bishops operating on an open board give him a slight positional advantage.

7.	B × Kt
8. B × B	Kt—K 2
9. Kt—R 4	

An artificial move which does not turn out particularly well, but it is difficult to find a satisfactory plan for White. If 9. P—K 4, Kt—Kt 3 (stopping Kt—R 4—B 5); 10. P—K Kt 3, Castles; 11. B—Kt 2, Kt—R 4; 12. Castles, P—K B 4; and Black has a strong initiative. White's trouble is that he has lost time in getting his Queen's Bishop to a square on which it is misplaced. As a result he cannot prevent Black from gaining the initiative.

9. . . . . . .   Q—Q 2 !

As often happens, one artificial move is best met by another. Black now threatens Kt—Kt 3, forcing an exchange of Kt's or an ignominious retreat to K B 3 and White cannot play 10. P—K 4 because of 10. . . . . Q—Kt 5 !

10. P—K Kt 3   Q—Kt 5

Rather over-elaborate. The simple 10. . . . . Kt—Kt 3; 11. Kt × Kt, R P × Kt; gave Black a fine game without any more ado.

11. Q—Kt 3   Kt—Kt 3
12. P—B 3

Now White manages to avoid the exchange of Kt's and retains some pressure on K B 5 by the manœuvre Kt—Kt 2, P—K 4, Kt—K 3. The effect of this is to reduce Black's King's side prospects for which reason Alekhine switches over to Queen's side operations.

12. . . . . . .   Q—Q 2
13. Kt—Kt 2   Castles
14. P—K 4   Q—Q 1

Freeing Q 2 for the K Kt which he intends to play to Q B 4 with the double object of Q side pressure and of allowing P—K B 4 or K B 3. Black's loss of time (Q—Q 2—Kt 5— Q 2—Q 1) is not so serious as one might expect as it has compelled White also to indulge in a good deal of marching and counter-marching

(11. Q—Kt 3 and 16. Q—B 2 also Kt—R 4—Kt 2—K 3).

15. Kt—K 3   Kt—Q 2
16. Q—B 2   P—Q R 4
17. B—Kt 2

There is little point in B—R 3 since after Kt—K 2 and Kt—Q B 4 White must either retreat to Kt 2 or else give up his one potential advantage, the two Bishops.

17. . . . . . .   Kt—B 4
18. Castles K R   B—Q 2
19. P—Kt 3

The normal method in positions of this type, where White hopes to dislodge the Kt by P—Q R 3 and P—Q Kt 4 (P—Q R 3 can never be played at once because of the reply P—R 5 !). However White has lost more time in the opening than Black and therefore the latter is able to forestall him. If White attempts to block the position by 19. P—Q R 4 then after 19. . . . . Q—Kt 1 !; 20. P—Kt 3, Q—R 2; 21. K R—K 1, Kt—K 2; followed later by P—K R 4, Black stands well since the Kt's are better than the Bishops, and his Pawn structure is sounder than White's.

19. . . . . . .   P—Q Kt 4 !
20. Q R—Q 1 ?

A clear error of judgment yielding up the Q R file and allowing Black permanent pressure on the Q's side. He should play 20. P × P, B × P; 21. K R—K 1, Kt—K 2; after which Black's advantage is much less marked than in the text though he retains the initiative on both wings.

20. . . . . . .   P—Kt 5
21. B—Q 2   Q—Kt 1
22. R—Kt 1

Admitting his error and preparing to meet Black's attack on the Q Kt P.

22. ......   P—R 5
23. P—R 4

23. P × P, B × P; 24. Q—Kt 2, Kt—Q 6; 25. Q—R 1, Q—Kt 3; 26. K—R 1, Q—B 4; followed by doubling the Rooks on the Q R file would leave White quite lost. The trouble about this attempt to get counter play on the K side is that Black has no weaknesses there and is already well on the way to exploiting White's very real weakness on Q Kt 3: thus Black is able to keep White tied up in defence on the Q side and is never in any danger on the K's wing. Notice the almost contemptuous way in which Alekhine denudes his K side !

23. ......   Kt—K 2

Threatening P—B 4 with an attack on both sides of the board and thus forcing White's reply which, however, leaves weaknesses on White's K B 4 and K R 4 which Alekhine exploits drastically later in the game.

24. P—Kt 4   P × P
25. P × P   R—R 6
26. P—R 5   Q—Kt 3
27. K—R 2   K R—R 1

Threatening 28. .... R—R 7; 29. R—Kt 2, R × R; 30. Q × R, R—R 6; winning.

28. R—Kt 2   P—Q B 3 !

Position after Black's 28th move

Excellent timing. Black seizes the moment when his own pieces are placed to the maximum advantage, and when White is uncomfortably tied down in defence, to open up the game: the text-move has the very subtle tactical idea, besides, of allowing the Black Queen to return *via* Q 1 to the K side with devastating effect—typical Alekhine !

29. P—B 4   K P × P
30. R × P   R—R 8
31. P × P ?

This and the next move shows that he has quite failed to appreciate his danger. 31. R—B 1! was much better, when the position can still be held.

31. ......   Kt × B P
32. Kt—Q 5 ?

Merely driving the Queen where it wants to go. He has to meet the threat of 32. .... Kt—Q 5 !; winning the Queen but 32. Kt—B 5 is a much better way of doing this. After 32. Kt—B 5, Kt—K 4; 33. B—K 3, Q—B 2; I can see no forced win for Black although he has much the better position. The text-move is a final and fatal error.

32. ......   Q—Q 1
33. B—K 3

To stop 33. .... Kt—Q 5.

33. ......   Q—R 5 ch

34. B—R 3   Kt—K 4
35. B × Kt   P × B
36. Q—K B 2

If 36. Q—K 2 the same combination as in the text can be played and if anything else 36. .... B or Kt × Kt P; wins.

Position after White's 36th move

36.	R—R 8 ch !
37. K × R	Q × B ch
38. Resigns	

38. K—Kt 1, R—R 8 ch; 39. Q—B 1, R × Q ch; 40. R × R, Kt—B 6 ch; 41. K—B 2, Q—R 7 ch; 42. K × Kt, Q × R; and wins easily. A game in the grand manner, with operations on both sides of the board by Alekhine—to be able to co-ordinate one's pieces and integrate such a game is the mark of a great master.

13

MONTEVIDEO 1939

Black: H. GOLOMBEK

Sicilian

1. P—K 4 ⸵	P—Q B 4
2. Kt—K B 3	P—Q 3
3. P—Q 4	P × P
4. Kt × P	Kt—K B 3
5. Kt—Q B 3	P—K Kt 3
6. B—K 2	B—Kt 2

The formidable Dragon variation, in which Black sets up a strong defensive formation on the K side, hoping to use his open Q B file and the long diagonal as the basis of a powerful Queen's side counter-attack. This game is strategically interesting and unusual in that it is White—who usually reckons to win on the K side, if at all, against the Sicilian—who gets the Queen's side attack.

7. Kt—Kt 3

If this Kt does not retreat, Black sooner or later forces a simplification by Kt—K Kt 5. Since White has an advantage in space and (normally) means to make a King's side attack he avoids this possibility.

7.	Kt—B 3
8. Castles	Castles
9. K—R 1	

White wants to play P—K B 4, but this move (or B—K 3) is a necessary preliminary since, if 9. P—B 4, P—Q Kt 4 !; and if 10. B × P (or Kt × P), Kt × P !; 11. B × Kt, Q—Kt 3 ch; with a good game. K—R 1 does not represent a loss of time as in almost all cases when White plays P—K B 4 in the Sicilian he wants to have the K on R 1 either to avoid Q—Kt 3 ch, to give a retreat for his Bishop on Kt 1, or to play R—K Kt 1 and P—Kt 4. There are considerable points in delaying B—K 3 since in a number of variations when the Bishop is on K 3 Black can play P—Q 4 with threat of P—Q 5 forking B and Kt.

| 9. ...... | P—Q R 4 |

This move, threatening P—R 5—R 6 practically forces White to reply in kind, whereupon Black can play his Kt to Q Kt 5 without being driven off by P—Q R 3. Q Kt 5 is a good square for the Black Knight, since after Kt—Q Kt 5 Black not only attacks the Q B P but also threatens P—Q 4, a key move in the defence which, once played in safety, gives Black immediate equality. The drawbacks to P Q R 4 are similar to its advantages; it gives White also a strong square on his Q Kt 5 and weakens the Black Queen's side Pawn structure.

10. P—Q R 4	B—K 3

A difficult position. This move does not turn out well, largely because White immediately threatens to attack the Bishop and Black has not the resource Kt—Q R 4 and B—B 5 available. I prefer 10. Kt—Q Kt 5; 11. P—B 4, P—Q 4; 12. P—K 5, Kt—K 5; 13. Kt × Kt, P × Kt; followed as soon as possible by ....P—K B 3. If here 14. P—B 3, Q × Q ch; 15. R × Q (15. B × Q, Kt—Q 6;), Kt—B 7; 16. R—Kt 1, B—K 3; etc. This line in my opinion (and this is an occasion on which I am very ready to admit to error !) gives equality.

11. P—B 4	Q—B 1

To prevent 12. P—B 5. If 11. ....B × Kt; 12. P × B, Kt—Q Kt 5; 13. B—B 3 followed by B—K 3 and Q R—B 1 with a fine game. If 11. ....P—Q 4; 12. P—K 5, Kt—K 1 (12. .... Kt—K 5; 13. Kt × Kt, P × Kt; 14. Kt—B 5 with advantage); 13. Kt—B 5, P—Kt 3 (best); 14. Kt × B, P × Kt; after which Black's Bishop is locked out of the game and his Queen's side Pawns are weak. Or finally 11. .... Kt—Q Kt 5; 12. Kt—Q 4, P—Q 4; 13. P—B 5, P × P; 14. P × P, B—Q 2; and White has a strong centralized position with excellent attacking chances on the K side.

12. B—K 3

White has played the opening very cunningly since he has now reached a position similar to a standard position arising from 9. B—K 3, the difference being that White's K is on R 1, not Kt 1, and Black's Q is on Q B 1, not Q 1. In this variation this is a gain for White since K—R 1 is a very desirable move whereas the Q is not well placed on Q B 1.

12.	B—Kt 5
13. B—Kt 1	

So that after the exchanges of the next few moves he will have immediate pressure on the K file.

13.	R—Q 1

If 13. ....Kt—Kt 5 (to prevent Kt—Q 5); 14. B—Kt 6 !

14. Kt—Q 5 !	B × B
15. Q × B	Kt × Kt
16. P × Kt	Kt—Kt 5
17. P—B 4	

At first sight Black seems to have a moderately satisfactory game but he finds it impossible to defend both his weak Pawn on K 2 and his Queen's side.

17.	Q—B 2

If 17. ....R—K 1 or Q 2; 18. B—Kt 6.

18. Kt—Q 4	K R—Q B 1

The Q R dare not leave the weak Q R Pawn.

19. P—Q Kt 3	Kt—R 3
20. Q R—K 1	R—K 1
21. P—K B 5	Kt—B 4
22. Q—B 3 !	

Position after White's 22nd move

Initiating the winning combination: the Black Rook must be o rced away from the protection of \ e K P.

22. ......   K R—K B 1

22. ....B × Kt; 23. B × B (23. P × P ?, B—B 3 !;), P—B 3 (23. P—K 4; 24. B P × P e.p., P × P; 25. B × Kt winning a Pawn); avoids the loss of the Pawn but leaves Black with much the worse position because of his weakness on the K file. After the text-move he is lost.

23. Kt—Kt 5   Q—Q 2
24. B × Kt   P × B
25. Q—K 3

Winning a Pawn and the game. One has the feeling that Black must have made a slip and could easily have avoided this dénouement, but it is very difficult to discover just what he should have done ! His 22nd move was wrong, but his position was unhealthy then anyway—his 10th move was probably the root cause of the trouble, but it is a small error to cost the game.

25. ......   K R—K 1
26. Q × B P   P × P
27. Q—B 7   Q R—Q 1
28. Q × R P

Now the ending is an easy win.

28. ......   P—K 4
29. Q—B 7   Q × Q
30. Kt × Q   R—K 2
31. Kt—Kt 5   P—K 5

Or 31. ....P—B 5; 32. R × B P, etc.

32. R × B P   P—K 6
33. R—K 2   R—K 5
34. P—Kt 3   B—R 3
35. K—Kt 2   Resigns

Black has no defence against the advance of the Q side Pawns.

14

CONSULTATION GAME, RIO DE JANEIRO 1939

White: ALEKHINE, W. CRUZ
Black: SILVA ROCHA, CHARLIER, O. CRUZ

Queen's Gambit Declined

1. P—Q 4   Kt—K B 3
2. P—Q B 4   P—K 3
3. Kt—Q B 3   P—Q 4
4. Kt—B 3

A quiet line, in which White puts less pressure on the centre than in the orthodox variation 4. B—Kt 5. As a result of this Black can afford an early counter-attack than in the normal lines.

4. ......   B—K 2

4. ....P—B 4; is also good and is perhaps the easiest way to equalise.

5. B—B 4   Castles
6. P—K 3   P—Q R 3 ?

The cause of the loss of the game.
6. ....P—B 4 !; is correct, equalising, e.g. 7. P × B P, B × P; 8.
P × P, Kt × P; 9. Kt × Kt, P × Kt;
10. B—Q 3, B—Kt 5 ch; 11. K—B 1
(11. Kt—Q 2, P—Q 5;), B—Q 3; and
although Black has an isolated Q P
White has had to move his King—
there is little in it either way.

7. P—B 5 !

Taking immediate advantage of
Black's error to establish a strangle-
hold on the position. If (as is the
case here) Black cannot effectively
break White's hold by P—K 4; he
will almost always lose through lack
of space.

7. ......   Q Kt—Q 2
8. B—Q 3   R—K 1

Threatening 9. ....B × P !; 10.
P × B, P—K 4; etc.

9. P—Q Kt 4   P—B 3

He wants to play P—Q Kt 3 but
must first prevent P—B 6.

10. P—K R 3

Not 10. Castles ?, Kt—R 4 !; and
White loses his valuable Q Bishop.
Kt—R 4 does not constitute a
danger until after White has castled
since Black will not dare to capture
on Kt 3 as long as White can utilise
the Rook file.

10. ......   P—Q Kt 3

Threatening 11. P × P, Kt P × P;
12. B × P, P × B; 13. P—K 4. •

11. B—R 2   P × P
12. Kt P × P   P—K 4

Position after Black's 12th move

A temporary Pawn sacrifice
enabling Black to free his game—
but only at the cost of fatal weaknesses in his Queen's side Pawn
position. However any other
method of play would allow White
to exploit his great advantage in
space and win at his leisure by
occupying the files on the Queen's
side and attacking the Q B and
Q R Pawns.

13. Kt × P

Not 13. P × P, Kt × B P !; 14.
P × Kt, B × P; 15. R—B 1, Q—R 4;
16. Q—Q 2 (16. Q—B 2, B × Kt ch;
17. Q × B, Kt × B ch), P—Q 5; and
Black has the advantage since if
14. Q Kt moves, Kt × B ch.

13. ......   Kt × Kt
14. B × Kt   B × B P
15. Castles

Best. Now Black's Q B P is left
very weak.

15. ......   B—Q 3
16. P—B 4   Q—K 2

Threatening 17. ....Kt—Q 2
which would force White to exchange
Bishops.

17. Q—B 2   P—Kt 3

18.	Kt—R 4	B—Kt 2
19.	Q R—Kt 1	R—R 2

If 19. ....R (either)—Kt 1; 20. Kt—B 5 and White wins at least a Pawn.

20. R—Kt 3

Not immediately R × B as after 20. R × B, R × R; 21. Q × P. Black gets a counter-attack by 21. .... R—Q 2 !; 22. B × Kt, Q × P ch; 23. R—B 2, R—B 2; 24. Q × B, R—B 8 ch;

20. ...... Kt—Q 2

Allowing the sacrifice, but there is no good move. If 20. ....R— Q B 1; 21. R × B, R × R; 22. B × P, etc. Black's game is positionally lost.

Position after Black's 20th move

21.	R × B !	R × R
22.	Q × P	B × B

It would be a little better to play 22. ....Kt × B; but after 23. B P × Kt, B—R 6; 24. Q × Q P Black would have little chance of saving the game.

23.	Q × R	B—Kt 2
24.	K—R 2	R—Kt 1

D

25.	Q × Q P	Q × P
26.	B—B 4	Q × P

After the Queen exchange the ending is a fairly easy win for White. 26. ....Q—K 2; would have enabled Black to offer a considerably longer resistance without affecting the ultimate result.

27.	Q × Q	B × Q
28.	R—Q 1	Kt—B 4
29.	R × B	Kt × Kt
30.	B × R P	Kt—B 4
31.	B—B 4	Kt—K 3
32.	R—K 4	R—Kt 5
33.	K—Kt 3	K—Kt 2
34.	B—Q 5	R—Kt 3
35.	K—B 3	R—Q 3
36.	B × Kt	P × B
37.	P—Q R 4	R—B 3
38.	P—R 5	P—R 4
39.	R—R 4	R—R 3
40.	K—K 4	P—R 5
41.	K—Q 4	K—B 3
42.	K—B 5	P—Kt 4
43.	P × P ch	K × P
44.	K—Kt 5	R—R 1
45.	P—R 6	K—B 4
46.	R × P	P—K 4
47.	R—Q R 4	Resigns

If necessary White can always give the Rook for the Black K P and win with his own K side Pawns.

15

BRILLIANCY PRIZE
MUNICH 1941

Black: H. ROHACEK

Ruy Lopez (Morphy Defence)

1.	P—K 4	P—K 4
2.	Kt—K B 3	Kt—Q B 3
3.	B—Kt 5	P—Q R 3
4.	B—R 4	Kt—B 3
5.	Castles	Kt × P

In the open form of the Morphy defence, Black gets greater freedom than in the close form 5. ....B— K 2, but at the cost of a slight loosening of his defensive position. The most typical games in this variation (of which Euwe is the great exponent) are those in which White builds up a King's side attack with a Pawn on K 5 as the spearhead, Black countering by an advance on the Queen's side where he gets 4 Pawns to 3.

6. P—Q 4	P—Q Kt 4
7. B—Kt 3	P—Q 4
8. P × P	B—K 3
9. P—B 3	B—K 2

The alternative 9. ....B—Q B 4; gives Black some attacking chances because of his superior development, but White, by careful play, can meet the attack adequately whereupon the position reacts against Black who requires the square Q B 4 for his K Kt or Q B P. 9. ....B—K 2; is certainly strategically correct.

10. P—Q R 4

Alekhine intends to make a speculative sacrifice of his K P (by Kt—Q 4) hoping to profit from the large number of more or less vulnerable pieces on the open K file. He plays P—Q R 4 first with the idea of either getting the open Q R file as well (as in the game) or else (if 10. ....P—Kt 5;) of undermining Black's grip on his (Black's) Q B 5. Objectively, this idea is not particularly good— Black should certainly be able to maintain equality—but the tense and complex position produced is just the type that Alekhine played to perfection.

10. ...... R—Q Kt 1

Too passive. He should play 10. ....P—Kt 5; and then if 11. Kt—Q 4, Kt × K P; 12. P—B 3,

Kt—B 4; 13. B—B 2, P—Kt 6 !; 14. B × P, Kt × B; 15. Q × Kt, Castles; with complete equality. 10. ....P—Q 5, suggested by Alekhine himself, is refuted by 11. R P × P, R P × P (11. ....B × B; 12. Q × B, R P × P; 13. Q × P !); 12. R × R, Q × R; 13. B × B, P × B; 14. R—K 1, Kt—B 4; 15. P × P followed by P—Q 5.

| 11. P × P | P × P |
| 12. Kt—Q 4 | Kt × K P |

He must accept the sacrifice otherwise White will get an overwhelming game by P—K B 4.

13. P—B 3

Not 13. P—K B 4 ?, B—K Kt 5 !; 14. Q—B 2, Kt—B 5; and Black has an excellent game.

| 13. ...... | Kt—B 4 |
| 14. B—B 2 | |

Now Black has not got the resource P—Kt 6 available and therefore cannot eliminate the White K B; further, the Rook is uncomfortably placed on Q Kt 1 because of the latent danger of a fork by Kt—B 6.

| 14. ...... | B—Q 2 |
| 15. P—Q Kt 4 | Kt—Kt 2 |

If 15. ....Kt—K 3; 16. P—B 4, Kt—B 5 (16. ....Kt—B 3; 17. Kt × K Kt, B × Kt; 18. P—B 5, B—B 1; 19. B—Kt 3 or 16. ....Kt × Kt; 17. Q × Kt, Kt—Kt 5; 18. Q × Q P !, Castles; 19. R—Q 1); 17. Kt—B 5, B—B 3 (17. ....P—Q B 3; 18. Kt × B, Q × Kt; 19. P—B 5 and 20. R—K 1); 18. Q × P. In every case White recovers the Pawn with an excellent game.

| 16. Q—K 2 | Kt—B 5 |
| 17. R—K 1 | K—B 1 |

Otherwise 18. B—Kt 5 will force a further weakening of his position.

18. B—B 4   Kt (2)—Q 3

18. .... B—Q 3; is rather better. If 19. B × B, Kt (2) × B; and the exchange has eased Black's position, and if 19. B—B 1 ?, Q—R 5; 20. P—Kt 3, B × P; with at least a draw.

19. Kt—Q 2

Position after White's 19th move

19. ......   P—Kt 4 ?

Those whom the Gods would destroy . . . Black's position, although difficult, is still quite defensible after 19. .... Kt × Kt; 20. Q × Kt, Kt—B 5; 21. Q—K 2, B—K B 3 (not 21. .... B—Q 3 ?; 22. B × B, Kt × B; 23. Q—K 5);— White's command of the board is worth the sacrificed Pawn but Black can hold the game.

20. Kt × Kt !   P × B

If 20. .... Kt × Kt ?; 21. B × B P ! and wins, and if 20. .... P (either) × Kt; 21. B—K 5, P—K B 3; 22. B—K Kt 3 Black has hopelessly weakened his position.

21. Kt—K 5   B—K B 3

Best. If 21. .... R—Kt 3 ?; 22. R—R 8 ! winning material however Black plays.

22. Kt (Q 4)—B 6   Q B × Kt
23. Kt × B   Q—B 1
24. Kt × R   Q × Kt

The game now reaches a critical stage for White. He has won the exchange, but there is a reaction (as so often happens in such cases) and he is forced to allow Black considerable counterplay. Alekhine handles the position with great coolness and accuracy.

25. Q—Q 2   Q—Kt 3 ch
26. K—R 1   Q—B 3
27. B—Kt 3 !   B × P
28. Q—B 1 !

28. K R—B 1, B × Q; 29. R × Q, P—Q 5; 30. R × P, B × P; would give Black some drawing chances. The text-move forces P—Q 5, opening the diagonal for White's Bishop and enabling White to build up a new attack.

28. ......   P—Q 5

If 28. .... Kt—B 4; 29. B × P, Kt—Kt 6 ch; 30. P × Kt, Q—R 3 ch; 31. K—Kt 1, B—Q 5 ch; 32. K—B 1, Q—R 8 ch; 33. K—K 2, Q × P ch; 34. K—Q 3 and wins.

29. Q × B P

Position after White's 29th move

29. ......   P—Q 6

This loses quickly, but the game is gone. If 29. ....Kt—B 5; 30. B × Kt, P × B; 31. Q—K 5, R—Kt 1; 32. P—Kt 5, Q—Kt 2; 33. Q—B 5 ch, K—Kt 2; 34. Q—Kt 5 ch, K—B 1; 35. Q—R 6 ch, R—Kt 2; 36. Q—R 6 ! !, Q × Q; 37. P × Q, R—Kt 1; 38. P—R 7, K—Kt 2; 39. K R—Q Kt 1 !; followed by R—Kt 8 winning (Alekhine), a beautiful variation. Or 29. ....B × Q R; 30. Q—B 6, R—Kt 1; 31. B × P, P—Q 6; 32. R × B and wins. The best chance is 29. ....B × K R; 30. R × B (best), Q—B 6; 31. Q—K 5, R—Kt 1; 32. B—Q 5 !, Q—B 7 !; 33. P—Kt 4, P—Q 6; 34. R—R 1, Kt—K 1 !; 35. R—R 8, Q—Q 8 ch; 36. K—Kt 2, Q—K 7 ch; 37. Q × Q, P × Q; 38. K—B 2, K—Kt 2; 39. K × P, Kt—Q 3; 40. R × R ch, K × R; 41. K—Q 3 and White wins comfortably, e.g. 41. ....K—Kt 2; 42. K—Q 4, K—B 3; 43. P—B 4 followed by K—B 5.

30. K R—Q B 1   P—Q 7
31. R—B 2   Q—R 3

A very forlorn hope !

32. R—Q 1   B—Kt 2
33. R × B P   Resigns

An interesting and rather unusual game.

16

MUNICH 1941

White: P. LEEPIN

English

1. P—Q B 4   P—K 4
2. Kt—Q B 3   Kt—K B 3
3. P—K Kt 3   P—Q 4

4. P × P   Kt × P
5. B—Kt 2

For general comments on this opening see Game No. 11 (Czerniak-Alekhine).

5. ......   Kt—Kt 3
6. P—Q R 4

Premature: this move is better delayed until after Black has moved the K B.

6. ......   P—Q R 4

Otherwise White will play P— R 5—R 6.

7. P—Q 3   B—Q Kt 5

As a result of White's 6th move Black now gets this strong post for his Bishop.

8. Kt—B 3   Kt—B 3
9. Castles   Castles
10. B—K 3   B—Kt 5
11. R—B 1

11. P—R 3 is preferable since if 11. ....B—K 3; 12. Kt—K Kt 5 followed (if Bishop moves) by P—B 4 and there is no other entirely satisfactory square for Black's Bishop.

11. ......   P—B 4

Setting a subtle trap...

12. Kt—K Kt 5

...into which White falls. 12. P— K R 3 is correct. If 12. ....B × Kt; 13. B × B, P—B 5; 14. Q B × Kt with equality and if 12. ....B—R 4; 13. Kt—K Kt 5 ! and now 13. .... P—B 5; is not playable because of 14. Kt—K 6, Q—K 2; 15. Q B × Kt, Q × Kt ? ?; 16. B—Q 5.

12. ......   P—B 5 !
13. Q B × Kt   Q × Kt

14. B × B P

White has now won a Pawn, but at the cost of the game.

14. ...... Q—R 4

Better than 14. ....Kt—Q 5; which can be met by 15. P—B 3. If now 15. P—B 3, B—B 4 ch; 16. K—R 1, P × P; and wins at once.

15. B × Kt

If 15. B—B 3, B × B; 16. P × B, R—B 3; and Black wins easily. Or 15. R—K 1, Kt—Q 5; 16. P—B 3, P × P; 17. P × P, B—Q B 4!; and wins.

15. ...... P × B
16. R—B 2

Or 16. R—K 1, P × P; 17. RP × P, R × P!; 18. K × R, B—B 4 ch; and wins.

16. ...... B × Kt
17. R × B

If 17. P × B, P—B 6!; and White must give up the Queen to avoid mate.

17. ...... B × P
18. Q—Kt 3 ch K—R 1
19. R—K 1

Position after White's 19th move

19. ...... Q—R 6!

An elegant final touch.

20. B × P

Or 20. R × B, P—B 6.

20. ...... P—B 6
21. Resigns

A slight game, but typical Alekhine!

17

MUNICH 1941

White: G. KIENINGER

Ruy Lopez (Classical Defence)

1. P—K 4   P—K 4
2. Kt—K B 3   Kt—Q B 3
3. B—Kt 5   B—B 4

Theoretically this is very slightly inferior to the more usual lines, because it does not give sufficient support to the Black centre in consequence of which White can secure the control of the centre. In order to do this, however, he must play with vigour and be prepared to enter into complications: if he plays quietly Black will have no difficulty in equalising since, apart from his temporary insecurity in the centre, his pieces are well posted. It is, therefore, an excellent defence for a player such as Alekhine to play occasionally against a weaker player, since the latter (as in this game) is likely to shirk the hazards involved in the correct line and to play timidly.

4. P—B 3   Q—B 3

4. ....B—Kt 3; 5. P—Q 4, P × P; 6. P × P, Q Kt—K 2! (to exploit the position of the W B on Kt 5); 7. Kt—B 3, P—Q B 3; 8. B—Q 3, P—Q 4; 9. P—K 5, B—Kt 5; 10. B—K 3, Kt—B 4; is Black's strongest line and leaves White with a minimal advantage. In this variation, however, Black has all the strange moves to play, and White's play is straightforward. Alekhine chooses instead a line throwing the onus on White.

5. Castles

Wrong. He should play 5. P—Q 4, P × P; 6. P—K 5!, Q—Kt 3 (6. ....Kt × P ?; 7. Q—K 2, etc.); 7. P × P, B—Kt 5 ch; 8. Kt—B 3, P—Q 4; 9. Castles, Kt—K 2; 10. Q—Kt 3, B × Kt; 11. P × B and White's two Bishops, open lines and strong centre give him a marked positional advantage.

5. ......   K Kt—K 2
6. P—Q 3

Now if 6. P—Q 4, P × P; 7. B—Kt 5, Q—Kt 3; 8. B × K Kt, Kt × B; 9. P × P, B—Kt 3; 10. Kt—B 3, Castles; Black has little if any the worse of it, his two Bishops practically compensating for his disadvantage in space. It would, however, be a shade stronger for White than the line played.

6. ......   P—K R 3
7. Q Kt—Q 2   Castles
8. Kt—B 4   Kt—Kt 3
9. P—Q 4

This is a case of better never than late: having missed at least one excellent opportunity of P—Q 4 White now plays it at a most inappropriate moment. He should play 9. P—Q Kt 4, B—Kt 3; 10. P—Q R 4, P—R 3; 11. Kt × B, P × Kt; 12. B—B 4, P—Q 3; 13. B—K 3, Kt—B 5!; and White cannot continue 14. B × P ? because

of 14. ....B—R 6!; 15. Kt—K 1, Q—Kt 3; 16. Q—B 3, B—Kt 5; 17. Q—K 3, B—K 7. The position (after 13. .... Kt—B 5!;) would be about level, Black having a considerable initiative to compensate him for his weakened Pawn formation.

9. ......   P × P
10. B × Kt   Q P × B !
11. Kt × P

No doubt White had intended to play here 11. P × P and found when he reached the position that after 11. P × P, R—Q 1!; 12. B—K 3, B—K Kt 5; he would have a lost game, e.g. 13. Q—B 2, B × Kt; 14. P × K B, Kt—R 5!; 15. P—K Kt 3, Q—K 3!; and wins—or if 13. P—K 5, Q—K 3!; and wins at least a Pawn. After the text-move, Black gets an advantage in space which his two Bishops and superior development enable him to exploit in an overwhelming manner.

11. ......   R—K 1
12. Kt—Kt 3   B—B 1
13. Q—B 2 ?

After this White's game goes rapidly downhill. 13. P—K B 3 is essential, though after 13. .... B—K 3; 14. Q—K 2, Q R—Q 1; Black has a considerable positional pull.

13. ......   Q—K 3 !

Far stronger than the more obvious B—K 3, which could be met with Kt—K 3. Now the double attack on Kt and K P forces White to obstruct himself in horrible fashion.

14. Kt (4)—Q 2   Kt—R 5
15. P—B 3   P—Q B 4 !

Taking away White's last good square, Q 4.

16. R—Q 1

16. R—B 2 is better, but Black's better development and two Bishops give him sufficient positional advantage to win in the long run anyway. He now settles matters by a farsighted sacrifice.

Position after White's 16th move

16. ......   Kt × Kt P !
17. K × Kt   Q—R 6 ch
18. K—Kt 1

If 18. K—R 1, B—Q 3; 19. P—K B 4, B—B 4 !; 20. R—K 1, B × P; 21. Kt—B 1, B × P ch !; and wins.

18. ......   B—Q 3
19. Kt—B 1   Q × P
20. R—Q 3

If 20. Q—Q 3, Q × Q; 21. R × Q, P—B 5; and wins.

20. ......   Q × P
21. R—Q 2

21. ....P—B 5; was threatened.

21. ......   Q—K R 5 !
22. R—Kt 2

If 22. R—B 2, B—R 6; 23. B—Q 2, R—K 3, threatening R—Kt 3 ch followed by Q × R and

Black wins. White is unable to complete his development without loss of material.

22. ......   B—R 6
23. Q—B 2   Q—K 5

Simplifying into a winning ending.

24. B—Q 2   Q × R ch
25. Q × Q   B × Q
26. K × B

Position after White's 26th move

The end-game is hopelessly lost for White, not so much because of his material disadvantage as because he cannot find any good posts for his minor pieces: the outcome in Rook and minor-piece endings very often depends on whether or not the player with the minor pieces (particularly if they are Knights) can find strong squares for them in the centre.

26. ......   R—K 7 ch
27. K—B 3   Q R—K 1
28. R—Q 1   P—Q Kt 3
29. Kt—B 1   R (7)—K 3
30. P—Kt 3   P—B 5 !

A temporary sacrifice, smashing White's Q side Pawns.

31. P × P

If 31. P—Kt 4, P—Q Kt 4; and White is completely tied up, Black winning at his leisure by the advance of K side (and, if necessary, Q side) Pawns.

31.	R—B 3 ch
32. K—Kt 2	R—K 5
33. Kt—K 3	B—B 4
34. R—K 1	B × Kt
35. R × B	R—Kt 5 ch
36. R—Kt 3	R × P
37. R—B 3	R—Q 3
38. B—B 4	R—Q 8
39. Kt—K 2	R—Q R 8
40. K—Kt 3	P—Q B 4

Merciless: the Knight is not to be allowed to come into the game.

41. R—K 3	R × R P
42. P—K R 4	P—Q Kt 4
43. P—R 5	P—Kt 5

44. Resigns.

After 44. P × P, P × P; White has no chance.

18

SALZBURG 1942

White: P. KERES

King's Gambit

1. P—K 4	P—K 4
2. P—K B 4	

This game was played in the last round of the tournament. Alekhine having 6½/9, Keres 6/9, and the other competitors being out of the running. Keres therefore had to go all out for a win, which explains his somewhat rash play.

2.	P × P

While it is somewhat safer for the average player to decline the gambit

by 2. .... P—Q 4 or 2. .... B—B 4, it is generally thought to be fundamentally sounder to accept it.

3. Kt—K B 3	Kt—K B 3

If 3. .... P—Q 4; 4. P × P, Kt— K B 3; 5. P—B 4!, P—B 3; 6. P—Q 4, P × P; 7. B × P and White's central Pawns give him good chances. The text-move avoids this line—if White replies 4. Kt—B 3, P—Q 4; 5. P × P, Kt × P; Black has nothing to fear, and the alternative 4. P—K 5 (as played) gives Black at least equality.

4. P—K 5	Kt—R 4
5. Q—K 2 ?	

This in conjunction with White's 7th move is a new idea in this variation—but not a very good one. Since the normal line 5. P—Q 4, P—Q 4; 6. P—B 4, Kt—Q B 3; 7. P × P, Q × P; 8. Kt—B 3, B— Q Kt 5; gives Black a satisfactory position with a Pawn plus Keres decides to delay Black's P—Q 4 and to prepare for Queen's side castling. Black, however, simply continues with his development, is able to play P—Q 4 as soon as he really needs to, and White's unnatural Queen move recoils on his own head.

5.	B—K 2
6. P—Q 4	Castles
7. P—K Kt 4 !?	

A corollary of 5. Q—K 2 with the following objects: (1) to permit the development of the Bishops; (2) to give White open lines for a King's side attack. If White does not play this move he will have to move his Queen again to develop the K B, and the Pawn on K B 5 will exercise a cramping effect on his whole game. The disadvantage of opening files in this way, *i.e.* by Pawn sacrifices that do not disturb the opponent's Pawn formation is that one has then no Pawns left with which to storm the King's position: for this reason Alekhine finds comparatively little difficulty in defending himself.

7. ......   P × P e.p.
8. Kt—B 3

Position after White's 8th move

8. ......   P—Q 4 !

Avoiding the tempting 8. .... B—R 5; 9. P × P !, Kt × P (9. .... B × P ch; 10. K—Q 1, Kt—B 5; 11. Q—K 4, Kt—Kt 3; 12. Q—Kt 4, B—B 7; 13. Q—R 5, P—K R 3; 14. Kt—K 4, winning easily); 10. Q—R 2, Kt × R; 11. Kt × B with a highly critical position in which White has good prospects.

9. B—Q 2

If 9. B—K 3, P—K B 4; 10. Castles, P—B 5; 11. B—Q 2, Q Kt—B 3; threatening 12. .... B—K Kt 5; and Black has a winning advantage. If here 10. P × P e.p. then the spearhead of White's attack (the Pawn on K 5) has gone and Black's extra material will give him a comfortable victory.

9. ......   Kt—B 3
10. Castles   B—K Kt 5
11. B—K 3

Necessary (to prevent 11. .... Kt × P;) and now 11. ....P—B 4; is not so menacing because of 12. P—K R 3, B × Kt; 13. Q × B.

11. ......   P—B 3 !
12. P—K R 3   B—K 3
13. Kt—K Kt 5 !

The only move to make a fight for the game, though not sufficient against Alekhine's accurate counterplay. Otherwise Black will play P—B 4—B 5 with an overwhelming game.

13. ......   P × Kt
14. Q × Kt   P—K Kt 3
15. Q—K 2   P—Kt 5 !

Forcing a further exchange of minor pieces and reducing White's already small chances of a successful attack.

16. P × P   B—Kt 4
17. K—Kt 1   B × B
18. Q × B   B × P
19. Q—R 6   R—B 2
20. B—Kt 2   Kt—K 2

Of course not 20. ....B × R; 21. B × P threatening Q × R P ch.

21. Q R—B 1   R—Kt 2

Note how snugly Black hides amongst his Pawns and White has nothing with which to dig him out.

22. Q—B 4   B—K 3
23. Kt—K 2

Or 23. Q × P, Kt—B 4; 24. Q—Q 3, Q—Kt 4; with a winning game.

23. ......   Kt—B 4
24. B—R 3

24. Kt × P, Kt × Kt; 25. Q × Kt again leaves Black with a win-ending, and White must try to create complications.

24. ......   Q—Q 2

Position after Black's 24th move

25. R (B 1)—Kt 1

Not 25. B × Kt (intending 25. ....
B × B; 26. Kt × P) because of 25.
....P—Kt 7 !;

25.	R—K B 1
26. Q—Q 2	Kt × P !

This neat little combination finally
destroys any chance White might
have had.

27. Q × Kt	B × B
28. R × P	B—B 4
29. Q × P	P—Kt 3
30. Q—R 3	P—B 4
31. Q—Kt 3	B—K 5
32. R—Q 1	Q—B 4
33. Kt—B 3	P—B 5
34. Q—R 4	Q × P
35. R—K 3	

A blunder under time pressure,
but the game is over in any case.

35.	B × P ch
36. Q × B	Q × R
37. Kt × P	Q—B 4
38. Q—B 3	P—R 4
39. P—R 3	R—B 4
40. Kt—B 6 ch	R × Kt
41. Q × R	Q—B 4 ch
42. Q × Q	P × Q
43. K—B 2	K—R 2

44. K—B 3	R—Kt 5
45. R—Q 7 ch	K—Kt 3
46. R—Q 6 ch	K—Kt 4
47. R × P	P—R 5
48. R—Kt 8	P—R 6
49. R—Kt 8 ch	K—B 5
50. R—K R 8	K—Kt 6
51. R—R 5	P—R 7
52. Resigns	

A game showing that, when
necessary, Alekhine could defend
with as much skill as he could
attack: Keres never had a chance
after his unsound opening tactics.

19

SALZBURG 1942

White: E. D. BOGOLJUBOW

Queen's Pawn

1. P—Q 4	Kt—K B 3
2. B—Kt 5	

An innocuous opening, allowing
Black easy equality.

2.	P—Q 4
3. P—Q B 3	

This move is far too passive.

3.	Kt—K 5
4. B—R 4	Q—Q 3

4. ....P—K Kt 4; 5. B—Kt 3,
P—Kt 5; is the natural and best
line of play and would leave Black
with a slight positional plus.

5. Kt—Q 2	B—B 4

If 5. .... Q—K R 3; 6. Kt × Kt,
Q × B; 7. Kt—Kt 3, P—K 3;
8. Kt—B 3, Q—Q 1; 9. P—K 4 !,
P × P; 10. Kt × P and White's
advantage in space and develop-

ment rather more than compensates for the two Bishops.

6. K Kt—B 3   Kt—Q 2
7. Q—Kt 3   Castles Q R

Unnecessarily compromising. The simplest line is 7. ....Q—Q Kt 3; since if 8. Q × P, Kt × Kt; 9. Q × B, Q × P; 10. R—Q 1, Kt—B 5; 11. Q—Q 3, Q × R P; etc. Alternatively Black could play 7. .... P—K B 3; holding K 4 and threatening Kt—Kt 3 followed by P—K 3, Q—Q 2, B—Q 3 and Castles K R or Q R according to circumstances. If then 8. Q × Kt P, R—Q Kt 1; 9. Q × R P, R × P; 10. Kt × Kt, P × Kt; 11. Kt—Q 2 (11. B—Kt 3, Q—B 3), Q—B 5; 12. Kt—B 4, R—B 7 ! and wins.

8. Kt × Kt   B × Kt
9. B—Kt 3   Q—Q B 3 ?

After this Black's game is very difficult. Correct was 9. .... Q—Q Kt 3; 10. Kt—Q 2, B—Kt 3; 11. P—K 3, P—K 3; and if 12. P—Q B 4, B—Kt 5; with a tenable though rather inferior game.

10. Kt—Q 2   B—Kt 3
11. P—K 3   P—K 3
12. P—Q B 4   Q—Kt 3

A sad necessity, otherwise with Q R—B 1 White will get up an overwhelming attack.

13. P—B 5 !   Q—R 4

If 14. ....Q × Q; 15. P × Q followed by P—Q Kt 4, B—K 2, Castles K R and doubling Rooks on the Q R file with a winning game.

14. P—Q R 3 !

Threatening 15. Q—Kt 4, Q × Q; 16. P × Q with a similar position to that of the previous note, and also threatening 15. Q—Q 1 followed by 16. P—Q Kt 4.

14. ......   P—K 4 !

Meeting the threat of Q—Kt 4

since now after 15. Q—Kt 4, Q × Q; 16. P × Q, P × P; 17. P × P, R—K 1 ch; or 17. R × P, P × P; 18. P × P, K—Kt 1; with good counterplay in either case.

15. Q—Q 1   P—Q B 3
16. P × P ?

It is astonishing that such a strong player as Bogoljubow should make such a mistake, throwing away his advantage. He should play 16. P—Kt 4, Q—B 2; 17. B—K 2 followed by Castles with a winning Queen's side attack.

16. ......   Q × P
17. R—B 1

17. B—K 2, followed by 18. Castles is slightly better. White's King is not comfortable on K 1 and he should get it away as soon as possible.

17. ......   Q—Kt 3
18. B—K 2 ?

But now he must play 18. P—Kt 4, R—K 1; 19. Kt—B 3, P—B 3; 20. P × P, Kt × P; 21. B—Q 3, Kt—K 5; 22. Castles, Kt × B; 23. R P × Kt, B—Q 3; a difficult position with approximately equal chances.

18. ......   Kt—B 4

The immediate 18. ....Q × P; would be equally strong since 19. P—K 6 (threat 20. R × P ch and 21. B—R 6 ch) could be met by 19. ....Kt—B 4 !; 20. Kt—Kt 3, Kt × P !

19. P—Kt 4

If 19. Castles, Q × P, and White has lost a Pawn without compensation. This would, however, have been a slightly cheaper way out than that actually adopted.

19. ......   Kt—Q 6 ch
20. B × Kt   B × B
21. Kt—Kt 3   B—B 5
22. Kt—Q 4   P—Q R 4 !

Compelling White to give up the exchange since 23. P × P, Q × P ch; 24. Q—Q 2, Q × P; 25. R—Q Kt 1, B—B 4; leaves White a Pawn down and in a clearly hopeless position.

23. Q—Kt 4 ch R—Q 2
24. R × B   P × R
25. Castles   P—Q B 4 !

Allowing the Black Queen to play to the King's side, breaking the force of the White attack.

26. P × R P   Q—Kt 3

Position after Black's 26th move

Now the game seems to be over since White must apparently exchange Queens, leading to a hopelessly lost end-game, or else lose a piece. Bogoljubow, however, finds an extraordinary resource.

27. P—R 6 !   Q × P

If 27. ....Q × Q; 28. P—R 7 or 27. ....P × P; 28. Q—B 3 ! with excellent attacking chances in either case. Unfortunately Black has the simple reply Q × P available but this gives White time to extricate his Knight and avoid the exchange of Queens.

28. Kt—K 2   Q—K 3
29. Q—K 4   P—B 4
30. Q—B 2   P—K Kt 4
31. P—B 4   P—Kt 5 ?

A weak move made under time pressure. The right line was 31. ....B—K 2 since White cannot play either (1) 32. P × P, B × P; 33. Kt—B 4, Q × P !; 34. Kt—Kt 6, B × P ch; 35. K—R 1, Q × B; 36. Kt × R, Q—K 4; or (2) 32. P—K 4, R—B 1; 33. B P × P, B × P; 34. P × P, B—K 6 ch; 35. K—R 1, R—Q 7; 36. Q—K 4, Q × B P; Black winning in both variations. After the text-move White is able to get two passed Pawns and should have equalised the game.

32. P—K 4 !   R—K B 2
33. P × P   R × P
34. B—R 4 ?

Too slow. 34. Q—K 4 ! should be played and would have given White at least equal chances. If 34. ....B—K 2; 35. R—Kt 1. Or 34. ....B—Kt 2; 35. R—Kt 1, R—B 2; 36. R—Kt 5, R—B 2; 37. P—B 5. Or 34. ....P—R 4; 35. B—R 4, B—R 3; 36. Kt—Kt 3.

34. ......   B—R 3 !
35. Q—K 4

If 35. B—K 7, Q × P !; 36. P × Q, B—K 6 ch; 37. R—B 2, R × R; and wins.

35. ......   K R—B 1
36. P—Kt 3

Position after White's 36th move

Now White threatens R—Q 1—Q 6 followed by Q × B P with an excellent game. Alekhine finds a typical and extremely fine resource.

36. ......   Q—Q 2 !
37. R—B 1

If 37. Q × P, R × K P !; 38. P × R, B—K 6 ch; and wins.

37. ......   R—K 1 !
38. K—Kt 2 ?

If 38. R × P, R (1) × P !; 39. P × R, Q—Q 8 ch; 40. K—Kt 2, Q—B 8 mate. Or 38. Q × P, R (1) × P; etc., as in the previous note. Disconcerted, no doubt, by these invisible protections for the Q B P, Bogoljubow fails to find the best move, 28. R—B 2, after which his game is by no means lost, though after 28. .... K—Kt 1; threatening Q—Q 6, Black has a clear advantage.

38. ......   R (1) × P
39. P × R   B × R
40. Kt × B   Q—K 3 !

Now the King's Pawn falls and in spite of having two pieces for the Rook White is lost. The threat is 41. ....R × P; 42. Q × R P, Q—Q 4 ch; 43. K—Kt 1 (43. K—B 2, Q—B 6 ch), R—K 8 ch; 44. K—B 2, Q—Q 7 ch; 45. Kt—K 2, Q × Kt mate.

41. P—R 3   P × P ch
42. K—R 2   R—B 7 ch
43. K—Kt 1   R—Kt 7 ch
44. K—R 1

Or 44. K—B 1, Q—B 2 ch; 45. B—B 6 (45. Q—B 4, Q × Q ch; 46. P × Q, R—B 7; 47. Kt—K 2, R × Kt !; and wins), Q—Q 2; 46. Q—K 1 (46. Q—B 3, Q—Q 7;), Q—Q 5; 47. Kt—K 2, Q—K 6; and wins.

44. ......   Q—Q 2
45. Q—B 3   Q—Q 5
46. Q—B 8 ch

If 46. Q—B 1, R—K B 7; 47. Q—K 1, Q—Q 4 ch.

46. ......   K—B 2
47. Q—K 7 ch   K—Kt 3
48. Q—Q 6 ch   Q × Q
49. P × Q   K—B 3
50. B—K 7   R—Q B 7
51. B—Kt 5   K × P
52. P—R 4   P—R 4
52. Resigns

Final Position

White's minor pieces can do nothing so Black can play his King round to Q R 4, capture the R P and Queen the Q Kt P. An exceedingly interesting game in spite of mistakes on both sides.

20

SALZBURG 1942

Black: P. KERES

Ruy Lopez

1. P—K 4   P—K 4
2. Kt—K B 3   Kt—Q B 3
3. B—Kt 5   P—Q R 3
4. B—R 4   Kt—B 3
5. Castles   B—K 2
6. Q—K 2

The Worrall attack, in which White plays Q—K 2 and R—Q 1 instead of R—K 1. The chief advantage of this formation is that from K 2 the White Queen brings pressure to bear on the Black Q side Pawns — once Black has played P—Q Kt 4, White always has the awkward threat of P—Q R 4. The chief disadvantage is that the line is still slower than the normal one (in which White's Q side development is quite slow enough anyway) and White is always liable to have his strategical plans upset by a tactical counter-stroke based on Black's superior development.

6.	......	P—Q Kt 4
7.	B—Kt 3	P—Q 3
8.	P—B 3	

The "thematic" move 8. P—Q R 4 is adequately met by 8. .... B—Kt 5; 9 P—B 3 (9. P × P ?, Kt—Q 5;), Castles. See Game No. 21 (Alekhine-Schmidt) for an example of this variation.

| 8. | ...... | Castles |
| 9. | R—Q 1 | |

If 9. P—Q 4, B—Kt 5; 10. R—Q 1, P × P; 11. P × P, P—Q 4 !; 12. P—K 5, Kt—K 5; with equality. White transposes moves in order to avoid this variation.

9. ......   Kt—Q R 4

If 9. .... B—Kt 5; 10. P—Q 3 ! followed by P—K R 3 and P—K Kt 4 with an excellent game. Black cannot reply 10. .... P—Q 4 ?; because of 11. P × P, Kt × P; 12. Q—K 4, B—K 8; 13. Kt × P. The usual Lopez rule applies: B—Kt 5 is not good for Black *before* White has played P—Q 4 because of the reply P—Q 3 ! leaving the Bishop misplaced.

10.	B—B 2	P—B 4
11.	P—Q 4	Q—B 2
12.	B—Kt 5	

It is more usual to leave the B on Q B 1 and to play the Q Kt round to the K side. The ideas behind the text are (1) that when the White Q Kt gets to K 3 (*via* Q 2 and K B 1) White will threaten B × Kt followed by Kt—Q 5, (2) Q R—Q B 1 will be possible earlier than usual. However, the Bishop is not really particularly well placed on Kt 5 and it is more important to get the Q Kt round to K 3 as soon as possible.

12. ......   B—Kt 5

For now Black could have played 12. ....B P × P !; 13. P × P, B—Kt 5; threatening 14. .... B × Kt; breaking up White's King's side. If 14. Kt—B 3, P—Kt 5 !; 15. B × Kt, P × Kt; 16. B × B, P × P; 17. Q R—Kt 1, Q × B; 18. R × P, Kt—B 3; with a good game ; and if 14. B—Q 3, Kt—B 3. In every variation Black has a fully equalised position.

| 13. | P × K P | P × P |
| 14. | Q Kt—Q 2 | K R—Q 1 |

14. ....Kt—R 4; at once gives Black a rather easier game. If 15. P—K R 3, B—K 3; 16. B × B, Kt—K B 5 !; 17. Q—B 1, Q × B; with a satisfactory position, 18. Kt × P being met by 18. ....B × R P. If here 16. Kt—B 1, B × B; 17. Kt × B, Kt—K B 5; 18. Q—K 1, B—B 5; 19. Kt—K 3, P—B 3; 20. Kt—B 3, B—K 7. I can see no way in which White can gain the advantage—the variations are similar to those that arise in the actual game with the important difference that in the game White has gained a very valuable move.

15. Kt—B 1   Kt—R 4

If 15. .... Kt—B 5; 16. B—Kt 3, Kt—Q R 4; 17. B × Kt, B × B; 18. B—Q 5 followed by Kt—K 3 with the better game. If Black does nothing in particular then 16. Kt—K 3, B—K 3; 17. Kt—R 4 and White has the advantage because of his pressure on K B 5 and Q 5.

Position after Black's 15th move

16. P—K R 3 !   B—K 3

Best. If 16. .. B × B; 17. P × B, Kt—B 5; 18. Q—K 1, B—K 2; 19. P—K Kt 3, Kt—R 6 ch; 20. K—Kt 2, Kt—Kt 4; 21. Kt —K 3 with much the better game.

17. Kt—K 3   P—B 3 !
18. Kt—R 2

Better than 18. B—R 4, Kt— K B 5; and Black has a good game.

18. ......   P—Kt 3

After 18. .... P × B; 19. Q × Kt White has a clear-cut advantage since sooner or later he will play Kt—Q 5 forcing Black to capture, and after the exchange Black will not be able to do anything with his 4 Pawns to 3 on the King's side.

19. B—R 6   B—B 1
20. B × B   K × B ?

Black should play 20. .... Kt—K B 5 !; 21. Q—B 3, R × B !; 22. P—K R 4, Kt—B 5; 23. P—K Kt 3 (not 23. Kt × Kt, B × Kt; 24. P—K Kt 3, B—K 7 !;), Kt × Kt; 24. Q × Kt, Kt—R 4; with an equal game. After missing this chance, he is not given another !

21. P—K Kt 3 !

Preventing Kt—K B 5 once and for all. Black cannot play 21. .... B × P; because of 22. Kt—Q 5, Q— Kt 2; 23. P—K Kt 4, Kt—B 5; 24. Kt × Kt, P × Kt; 25. Q—B 3 winning.

21. ......   R × R ch

This exchange helps White whose Bishop (with a masked threat of B × Kt) is well placed on Q 1. The best line was 21. .... Kt—Q B 5; 22. Kt—Q 5, B × Kt; 23. P × B, Kt—Q 3; and although Black's game is undeniably inferior he has better drawing chances than as played. White's advantage (in this variation and in the actual game) consists in the following: (1) he cannot be prevented from getting a passed Q P; (2) Black's King's side is somewhat weakened and his K Kt displaced; (3) Black's Queen's side is open to attack by P—Q R 4. None of these weaknesses separately seems very serious—it takes an Alekhine to exploit them.

22. B × R   R—Q 1

Here again Kt—Q B 5 is better. The text results in White gaining command of the Q R file which is of more value to him than the Q file is to Black.

23. P—Q R 4   Kt—Q B 5
24. P × P   P × P
25. Kt—Q 5 !

Position after White's 25th move

Another fine move. Black cannot safely accept the offered Pawn.

25. ......   Q—Q Kt 2

If 25. ....B × Kt; 26. P × B, R × P; 27. Q—K 4!, R—Q 1; (27. ....R—Q 7; 28. B × Kt, P × B; 29. Kt—B 3 and the Rook must retreat since if 29. ....R × Kt P ?; 30. Q—R 8 ch, K—Kt 2; 31. R—R 7); 28. B × Kt, P × B; 29. Q—B 3, Q—K B 2; (29. ....K—Kt 2; 30. Q × P, Kt × P; 31. Kt—Kt 4 winning back at least the sacrificed Pawn with a strong attack and the better game); 30. Q—B 6, Kt × P; 31. Q × P ch, K—Kt 1; 32. Q × P with much the better game.

26. P—Kt 3   Kt—Q 3
27. P—Q B 4   P × P
28. P × P   B × Kt
29. K P × B

The first stage of the middle-game (which might be said to have begun on White's 14th move) is over and White has achieved his aims with a decisive or almost decisive advantage. White's Bishop is better than Black's Knight, his passed Pawn is invulnerable and Black has a weak Q B P and a King's side majority with little future. The next stage sees White

gradually increasing his advantage until Black, under pressure, loses a Pawn by a blunder.

29. ......   Kt—Kt 2
30. Kt—Kt 4   Q—K 2
31. B—B 2   K Kt—K 1

31. ....Kt—B 2; followed by P—B 4 might be a little better.

32. P—R 4

Preventing any sort of Pawn rush by Black.

32. ......   P—K 5

This turns out badly but if Black does nothing White will play Kt—K 3 followed by R—R 6, Q—Q 2 and Q—R 5 with a powerful Queen's side attack.

33. Kt—K 3   Q—K 4 ?

Blundering in a bad position, as so often happens.

34. R—R 7   K—Kt 1 ?

34. ....K Kt—Kt 2; is essential, but after Q—K 1—R 5 White has a winning game.

35. Kt—Kt 4   Q—Q 5

Position after Black's 35th move

36. B × P !   P—B 4

36. .... Kt × B ? ; 37. Kt—R 6 ch,
K—R 1 (37. .... K—B 1 ? ? ;
R—B 7 mate) ; 38. Kt—B 7 ch
and 39. Kt × R. A similar line wins
against 36. .... Q × B.

37. Kt—R 6 ch	K—R 1
38. B—B 2	Q—B 3
39. Q—K 6	Q × Q
40. P × Q	

Now comes the final stage—
winning a won ending.

| 40. ...... | R—B 1 |
| 41. Kt—B 7 ch | Kt × Kt |

After 41. .... K—Kt 1 ; 42.
Kt—K 5 the ending is of course
also won.

| 42. P × Kt | Kt—Q 3 |
| 43. B—Q 3 | K—Kt 2 |

If 43. .... R—B 1 ; 44. R—B 7
and if 43. .... P—R 4 (or P—R 3) ;
44. R—Q 7 ! (44. R—B 7, K—
Kt 2 !;), Kt—K 5 ; 45. B × Kt,
P × B ; 46. R—B 7, R—B 1 ; 47.
K—B 1 !, K—Kt 2 ; 48. K—K 2,
R × P ; 49. R × R ch, K × R ; 50.
K—K 3 winning.

44. P—B 8 = Q ch	K × Q
45. R × P	K—Kt 1
46. R—Q 7	Kt—K 1
47. P—R 5 !	P × P

If 47. .... Kt—B 3 ; 48. R—Q 6,
K—Kt 2 ; 49. P × P, K × P ; 50.
P—Kt 4 ! winning a second Pawn.

48. B × P	R—R 1
49. B—K 6 ch	K—R 1
50. R—Q 5	Kt—B 3
51. R × P	K—Kt 2
52. K—Kt 2	R—R 7
53. B—B 5 !	

Preparing a very neat finish—
there are of course many ways of
winning now.

E

| 53. ...... | R—R 6 |
| 54. R—B 7 ch | K—R 3 |

54. .... K—Kt 1; last a little
longer—Keres probably allowed this
quick end deliberately.

| 55. R—B 7 | R—R 3 |
| 56. P—B 4 | |

Reducing Black to complete help-
lessness, White can now play his
King round to the Q side, winning
with the utmost ease.

| 56. ...... | P—R 5 |

This saves trouble.

| 57. P—Kt 4 | Resigns |

White threatens P—Kt 5 ch and
Black dare not move the Knight
because of R—R 7 mate. An
exceedingly difficult game — certainly the hardest to annotate of any
in the book.

21

SALZBURG 1942

Black: P. Schmidt

Ruz Lopez

1. P—K 4	P—K 4
2. Kt—K B 3	Kt—Q B 3
3. B—Kt 5	P—Q R 3
4. B—R 4	Kt—B 3
5. Castles	B—K 2
6. Q—K 2	

See Game No. 20 (Alekhine-Keres)
for general comments on this
variation.

6.	P—Q Kt 4
7. B—Kt 3	P—Q 3
8. P—Q R 4	

The alternative is the quieter move 8. P—B 3. (See Game No. 27, Alekhine-Junge, and Game No. 20, Alekhine-Keres.) The text-move attempts to exploit immediately the weakness of the Black Q side Pawns: its disadvantage is that it is not a developing move and Black by rapid development is able to get up a considerable counter-attack which enables him to maintain equality.

8. ......   B—Kt 5 !

If 8. ....R—Q Kt 1; 9. P × P, P × P; 10. P—B 3 and White's command of the Q R file and better Pawn position gives him the advantage. If 8. ....P—Kt 5 ?; 9. Q—B 4 !, P—Q 4; 10. Q × Kt ch, B—Q 2; 11. Q—Kt 7, B—Q B 4; 12. Kt × P !, R—R 2; 13. Kt—B 6, R × Q; 14. Kt × Q, K × Kt; 15. P—K 5 with a winning advantage.

9. P—B 3   Castles
10. R—Q 1

If 10. P × P, P × P; 11. R × R, Q × R; 12. Q × P, Kt—R 2 !; 13. Q—K 2, Q × P; and Black has an excellent game (Fine-Keres, AVRO, 1938). It is instructive to see how Black's superior development counterbalances his Pawn weakness.

10. ......   P—Kt 5

Now this is safe (Black having castled) and White can no longer force open the Q R file.

11. P—R 5 !

If 11. P—Q 4, K P × P; 12. P × P, P—Q 4 !; 13. P—K 5 (if 13. P × P, Kt—Q R 4 !; 14. B—B 2, Q × P;), Kt—K 5; with equality. The text threatens this line because after 12. P—Q 4, K P × P; 13. P × P, P—Q 4; 14. P × P !, Kt × P; 15. Q—B 4 and wins. It also opens

Q R 4 for B or R—a subtle and powerful move difficult to meet.

11. ......   P—Q 4 ! ?

Schmidt attempts to solve his problems in a manner typical of his enterprising style. At the cost of two Pawns he gets a dangerous attack which is, however, not quite good enough. The best line is 11. ....B—K 3 !; 12. B × B (12. B—B 2 ?, P—Kt 6 !;), P × B; 13. P—Q 4, K P × P; 14. Kt × P, Kt × Kt; 15. P × Kt with a slight advantage to White.

12. P × P

Compare the Alekhine-Junge game after 8. ....P—Q 4. White cannot very well now play 12. P—Q 3, because of 12. .... P—Q 5 !; and White must either allow Black Q 5 for his Kt or play one of the obviously unsatisfactory moves 13. P—B 4 or P × Kt P.

12. ......   P—K 5

Not 12. ....Kt × P; 13. Q—B 4, B × Kt; 14. P × B, Kt—B 5; 15. Q × Q Kt, B—B 4; 16. K—R 1 !, B × P; 17. P—Q 4, Q—R 5; 18. B × Kt, P × B; 19. Kt—Q 2, B—Kt 6; 20. Kt—B 1 and wins.

13. P × Kt   B—Q 3
14. P—Q 4   R—K 1

Position after Black's 14th move

15. B—K 3

If 15. B × P ch, K × B; 16.
Q—B 4 ch, K—Kt 3 !; an extra-
ordinary position in which almost
anything might happen ! e.g. 17.
Kt—R 4 ch, K—R 4; 18. P—B 3,
B—K 3; 19. Q—K 2, K × Kt;
20. Q—K 3, P—R 3; and if
21. P × P, B × P ch; 22. K—R 1,
B—Kt 6. Or 17. Kt—Kt 5,
Kt—Q 4 ! (threat P—K 6); 18.
P—B 3, P × P; 19. Kt × B P, B ×
Kt; 20. P × B, Q—R 5 (19. Q—Q 3
ch, B—B 4; 20. Q × P, P—R 3;
21. Kt—R 3, Q—R 5).

15.	P × Kt
16. P × P	B—R 4
17. Kt—Q 2	Kt—K 5 !

Threatening Q—R 5, and the only
way of continuing the attack.

18. B × P ch !	K × B
19. Q—B 4 ch	K—B 1
20. P × Kt	

Not 20. Kt × Kt, R × Kt !; 21.
P × R, Q—R 5; with a winning
attack, since if 22. P—K 5, B × P;
and the Bishop cannot be recaptured.

20.	Q—R 5

If 20. ....B × R; 21. R × B,
Q—R 5; 22. K—B 1 !, Q × P;
23. P—K 5 and White should win.
This would, however, be a better
chance than the line played.

21. P—K 5	B × R
22. P × B	

For now Black does not win the
K R Pawn, an important difference.

22.	Q—Kt 5 ch
23. K—B 1	B P × P ?

He should first play Kt P × P,
which would save him a Pawn and

prevent the entry of the W R later
via the third rank.

24. P—Q 5	Q—R 6 ch
25. K—K 1	B—B 7

25. ....B—Kt 5; is a little
better but the White Pawns are
too strong whatever Black does.

26. P × P	R × B ch

If 26. ....B—B 4; 27. R—R 3
and wins on the Q side without much
trouble.

27. P × R	Q × P ch
28. Q—K 2	Q—R 3

Or 28. .....Q—Kt 4; 29. Kt—B 3,
Q × P (best); 30. Q × B, Q × Kt;
31. Q—B 2, Q × Q ch; 32. K × Q,
K—K 2; 33. K—K 3, P—Q 4;
34. K—Q 4, K—Q 3, 35. R—Q B 1
and White wins. If 28. .....Q else;
29. Q—B 2 ch or Q—B 3 will force
the exchange of Queens.

Position after Black's 28th move

29. R—R 3 !

Decisive; 29. ....R—K 1 ?;
30. R—B 3 ch is fatal for Black, so
his attack has gone and he is left
two Pawns down and in a bad
position.

29.	......	B—B 4
30.	R—K 3	P—Kt 3
31.	Q—B 2	R—Kt 1
32.	Kt—B 4	R × P
33.	Kt × P	Resigns

If 33. .... R × P ?; 34. R—K 8 ch, K—Kt 2; 35. Q × R mate so Black has nothing left. A lively game.

22

MUNICH 1942

White: K. JUNGE

Catalan

1.	P—Q 4	Kt—K B 3
2.	P—Q B 4	P—K 3
3.	P—K Kt 3	P—Q 4
4.	B—Kt 2	

Black is faced with two problems in the Catalan: (1) the development of the Q B—Black's chief tactical problem in all the Queen's side openings; (2) the defence of his Queen's side Pawns against the pressure exerted by the White K B. If Black plays purely passively he is liable to get a lifeless and cramped position—on the other hand if he counters in the centre with P—B 4 and Kt—B 3 his Q and Q Kt Pawns may get into trouble.

4.	......	P × P
5.	Q—R 4 ch	B—Q 2
6.	Q × P	B—B 3

Alekhine adopts a line which simultaneously solves both his problems by allowing him to challenge Bishops: its only drawback is that by obstructing the Q B P Black has prevented himself from contesting the centre for some time. White accordingly prepares to play P—K 4,

if he can do this without any compensating drawbacks he will have the better game.

7.	Kt—K B 3	Q Kt—Q 2
8.	Kt—B 3	Kt—Kt 3
9.	Q—Q 3	B—Kt 5
10.	Castles	Castles
11.	B—Kt 5	

In order to force P—K 4 White must either allow Black the two Bishops or else permit an exchange of Bishops by 10. Kt—K 5, B × B, 11. K × B. The latter line would allow Black fairly easy equality since he could play R—Q B 1 and P—Q B 4, so Junge (a very dangerous attacking player) takes the more enterprising and more dangerous line.

11.	......	P—K R 3
12.	B × Kt	Q × B
13.	P—K 4	

Position after White's 13th move

This plausible move is premature. It would be better first to play P—Q R 3, before Black has the square K B 1 available for retreat. If in reply 13. ....B—Q 3; 14. P—K 4! with a fine game and if 13. ....B—K 2; 14. Kt—K 5, B × B; 15. K × B threatening Kt—K 4 and retaining the initiative with a little the better of the game.

13. ......   K R—Q 1 !

A very strong move, putting pressure on the White centre and preparing squares for the temporary retreat of the Bishops.

14. Q R—Q 1

Also plausible but incorrect; it is essential to get the Queen away from the Black Rook immediately by 14. Q—K 2. If then 14. .... B—K 1; 15. P—Q R 3, B—B 1; 16. P—Q Kt 4 and White can restrain the Black Q B P.

14. ......   B—K 1 !
15. P—Q R 3   B—B 1

Suddenly White finds himself on the defensive. Black threatens P—B 4 and if 16. P—Q Kt 4, then 16. ....P—B 4!; just the same. The next move is White's only way of delaying this advance.

16. Q—K 3   Q R—B 1
17. B—R 3

In order to meet 17. ....P—B 4; with 18. P—Q 5.

17. ......   R—Kt 1
18. K R—K 1

If 18. P—Q Kt 4, Kt—B 5; 19. Q—B 1, P—Q R 4 !; and Black has the better game.

18. ......   Kt—R 5 !
19. P—K 5 ?

After this White has a definitely inferior game. The idea is still to prevent P—B 4; if 19. Kt × Kt, B × Kt; 20. Q R—B 1, P—B 4; 21. P × P, Q × P;—so White avoids this variation by first playing P—K 5. As, however, he ultimately has to submit to P—B 4 in less favourable circumstances he would do better to allow it now by

19. Kt × Kt, B × Kt; 20, Q R—B 1, P—B 4; 21. P—K 5, P × P; 22. Kt × P with equality.

19. ......   Q—K 2
20. Kt × Kt   B × Kt
21. Q R—B 1   P—Q Kt 3
22. B—B 1

If 22. P—Q Kt 4, P—Q R 4 !; with advantage. White prepares to support his Q side Pawns with the Bishop.

22. ......   P—Q B 4
23. P—Kt 3   B—B 3

Note how much the premature advance of P—K 5 has weakened White's hold on the central squares. Now he is forced to exchange Pawns with a miserable game.

24. P × P   P × P
25. B—B 4   Q—Kt 2
26. R—B 3   R—Q 2

Black now occupies the Q file in force; White counters this by preparing to challenge the file. The trouble is that White is in danger on the Q side as well as on the K side and at the critical moment Black is able to exploit this Q side weakness (31. .... Q—R 4;) to force an entry for his Queen.

27. R(1)—Q B 1   R (1)—Q 1
28. Kt—K 1   R—Q 5
29. P—B 3

Black threatened 29. ....R—K 5; winning the Queen (30. Q—B 3, R × Kt ch;).

29. ......   B—K 2
30. R—Q 3   Q—Kt 3
31. R (1)—Q 1   Q—R 4 !
32. Kt—B 2   B—K Kt 4
33. Q—K 2

33. P—B 4 leaves White very weak on the long diagonal, but would be a little better than the text.

33. . . . . . .   R × R

Position after Black's 33rd move

34. R × R

If 34. B × R, Q—B 6; 35. Kt—R 1 (35. P—Q Kt 4, P—B 5; 36. B—K 4 (forced), R × R ch; 37. Q × R, B × B; 38. P × B, Q × KP; winning a Pawn), R—Q 4; 36. P—B 4, B—Q 1; 37. B—B 4, R × R ch; 38. Q × R, B—R 4; and Black has a winning attack, *e.g.* 39. Kt—B 2, B—K 5; and the Kt must return to R 1 whereupon Q—Kt 7 and B—Q B 6 wins—or 39. B—Q 3, Q—Kt 7; winning a Pawn at least—or 39. P—Q R 4, B—B 6; and White is mated or loses a piece.

34. . . . . . .   B—B 8 !
35. Q—Q 1   R × R
36. Q × R

Indirectly protecting the Q R P since if 36. . . . . B × R P; 37. Kt × B, Q × Kt; 38. Q—Q 8 ch, K—R 2; 39. B—Q 3 ch, P—Kt 3; 40. Q—K 7. Black very ingeniously circumvents this counter-attack.

36. . . . . . .   B—Kt 7 !
37. P—B 4   B × R P
38. Kt × B   Q—K 8 ch !

The point of the 36th move White must now retreat his Queen.

39. Q—B 1   Q—K 6 ch
40. Q—B 2   Q—B 8 ch
41. Q—B 1   Q × Kt
42. P—B 5   B—Q 4
43. B × B

43. P × P, B × P; is equally hopeless. White makes a last effort with his centre Pawns which Black has little difficulty in meeting.

43. . . . . . .   P × B
44. P—K 6   Q × P
45. Q—K 1

Of course not 45. P—K 7, Q—K 6 ch; the text, however, threatens P—K 7 winning.

45. . . . . . .   K—B 1
46. P × P   Q—Kt 1
47. K—Kt 2   P—Q 5
48. Q—K 6   Q—Q 1
49. Q—B 4   Q—Q 3
50. Q—R 4

Otherwise Black simply advances his Q P.

50. . . . . . .   Q—Q 4 ch
51. K—Kt 1   Q × P (B 2)
52. Resigns

Although not so spectacular as some of his games, this is undoubtedly one of Alekhine's best—it is difficult to improve on a single move, and he took the maximum advantage of the few errors which Junge made.

23

MUNICH 1942

Black: P. KERES

Queen's Pawn (Queen's Indian Defence)

1. P—Q 4   Kt—K B 3
2. Kt—K B 3   P—Q Kt 3

Against Kt—K B 3 on second or third move, the immediate Queen's side fianchetto is an excellent line, since Black is able to gain control of K 5. In the variations in which White plays P—Q B 4 and Kt—Q B 3 on the other hand is weak, as White is able to prevent Black from occupying K 5 and can get a dominating position in the centre.

3. P—B 4   B—Kt 2
4. P—K Kt 3   P—K 3
5. B—Kt 2   B—K 2

Best. 5. . . . B—Kt 5 ch; 6. B—Q 2, Q—K 2; 7. Castles, B × B ch; 8. Q × B is better for White since White's Queen Bishop is rather difficult to develop satisfactorily in this variation, whereas the Black K B is a good defensive piece and can often be effectively played to K B 3 after Black has played Kt—K 5.

6. Castles   Castles
7. P—Kt 3

If 7. Kt—B 3, Kt—K 5; 8. Q—B 2, Kt × Kt; 9. Q × Kt, P—B 4; 10. R—Q 1, B—B 3; with equality. The text-move is played to avoid this simplification and to solve the problem of the White Q B.

7. . . . . . .   P—Q 4

However, Black could have taken advantage of White's momentary weakness on the Black long diagonal to free his game by 7. . . . . P—B 4 ! The general rule in these positions is that P—B 4 is good if White cannot reply P—Q 5 and here he cannot, for if 8. P—Q 5, P × P (not 8. . . . . Kt × P ! ?; 9. Kt—K 5 ! and wins a piece); 9. Kt—R 4 (9. Kt—K 5, P—Q 3; 10. Kt—Q 3, Q—B 2;), Kt—K 5 !; with advantage to Black. The text-move is not bad, but gives Black a rather less easy game.

8. Kt—K 5   P—B 3

And here 8. . . . . P—B 4; would certainly be better. After 8. . . . . P—B 4; 9. P × B P, Kt P × P; 10. P × P, P × P; Black is left it is true with "hanging Pawns" (which was probably why Keres rejected the line) but, as Alekhine himself showed with Black in the 23rd game of his 1937 match with Euwe, he can maintain equality. The Euwe-Alekhine game continued 11. Kt—Q B 3, Q Kt—Q 2; 12. Kt—Q 3, Kt—Kt 3; 13. P—Q R 4, P—Q R 4; 14. B—R 3, R—B 1; with equal chances.

9. B—Kt 2   Q Kt—Q 2
10. Q Kt—Q 2   P—B 4

Now if White exchanges Pawns, he cannot put the Black centre under immediate pressure by Kt—B 3. He can (and does), however, hold the centre by P—K 3 retaining an advantage in space: it was not worth Black's while to play in this over cautious manner.

11. P—K 3   R—B 1
12. R—B 1   R—B 2
13. Q—K 2   Q—R 1 ?

He should play 13. . . . . Q—Kt 1; followed by . . . . K R—B 1. The text-move leaves the R on B 2 unprotected, of which Alekhine takes instant advantage.

14. B P × P   Kt × P

If 14. . . . . K P × P; 15. P × P, P × P (15. . . . . Kt or B × P; leaves him with a very bad Q P and enables White to occupy Q 4 with much the better game); 16. Kt × Kt, Kt × Kt (16. .... R × Kt; 17. B × Kt and wins a Pawn); 17. P—K 4, P × P (17. .... P—Q 5 ?; 18. B × P); 18. B × P, with the better end-game, Black having two weak Pawns. This would, however, be a little better than the line played.

| 15. P—K 4 | K Kt—B 3 |
| 16. P—Q Kt 4 ! | |

Exploiting to the full the vulnerable position of the Rook on Q B 2.

16.	K R—B 1
17. Q P × P	P × P
18. P—Kt 5	P—Q R 3 ?

This manœuvre opening the R file is immediately fatal and is a surprising error of judgment for a master of Keres' strength. Best was 18. .... Kt × Kt; 19. B × Kt, R—Q 2; 20. K R—K 1 followed by Kt—Kt 3 or B 4. White's superior Pawn formation then gives him an appreciable advantage but there is a great deal of play left in the game.

| 19. P—Q R 4 | P × P |
| 20. P × P | Q—R 7 |

Obviously overlooking the reply, but his game is now very bad in any event.

Position after Black's 20th move

| 21. Kt (5)—B 4 ! | Q—R 1 |
| 22. B × Kt | P × B |

However he plays he loses the exchange. If 22. .... B × B; 23. P—Kt 6 or if 22. .... Kt × B; 23. Kt—Kt 6.

23. P—Kt 6	R—B 3
24. P—K 5	R × P
25. Kt × R	Kt × Kt
26. B × B	Q × B
27. P × P	B × P
28. Kt—K 4	B—K 2

If 28. .... B—Kt 2; 29. Kt—Q 6 and if 28. .... Q—K 2; 29. Q—R 6, R—Kt 1; 30. R—Kt 1, Kt—Q 2; 31. R × R ch, Kt × R; 32. Q—B 8 ch winning a piece.

| 29. Q—Kt 4 ch. | K—R 1 |

29. .... K—B 1; is better but after 30. Kt—Kt 5, B × Kt; 31. Q × B White must win.

| 30. Q—B 4 | |

Threatening 31. Q × P and 31. Kt × P. If 30. Kt × P ?, R × Kt; 31. Q—Q 4 ch, P—K 4; and Black wins a piece.

| 30. ...... | B—B 1 |
| 31. Kt × P | Q—B 2 |

If now 31. .... R × Kt; 32. R × R, B × R; 33. Q—K 5 ch. The textmove loses another Pawn, but whatever Black plays White wins easily.

| 32. Kt × P | Q × Q |
| 33. Kt × Q | Resigns |

This was the decisive game in the tournament.

24

MUNICH 1942

Black: G. BARCZA

Ruy Lopez (Morphy Defence)

1. P—K 4   P—K 4
2. Kt—K B 3   Kt—Q B 3
3. B—Kt 5   P—Q R 3
4. B—R 4   Kt—B 3
5. Castles   B—K 2
6. Kt—B 3

An unusual line which is less
strong than 6 R—K 1 or 6 Q—K 2.
Its chief drawbacks are (1) that it
allows Black to force off White's
K B early in the game, (2) that it
prevents the formation of the
typical Lopez centre by P—B 3 and
P—Q 4. However, it has certain
advantages—it gives White a more
rapid development than he gets in
the orthodox lines and (as this game
shows) he can cause Black considerable trouble by an early Kt—Q 5.
(See Game No. 21, v. Schmidt, for
another example of this variation.)

6. ......   P—Q Kt 4
7. B—Kt 3   P—Q 3
8. Kt—Q 5   B—Kt 5 ?

This move is rarely good in the
Lopez unless White has already
played P—Q 4, when it helps to put
pressure on the centre. If White
has not committed himself to
P—Q 4, he can gain time by
threatening the Bishop by P—K R 3,
keeping the choice between P—Q 4
and P—Q 3 open until he sees which
way the Bishop will retreat.

9. P—B 3   Castles

If 9. ....Kt × P; 10. Kt × B,
Kt × Kt; 11. P—Q 4 gives White
adequate compensation for the
Pawn.

10. P—K R 3

As remarked above, White will
not declare his intentions as regards
his Q P until Black shows what he
is going to do with the Bishop. If
in reply 10. ....B—R 4; 11.
P—Q 3 ! followed later by P—
K Kt 4 with a powerful King's side
attack.

10. ......   B—K 3

Natural, but 10. ....B—Q 2;
would be safer, maintaining a solid
though cramped and somewhat
inferior game.

11. P—Q 4

For now Alekhine, in typical
style, conjures up in this apparently
harmless position a long series of
tactical threats which wins him the
game. Black suffers from the in-
secure position of his Q Kt and
Q B and from his weakened
Q side Pawn formation. The text
threatens Kt × B ch followed by
P—Q 5.

11. ......   K—R 1 ?

Now if 12. Kt × B, B × B; 13.
Kt × Kt, B × Q; 14. Kt × Q, B × Kt;
15. Kt × P ch, R × Kt; 16. P × B,
Kt—R 4; 17. K—Kt 2, Q R—K B 1,
etc. However, 11. ....P × P; is
better. If, in reply, 12. P × P,
B × Kt; 13. B × B (13. P × B,
Kt—Kt 5; and 14. .....Q Kt × Q P;),
Kt × B; 14. P × Kt, Kt—R 4;
followed by P—Q B 4 with a fairly
satisfactory game. And if 12. Kt ×
P, Q Kt × Kt; 13. Q × Kt, P—B 4;
14. Q—K 3, Kt × Kt !; 15. B × Kt
(15. P × Kt, B—B 4;), B × B;
16. P × B, Q—Q 2; with equality.
Black may have been suffering from
the common delusion that it is
always a great score for the enemy
if one has to exchange Pawns in such

a position. Here it is necessary to liquidate the centre since the need for defence against P—Q 5 combined with the need for protection of the K P (which ties the Q Kt) is the cause of Black's trouble.

12. R—K 1   Kt—Q 2 ?

After this move, Black is probably lost. A similar line to that suggested in the previous note was still best, though less good, as White has gained a useful tempo.

13. B—B 2

Threatening 14. Kt × B (if 13. Kt × B, B × B;), Kt × Kt; 15. P—Q 5.

13. ......   P—B 3
14. P—Q R 4 !

Very strong since the normal reply R—Q Kt 1 fails against 15. P × P, P × P; 16. R—B 6 !, Kt—Kt 3; 17. Kt × Kt followed by P—Q 5.

14. ......   Kt—R 2

14. ....Kt—R 4; was the only chance, though, after 15. Kt—K R 4 with threats of 16. Kt × B, Q × Kt; 17. P—Q 5 followed by 18. Kt—B 5 and also of P—K B 4—B 5 and (in some cases) of Q—R 5, White has a clear superiority. Black's trouble is that he has the worse position on both sides of the board and no real counter chances.

15. P × Kt P   P × Kt P
16. B—K 3

Again threatening to win a piece, this time by 17. Kt × B, Q × Kt; 18. P—Q 5, B—B 2; 19. R or B × Kt.

16. ......   P—Q B 4
17. P × B P   P × P
18. R—R 6   B × Kt
19. P × B

Position after White's 19th move

19. ......   Q—B 1

If 19. ....Q—Kt 1; 20. P—Q 6, B—Q 1; 21. B—K 4.

20. Q—R 1   Q—Kt 2
21. P—Q Kt 4 !

If 21. P—Q 6 at once then 21. ....B—Q 1; followed by B—Kt 3. Black cannot answer the text by 21. ....K R—B 1; 22. P—Q 6, B—Q 1; 23. P × P, Kt × P; 24. B × Kt, R × B; because of 25. B—K 4 winning.

21. ......   K R—Q Kt 1
22. P—Q 6   B—Q 1
23. P × P   R—B 1
24. R—R 2   P—K 5

Hastening the end but the position is quite hopeless, since White's Pawns will win the game comfortably for him even if Black survives his immediate troubles.

25. B × P !   Q × B
26. B—Q 4   Q—Kt 3
27. R × Kt   R × R
28. Q × R   Kt—K 4
29. B × Kt   Resigns

If 29. ....P × B; 30. Kt × P followed by Kt—B 7 ch and Black must give up the Queen to avoid immediate mate. From move 11 onwards Black has been faced with an almost uninterrupted series of threats of material loss.

25

MUNICH 1942

Black: K. RICHTER

Caro Kann (by transposition)

1. P—K 4   P—Q 4
2. P × P   Kt—K B 3

This defence is better than its reputation. White has the choice between either (*a*) transposing into the Caro Kann as in the present game, or (*b*) attempting to hold on to his extra Pawn. In the latter case he has theoretically the better game, *e.g.* 3. P—Q B 4, P—B 3; 4. P × P, Kt × P; 5. P—Q 3, P—K 4; 6. Kt—Q B 3, B—Q B 4; 7. B—K 3, B × B; 8. P × B, Q—Kt 3; 9. Q—Q 2, B—K 3; 10. P—K 4 !, R—Q 1, 11. Kt—Q 5 and Black has not sufficient compensation for the Pawn. This type of game, in which one yields up the initiative for a Pawn, is not, however, congenial to Alekhine who prefers a variation in which he has the initiative even if objectively it is not so favourable. 3. B—Kt 5 ch, B—Q 2; 4. B—B 4 is less good for White as Black cannot be prevented from regaining the Pawn and equalising.

3. P—Q B 4   P—B 3
4. P—Q 4

See previous note: this transposes to the Panov attack in the Caro Kann.

4. ......   P × P
5. Kt—Q B 3   Kt—B 3
6. B—Kt 5   P—K 3

6. ....Q—Kt 3; 7. P × P, Kt × Q P; with equal chances is a good alternative. The line played is perfectly sound, and has the great advantage (against Alekhine !) of avoiding complications.

7. Kt—B 3   B—K 2
8. B—Q 3

Here White should play R—B 1. Botwinnik-Konstantinopolsky continued 8. R—B 1, Castles; 9. P—B 5 !, Kt—K 5; 10. B × B, Q × B; 11. B—K 2, B—Q 2; 12. P—Q R 3 and White has the better game. In such positions if White can maintain his Queen's side Pawns he almost always gets the upper hand. If Konstantinopolsky had played (as he should) 8. .... P × P, then the same position as in Alekhine-Richter would have been reached except that Botwinnik would have gained a useful tempo, his Rook being on Q B 1 instead of on Q R 1.

8. ......   Castles
9. Castles   P × P
10. B × P   P—Q Kt 3

The more aggressive 10. .... P—Q R 3 ; followed by P—Q Kt 4 and B—Kt 2 would be better. Black could then play Q—Kt 3 and R (either) to Q 1 with good play on the Q side.

11. P—Q R 3   B—Kt 2
12. Q—Q 3   Kt—Q 4

The plausible 12. .... Kt—Q R 4; 13. B—R 2, B × Kt; 14. Q × B, Q × P; loses because of 15. P—Q Kt 4, Kt—B 5; 16. Q R—Q 1, Q—K 4; 17. B—B 4, Q—K R 4 (best); 18. Q—Kt 7 ! and wins a piece.

13. B × Kt !   B × B

13. ....P × B; 14. B × B, Kt × B; leaves White with the superior game as he is better developed and his minor pieces are on much better squares than Black's which are rather misplaced.

14. B—K 4.

With the double threat of B × P ch and Q—Kt 5, so that Black's reply is forced.

14. ......   P—B 4
15. Kt × B   Q × Kt
16. B—B 3   K—R 1

Forestalling White's threat of Q—B 4, which would now be answered by 17. ....Q R—B 1; 18. Q × P ?, Kt × P; winning.

17. K R—K 1   Q R—Q 1

Black, who now threatens R × P or if 18. Q—Kt 5 or R × P, Kt × P !; seems to have fully equalised, but Alekhine finds an extraordinary move which enables him to retain the advantage in every variation.

Position after Black's 17th move

18. Q—B 1 !   R × P

If 18. ....K R—K 1; 19. Q R—Q 1 followed by Q—B 4 or Kt 5 with the better game.

19. Q—Kt 5 !   R—Q 3 ?

A blunder, losing the game. The only move is 19. .... Kt—Q 1

(19. ....R—K Kt 5; 20. B × R, Kt—Q 5; 21. Q—Q 7 ! wins); 20. B × B, Kt × B; 21. Q—K 5 !, R—K Kt 5; 22. P—K Kt 3, Kt—B 4; 23. Q R—Q 1 and White will regain the Pawn with good winning chances as he controls the central files.

20. Kt—K 4   Q—Kt 3
21. Kt × R

Good enough to win but not the best. After 21. B—R 5 !, Q × B; 22. Kt × R, Kt—Q 5; 23. Q—Q 3, Kt—B 6 ch (otherwise the extra material gives White an easy win); 24. P × Kt, B × P; 25. R—K 3, Q—Kt 5 ch; 26. K—B 1, Q—Kt 7 ch; 27. K—K 1, and wins easily.

21. ......   Kt—Q 5
22. B × B   Kt × Q
23. Kt × Kt   Q—B 3
24. Kt—B 3   P—K 4

It would be a little better to play R—Q 1 first. Now White succeeds in occupying the Q file and preventing Black from challenging it.

25. Q R—Q 1   P—K 5
26. R—Q 7   P—K R 4

Not 26. ....R—Q 1 ?; 27. Kt—Q 5, Q—Kt 4; 28. R × R ch, Q × R; 29. R—Q B 1 ! and wins.

27. P—R 3   P—R 5

Still not ....R—Q 1 ?; 28. Kt—Q 5, Q—Kt 4; 29. P—K R 4 ! Q × P; 30. Kt—K 7 ! and wins.

28. K R—Q 1   K—R 2
29. B—R 6   R—B 2
30. R (7)—Q 6   Q—Kt 4
31. R (6)—Q 5

Beginning a manœuvre to force Black to weaken his King's side by P—Kt 3.

31. ......   Q—B 5

32. Kt × P was threatened.

32. Kt—K 2	Q—Kt 4
33. Kt—Q 4	R—B 3
34. B—K 2 !	

Combining attack and defence. If 34. .... R—Kt 3 ?; 35. B—Kt 4, and wins.

34.	K—R 3
35. Kt—B 2	R—B 2
36. Kt—K 3	

White's pieces are now ideally posted and Black can no longer avoid P—Kt 3.

| 36. ...... | P—Kt 3 |

Otherwise White will force it by B—Kt 4.

37. B—B 4	Q—B 5
38. R—Q 6	R—B 2
39. P—Q Kt 3	K—R 2
40. P—R 4	Q—K 4
41. R—K 6	Q—B 6

The White Rooks and minor pieces dominate the board, and it is merely a question of how many moves Black can last.

42. Kt—Q 5	Q—B 7
43. R—K B 1 !	R—K Kt 2
44. P—B 3	P × P
45. R × P	K—R 3 ?

Immediately fatal, but 45. .... Q—B 8 ch (best); 46. R—B 1, Q—Kt 4; 47. Kt—B 6 ch, K—R 3; 48. B—Q 3 (threat 48. R × B P or B × P), P—B 5; 49. Kt—Kt 4 ch, K—R 2; 50. R—K 5, Q—Q 1; 51. R—R 5 ch, K—K 1 ; 52. B—B 4 ch, K—B 1 ; 53. R—R 8 ch, also loses, White winning the Queen.

| 46. Kt—K 3 | Resigns |

46. .... Q—B 8 ch; 47. R—B 1, Q any; 48. Kt × P ch and wins. A

beautiful example of how to play with three pieces against the Queen.

Final Position

26

MUNICH 1942

Black: B. RABAR

Catalan

1. P—Q 4	Kt—K B 3
2. P—Q B 4	P—K 3
3. P—K Kt 3	P—Q 4
4. B—Kt 2	P × P

For general comments on the opening see Games Nos. 33, 32, and 22 (Alekhine-Bogoljubow, Alekhine-Junge and Junge-Alekhine). Alekhine makes the following interesting comment on this game and the game with Bogoljubow: "Rabar loses because he tries to solve the problem of his Q B quickly, which loses him too much time, while Bogoljubow falls victim to his wish to simplify at all costs."

5. Q—R 4 ch	B—Q 2
6. Q × P	B—B 3
7. Kt—K B 3	B—Q 4

Up to here Black has played well, but this move which aims at freeing the Q side by P—Q B 4 is a little premature. While it enables him to get rid of the weak Q B P it has the grave disadvantage of opening up the game whilst he is still badly behind in development. More patient play by Kt—Q 2—Kt 3 and B—K 2 or Q Kt 5, according to circumstances, was correct.

8. Q—Q 3   P—B 4
9. Kt—B 3   B—B 3

If 9. ....P × P; 10. Kt × B, Kt or Q × Kt; 11. Castles! with much the better game since the White Bishops and Rooks will dominate the centre and Black's Queen's side.

10. Castles   Q Kt—Q 2

10. ....P × P; 11. Kt × P, B × B; 12. K × B, Kt—B 3; is better and would leave Black with quite a playable game although White's superior development gives him some advantage. As Black will have to exchange in the centre quite soon anyway, he should do so before getting his Knight on to an unfavourable square.

11. R—Q 1 !

Not 11. P—K 4, P × P; 12. Kt × P, Kt—B 4; 13. Q—K 3, Kt—Kt 5!; 14. Q—Q 2, Kt—K 4; 15. Kt × B, Kt × Kt; and Black would have a much better game than he actually gets.

11. ......   P × P

Now this is necessary since White threatens 12. P—K 4, P × P; 13. Kt × P, Kt—B 4; 14. Q—K 2 with complete control of the centre and retaining his two Bishops.

12. Kt × P   B × B
13. K × B   B—K 2

Not 13. ....Kt—B 4?; 14. Q—Kt 5 ch, Q—Q 2; 15. Kt × K P !, Q × Q; 16. Kt—B 7 ch with a Pawn ahead and a winning game.

14. Q—B 3   Q—Kt 3 ?

Fatal. 14. ....Q—Kt 1 must be played, after which White with P—Kt 3, B—Kt 2 and Q R—B 1 completes his development with a beautiful position, but Black's game is still tenable.

15. B—K 3 !   Castles K R

If 15. ....Kt—K 4; 16. Kt (4)—Kt 5 ! wins at least the exchange. Or if 15. ....Q × P; 16. Kt (3)—Kt 5 ! and Black cannot defend himself against both the threat of Kt—B 7 ch and that of K R—Kt 1.

16. Kt—B 5   B—B 4

If 16. ....Q—Q 1; 17. Kt × 5 ch, Q × Kt; 18. Q × P winning a Pawn.

17. Kt—Q R 4   Q—R 4
18. Kt × B   Kt × Kt

Position after Black's 18th move

19. Kt × P !

A pleasant if (for Alekhine !) somewhat conventional sacrifice, the real point of which appears on the next move.

19.	K × Kt
20. B—Q 4 !	

Far better than the apparently more forceful B—R 6 ch, which is met by ....K—Kt 3 ! and Black can defend himself (21. Q—B 4, Q Kt—K 5).

20.	Kt—K 5

If 20. ....Kt—Q 2; 21. B—B 3 followed by R × Kt.

21. Q × Kt	Q—K B 4
22. Q × Q	

Simple and effective: the ending is easily won.

22.	P × Q
23. Q R—B 1	K R—K 1
24. R—B 7	R × P
25. R × P	K—Kt 3
26. B × Kt	K × B
27. R—Q 6 ch	Resigns

Black might perhaps have continued a little longer, but he must lose, e.g. 27. ....K—Kt 2; 28. R (6)—Q 7, R—K B 1; 29. K—B 3; R—B 7; 30. R (Q 7)—B 7, R—Q 7; 31. K—K 3 driving the Rook from the seventh rank and winning easily.

27

CRACOW 1942

Black: K. JUNGE

Ruy Lopez

1. P—K 4	P—K 4
2. Kt—K B 3	Kt—Q B 3
3. B—Kt 5	P—Q R 3
4. B—R 4	Kt—B 3

5. Castles	B—K 2
6. Q—K 2	

See Game No. 20 (Alekhine-Keres) for general comments on this variation.

6.	P—Q Kt 4
7. B—Kt 3	Castles
8. P—B 3	P—Q 4

One of the features of the Lopez is that the development of White's Queen's side pieces is very slow. This leads in a number of variations to aggressive play by Black attempting to exploit this temporary weakness tactically (the Marshall attack in the 6. R—K 1 line and the Dilworth variation in the 5. .... Kt × P; line, for example). White's position is, however, very solid and in all these lines Black's attack, although dangerous, can be adequately defended and the game then reacts in White's favour. The text-move is better than most of the moves of its kind, but nevertheless the more solid move P—Q 3 is to be preferred (as played by Keres in Game No. 20).

9. P—Q 3 !

An excellent reply, avoiding the complications arising from 9. P × P and ensuring White a positional advantage since the opening of the Q file is in his favour (he can immediately occupy it). If 9. P × P then Black can either play (1) 9. .... Kt × P; 10. Kt × P, Kt—B 5; 11. Q—K 4, Kt × Kt; 12. P—Q 4 !, B—Kt 2 !; 13. Q × Kt (B 4) or Q 6; and Black has not quite enough compensation for the Pawn in theory, but has good practical chances, or (2) 9. ....B—Kt 5; 10. P × Kt, P—K 5; an extremely difficult position which has not had sufficient test in practical play to see who has the advantage.

9.	P × P

If 9. ....P—Q 5; 10. P × P,
Kt × P; 11. Kt × Kt, Q × Kt; 12.
B—K 3, Q—Q 3; 13. P—B 4 with
rather the better game. This, however, is Black's best line. If 9. ....
B—Kt 5; 10. P—K R 3 (10. P × P,
Kt × P; 11. Q—K 4, B—K 3!;
12. Kt × P, Kt × Kt; 13. Q × Kt,
B—Q 3; is dangerous for White),
B—R 4; 11. B—Kt 5, P × P; transposing into the line played. Or
9. ....Q—Q 3; 10. B—Kt 5, etc.
In every case Black will be forced,
by the combined pressure on his
K P and Q P, to play P × P or P—Q 5
and both moves react against him.
This position is worth considerable
study as it is an interesting example
of a not uncommon type—where
one player has a free and apparently
very satisfactory game but where
the fundamental insecurity of his
Pawn formation makes it difficult
for him to maintain equality.

10. P × P	B—Kt 5
11. P—K R 3	B—R 4
12. B—Kt 5	

Indirectly preventing 12. ....
Kt—Q R 4; since if now 12. ....
Kt—Q R 4 ?; 13. P—Kt 4, B—Kt 3;
14. Kt × P, winning a Pawn (if 14.
....B × P ?; 15. B × Kt, P × B;
16. Kt × P and wins).

| 12. ...... | Kt—K 1 |
| 13. B × B | B × Kt |

Forced. If 13. ....Q × B; 14.
P—Kt 4, B—Kt 3; 15. B—Q 5,
Q—Q 2; 16. Q Kt—Q 2 ! and Black
loses the K P. Or if 13. ....Kt × B;
14. P—Kt 4 again winning the K P.

14. Q × B	Kt × B
15. R—Q 1	Kt—Q 3
16. Kt—Q 2	P—B 3

Better 16. ....K—R 1 !; and if
17. Kt—B 1, P—K B 4; or 17.
B—B 2, P—Q B 3; in this latter
variation Black is obviously better
off than in the game as White does
not particularly want to retire the
Bishop. White has in any event

the better game since his Bishop is
a better piece than the opposing
Knight and he can attack the
weakened Q side Pawns at an
appropriate moment by P—Q R 4,
but Black's position was still quite
defensible. After the text it steadily
becomes more difficult for Black to
hold the game.

| 17. Kt—B 1 | Q—B 2 |
| 18. P—Q R 4 ! | |

In Alekhine's words "The opening
of the Q R file in the Ruy Lopez is
in every case favourable for White."

| 18. ...... | Q R—Q 1 |
| 19. Kt—Kt 3 | Kt (2)—B 1 |

White threatens 20. Q—K 2;
followed either by P × P and R—R 7
or (if 20. ....P—B 4;) by 21. P × P,
P × P; 22. B—Q 5 with much the
better game. It is very interesting
to see how White's Queen side
threats force the Black Knight over
to Q Kt 3, whereupon White wins
on the K side !

20. P × P	R P × P
21. Kt—B 5 !	Kt—Kt 3
22. Q—K 3 !	Kt × Kt

If 22. ....K Kt—B 5; 23. B × Kt,
Kt × B (23. ....P × B; still 24.
Q—B 5); 24. Q—B 5 and wins, e.g.
24. ....Kt × P; 25. R × R, R × R;
26. Kt—K 7 ch, K—R 1; 27. Kt × P,
R—Q B 1; 28. R—R 7.

| 23. P × Kt | P—B 4 |

Position after Black's 23rd move

Allowing a pretty finish, but the game was hardly to be saved. If 23. ....Kt—Q 4 (best); 24. B × Kt, R × B; 25. R × R, P × R; 26. R—R 7, Q—Q 3 (26. .... Q—Kt 1, 27. Q—Kt 5 ! !, K—R 1 !; 28. Q—K 7); 27. R—Kt 7, R—Kt 1; 28. Q—R 7, R × R; 29. Q × R and should win. If 24. ....P × B; 25. R—R 7, P—Q 5; 26. R × Q, P × Q; 27. R × R, P × P ch; (27. ....P—K 7; 28. R(7)—B 8 ! !, P = Q ch; 29. K—R 2, P—Kt 4 !; 30. P—B 6, P—R 4; 31. R × R ch, K—R 2; 32. R—K Kt 8 ! and wins); 28. K × P, R × R; 29. R—Kt 7 and wins.

| 24. P—B 6 ! | P × P |
| 25. Q—R 6 | P—B 4 |

If 25. ....R × R ch; 26. R × R, P—B 4; 27. Q—Kt 5 ch, K—R 1; 28. Q—B 6 ch, K—Kt 1; 29. R—Q 3, P—B 5; 30. R—Q 6, Kt—Q 2; 31. Q—K 7 and wins. Black must play P—B 4 as otherwise B—B 2 wins.

26. B × P ch !

A beautiful finishing touch.

| 26. ...... | Q × B |

If 26. ....K × B; 27. Q × P ch. Or 26. ....R × B; 27. Q—Kt 5 ch or 26. ....K—R 1; 27. Q—B 6 mate.

| 27. R × R | Kt—R 5 |

Or 27. ....R × R; 28. Q—Kt 5 ch.

| 28. P—Q Kt 3 | Resigns |

28. .... Kt × P; 29. R (1)—R 8. A most instructive game for all players, like myself, who are addicted to the Lopez.

F

28

PRAGUE 1942

Black: J. PODGORNY

Sicilian

| 1. P—K 4 | P—Q B 4 |
| 2. P—Q B 3 | |

For general comment on this variation see Game No. 10 (Alekhine-Zvetkoff).

2.	P—Q 4
3. P × P	Q × P
4. P—Q 4	Kt—Q B 3
5. Kt—B 3	B—Kt 5
6. B—K 2	P × P

Premature: moves of this type releasing tension should usually be postponed as long as possible. It would be better to play 6. .... P—K 3; 7. B—K 3 (threat P × P), P × P; 8. P × P, Kt—B 3; 9. Kt—B 3, B—Kt 5; and Black's position is preferable to that in the actual game since his extra move (Kt—K B 3) is more valuable than White's (B—K 3). Should White break up the centre by 7. P—B 4, Q—Q 2; 8. P—Q 5 Black can maintain equality by 8. ....P × P; 9. P × P, B × Kt; 10. B × B, Kt—Q 5; 11. Castles, Kt. × B ch; 12. Q × Kt, B—Q 3; 13. Kt—B 3, Kt—K 2.

7. P × P	P—K 3
8. Kt—B 3	B—Kt 5
9. Castles	Q—Q R 4

9. ....K B × Kt; 10. P × B, K Kt —K 2; 11. B—R 3 leaves White with a clear advantage in position.

| 10. P—Q R 3 | Kt—B 3 ? |

Position after Black's 10th move

The losing move. 10. . . . . B × Kt; 11. P × B, Kt—B 3 (11. . . . . Q × B P ?; 12. B—Q 2, Q—Kt 7; 13. Q—R 4 !, Q—Kt 3; 14. P—Q 5 !, B × Kt; 15. B × B, P × P; 16. R—K 1 ch, Kt—K 2; 17. B—Q Kt 4, K—B 1; 18. R × Kt !, Kt × R; 19. R—K 1, R—K 1; 20. Q—Q 7, Q—K B 3 (or Q 1); 21. R × Kt, R × R; 22. Q—Q 8 mate): 12. P—B 4 and while White's two Bishops give him rather the better game his Pawns are somewhat vulnerable and Black has therefore fair counter chances. Now White wins material by a splendid series of moves.

11. P—Q 5 ! P × P

If 11. . . . . Kt × P; 12. Kt × Kt, P × Kt; 13. Kt—Q 4 (threat Kt—Kt 3 followed by P × B), Kt × Kt; 14. B × B, Kt—B 3 (14. . . . . Kt—K 3; 15. B × Kt, P × B; 16. Q—R 5 ch, P—Kt 3; 17. Q—K 5 with a winning game since 17. . . . . Castles K R; is refuted by 18. P × B, Q × R; 19. B—R 6 !); 15. P × B !, Q × R; 16. Q—K 2 ch, K—B 1 (16. . . . . Kt—K 2 ?; 17. B—Kt 5); 17. P—Kt 5 !, Kt—R 4 (17. . . . . R—K 1 ?; 18. B—K 3 ! or 17. . . . . Kt—Q 5; 18. Q—K 5, Kt × P; 19. B—R 6 !); 18. R—K 1 ! (threat

mate in 3), P—R 4; 19. B—B 5 and wins for if 19. . . . . P—K Kt 3; 20. B—R 6 ch and if 19. . . . . P—B 3 ; 20. B—Kt 6.

12. P × B ! Q × R
13. Kt—Q 2 !

This unexpected move is the key to the whole combination. Black's reply is forced, since if the Bishop retreats Kt—Kt 3 wins the Queen.

13. . . . . . . B × B
14. Q × B ch Kt—K 2

If 14. . . . . K—B 1; 15. P—Kt 5, Kt—Q 5; 16. Q—Q 3 and if the Kt on Q 5 moves 17. Kt—Kt 3 wins the Queen.

15. R—K 1 Castles K R

The Knight clearly cannot be saved.

16. Kt—Kt 3 Q—R 3
17. Q × Q P × Q
18. R × Kt Q R—Kt 1
19. P—Kt 5 P × P
20. R × P

Although White's material advantage is not so very great the game is not difficult to win because Black cannot prevent him from posting his pieces in dominating central positions.

20. . . . . . . P—Kt 5
21. Kt—K 2 K R—B 1
22. P—B 3 R—R 1
23. R × R R × R
24. K—B 2 Kt—Q 2
25. Kt—B 4 Kt—Kt 3
26. K—K 3 R—Q B 1
27. K—Q 3 P—Kt 4

White was threatening 28. B—K 3, Kt—B 5; 29. B—Q 4, R—Q 1; 30. Kt—B 5 followed by Kt—R 6.

28. Kt—R 5 Resigns

A rather sudden resignation, but there is little to do. If 28. ....
P—R 3; 29. B—K 3, Kt—B 5; 30. B—Q 4 (threat Kt—B 6 ch), R—Q 1; 31. Kt—B 5 (threat Kt—Q 7 followed by Kt (5)—B 6 ch), K—B 1; 32. P—Q Kt 3, Kt—Q 3; 33. B—Kt 7 ch or Kt—R 6 winning easily in either case.

29

PRAGUE 1942

Black: T. Suchá

French Defence

1. P—K 4   P—K 3
2. Q—K 2

Tchigorin's move, delaying Black's P—Q 4 by pinning the K P (since 2. ....P—Q 4; 3. P × P, Q × P; 4. Kt—Q B 3 followed by P—K Kt 3 would give White an excellent game), and intending to set up a Pawn formation Q 3, K 4, K B 2, K Kt 3, K R 2 holding the centre but not yet attempting to dominate it. Compare the slow form of the Sicilian 2. Kt—Q B 3 where White sets up a somewhat similar formation. Vigorous counter-play in the centre is Black's correct line, as is usually the case when White adopts slow methods against one of the irregular defences. Treybal-Tartakower (Pistyan, 1922) continued 2. ....P—Q B 4; 3. Kt— K B 3, Kt—Q B 3; 4. P—K Kt 3, B—K 2; 5. B—Kt 2, P—Q 4; 6. P—Q 3, Kt—B 3; 7. Castles, Castles; 8. Kt—B 3, P—Q 5; 9. Kt—Kt 1, P—K 4; 10. Q Kt—Q 2, P—K R 3; 11. Kt—B 4 with approximately equal chances. In Alekhine-Suchá we have a good example of what happens when

Black neglects his opportunities in the centre.

2. ......   B—K 2
3. P—K Kt 3   P—Q 4
4. B—Kt 2   Kt—K B 3
5. P—Q 3   Kt—B 3

This, combined with his 6th move, is the source of all his subsequent troubles; the natural line here is 5. ....P—B 4, leading to a position similar to that in the preceding note.

6. P—K 5

If 6. Kt—K B 3, P × P !; 7. P × P, P—K 4 !; and Black has approximate equality.

6. ......   Kt—Q 2 ?

After this move Black has a difficult game: he should play 6. ....Kt—Q 5 !; 7. Q—Q 1, Kt— Q 2; 8. P—Q B 3, Kt—K B 4; 9. P—Q 4, P—B 4; with an equal game. Now he never succeeds in getting in his counter on the Queen's side.

7. Kt—K B 3   Castles
8. Castles   P—B 3 ?

Since this move and the subsequent exchange of Pawns in no way breaks White's hold on the centre but merely saddles Black with a very weak K P, it would be better to play 8. ....P—Q Kt 3; threatening B—R 3 and P—B 3, if in reply 9. P—Q 4, Kt—Kt 5 !; followed by P—Q B 4. White's best is 9. P—Kt 3, B—R 3 (or Kt 2); 10. B—Kt 2 whereupon Black must laboriously attempt to undo the damage done by his 5th and 6th moves with R—Q B 1, Q Kt—Kt 1, B 4 or Kt 5 and P—Q B 4. White still has the better of it, but Black has more chance than in the actual game.

9. P—Q 4   P × P

9. ....P—B 4; blocking the position is better.

10. P × P   R—B 2

10. ....P—Q Kt 3; is still best though the weakness on K 3 now makes it more dangerous to move the Q B away.

11. P—Kt 3   Kt—B 1
12. B—Kt 2   Kt—Kt 3
13. Q Kt—Q 2   Q—B 1

Evacuating the Q file before a White Rook arrives there: the move is purely defensive as Black has no prospects on the K B file.

14. P—B 4

Position after White's 14th move

14. ......   P × P

A deplorable necessity as 15. P × P, P × P; would leave White's King's side Pawns too strong. The simplifying 14. ....B—R 6; loses because of 15. B × B, Q × B; 16. P × P, P × P; 17. Kt — Kt 5, R—Q 2 (otherwise 18. B × P ch); 18. Q—R 5, Kt—B 1 (18. ....P—K R 3; 19. Q × Kt, P × Kt; 20. Q × P); 19. B × P ch ! and wins.

15. Kt × P   B—Q 2
16. P—K R 4   R—Q 1

17. Kt—Kt 5   B × Kt
18. P × B   Q—B 4

A useless excursion, but Black is now helpless: White's 2 Bishops and superior Pawns' position give him a strategically won game.

19. Q R—B 1   Q—K 2.

20. Kt—Q 6 was threatened.

20. P—B 4   Kt—B 1
21. B—Q R 3   Q—K 1
22. K R—Q 1   P—K Kt 3

Further weakening his position, but White can always force the move by B—K 4 and Q—R 5.

23. Q—K 3

Not directed primarily against the Q R P, but protecting Q 4 so that when he plays Kt—Q 2 Black shall not be able to play Kt—Q 5 followed by B—B 3 or Kt 4.

23. ......   P—Q R 3
24. Kt—Q 2   B—B 1
25. Kt—K 4   Kt—Q 2

It would be a little better to play 25. ....R × R ch; 26. R × R, Kt—Q 2; but White can then win by Q—Q B 3 followed by Kt—B 2— Kt 4 and Black's Queen's side Pawns will fall if nothing worse befalls him.

26. R—Q 2   Kt—K 2

This allows an immediate win but there is no defence against the threat of 27. Q R—Q 1; 28. Q—K 1 and 29. Kt—B 6 ch, Kt × Kt; 30. B × Kt winning a Rook.

27. R × P   Kt—Q 4

Position after Black's 27th move

28. R × Kt !	P × R
29. Kt—Q 6	Q—K 2
30. B × P	Resigns

White can win material in several ways.

30

PRAGUE 1942

White: DR FLORIAN

Philidor's Defence

1. P—K 4	P—K 4
2. Kt—K B 3	P—Q 3
3. P—Q 4	Q Kt—Q 2

The "Hanham" variation of Philidor's defence against which White should by normal development get a marked positional advantage, since Black is left with a cramped game without any compensation.

4. P—B 4

But this move, which deprives the White K Bishop of its natural square, is inferior. The correct line is 4. B—K B 4, P—Q B 3; 5. P—Q R 4! (preventing the freeing manœuvre P—Q Kt 4), B—R 2; 6. Kt—B 3, K Kt—B 3; 7. Castles, P—K R 3; 8. P—Q Kt 3 and White has excellent attacking chances on the King's side. After the text-move, the position resembles that of a King's Indian Defence to the Queen's, except that Black has not played Kt—K B 3 and has therefore the possibility of playing P—K B 4 or B 3 earlier than in the normal variations.

4.	P—K Kt 3
5. B—Kt 5	

There is little point in this finesse: White would do better to proceed quietly with his development by Kt—B 3, P—K Kt 3, B—Kt 2 and Castles.

5.	P—B 3

This move and the following Knight manœuvre is often seen in similar variations in the Steinitz defence to the Lopez and gives Black a very solid central position against which it is extremely difficult for White to make headway —Black contents himself in the early stages with a cramped but firm position and later threatens to break out with P—K B 4.

6. B—K 3	Kt—R 3
7. P—K R 3	Kt—B 2
8. Kt—B 3	B—Kt 2
9. Q—Q 2	Kt—B 1
10. Castles	

This is White's best line, threatening to break the Black centre to some extent with P—B 5.

10.	P—Kt 3

The immediate 10. .... Kt—K 3; is better. After 11. P—Q 5, Kt—B 4; 12. P—Q Kt 4, Kt—Q 2; Black's position remains very solid and he has good counter chances on the Queen's side, *e.g.* 13. P—B 5, P—Q R 4 !; and I prefer Black. And if 11. P—B 5 ?, P × Q P; 12. B × P, P × P; winning a Pawn safely.

11. P—B 5 !	Kt—K 3
12. Q P × P	B P × P
13. B—Kt 5 ch	

It would be a shade better to play at once 13. Q—Q 5, B—Q 2; 14. P × Q P, P × P; leaving White with the better game owing to the weakness of the Black Q P. 13. .... R—Q Kt 1; 14. B—Kt 5 ch, K—B 1 (14. .... B—Q 2 ? ?; 15. Q × Kt ch); 15. P × Q P is of course much worse for Black.

13.	B—Q 2
14. Q—Q 5	Castles
15. P—B 6	

A positional error. 15. P × P, P × P; would still leave White with a slight advantage. The Pawn on B 6 does not seriously obstruct Black, and White has no longer any possibilities on the Q file.

15.	B—B 1
16. P—K R 4	P—K R 3
17. B—Q B 4	

With the faulty idea of playing the Bishop to Q 5: it would be better simply to retire the Q at once. White has however no longer got a good game: he can make no headway on the K side. Black can advance the Q side Pawns and ultimately the P on Q B 6 will be endangered by Q—K 1 and K Kt—Q 1.

17.	Kt—B 4
18. Q—Q 2	B—K 3
19. B—Q 5	

There is nothing satisfactory; if 19. B × B, Kt × B; 20. Kt—Q 5

then 20. ....Q—K 1; 21. Q—B 2, K Kt—Q 1, etc.

| 19. ...... | B × B |
| 20. P × B | P—K 5 ! |

Position after Black's 20th move

21. B × Kt

Declining the Pawn sacrifice is no better, *e.g.* 21. Kt—Q 4, Kt—K 4 !; 22. Q—B 2, Kt (K 4)—Q 6 ch; 23. K—B 1, Q—K 2; followed by the advance of the Q side Pawns with much the better game.

21.	Kt P × Kt
22. Kt × P	R—Kt 1
23. Kt—B 3	Kt—K 4

Black's Pawn sacrifice has miraculously transformed the position and all his pieces have sprung to life.

| 24. Kt × Kt | B × Kt |
| 25. Q—B 2 | |

25. Q × P ? ?, B—B 5 ch;

25.	Q—B 3
26. P—R 5	P—Kt 4
27. K R—K 1	

Naturally White would have no chance after 27. Q—Kt 6 ch, Q × Q;

28. P × Q, R × B P. If 27. P—B 3, R—Kt 5 !; and White has no defence against the threat of 28. .... K R—Kt 1; since if 28. Kt— R 4 ?, Q—B 5 ch; or 28. R—Q 2 ?, B—B 5.

| 27. ...... | Q × P |
| 28. Q—Kt 6 ch | |

This takes the Queen out of play. 29. R—K 2 at once was better, though in any case Black has probably a winning positional advantage.

28.	B—Kt 2
29. R—K 2	Q—B 5 ch
30. Q R—Q 2	

Fatal, but after 30. K—Kt 1, Q—B 4 ch; 31. Q × Q, R × Q; 32. R—Q B 2 (32. R—K 3, R—B 7; or 32. Kt—R 4, R—B 5;), P—Kt 5; 33. R—R 1, B × Kt; 34. R × B, R × Q P; Black still wins.

Position after White's 30th move

| 30. ...... | R × P ! |
| 31. Q—K 4 | |

Forced. If 31. K × R, Q—Kt 5 ch; 32. K—B 1, Q × Kt ch; 33. K—Q 1 (33. R—B 2, R—B 8 ch; or 33. Q—B 2, Q—R 8 ch; 34. Q—Kt 1, R—B 8 ch), R—B 8 ch; 34. R—K 1, Q—R 8 ch; 35. K—B 2, R × R winning at once.

31.	R—Kt 5
32. Q × Q	R (1) × Q
33. R—Q 3	Q R—B 5
34. K—B 2	K R—Q 5
35. R—B 3	B—K 4
36. R × B	

A pointless sacrifice which hastens the end. 36. K—Kt 3 (to prevent R × Q P) would avert immediate disaster but a Pawn behind with the inferior position White has no chance in the long run.

36.	P × R
37. R—Q 3	P—K 5
38. R—K 3	R × P
39. R × P	R × R
40. Kt × R (K 4)	R—K 4
41. Kt—B 3	R—K 3
42. Kt—Q 5	K—B 2
43. Kt × P (B 7)	R × P
44. Resigns	

31

PRAGUE 1942

Black: L. PACHMAN

Queen's Pawn (Nimzowitsch Defence)

1. P—Q 4	Kt—K B 3
2. P—Q B 4	P—K 3
3. Kt—Q B 3	B—Kt 5
4. Q—B 2	

Nowadays the rather more non-committal move P—K 3 is generally preferred and does seem on the whole to make it more difficult for Black to find a satisfactory plan. It is, I believe, a general principle in the Queen's side openings that the quieter the line adopted by White (within reason !) the harder it is for

Black to equalise and free his game. See Game No. 12 for a full discussion of the opening.

4. ......   Kt—B 3

The Milner-Barry or Zurich variation in which Black plays for an early P—K 4. There are two main systems of play against it. (1) An early advance of the Queen's side Pawns combined with a Queen's side fianchetto: this is strategically very strong but has some tactical disadvantages as White gets behindhand with his development. Some brilliant games have been won by both White and Black in this line but general opinion is that White should survive his tactical troubles and emerge with rather the better game. (2) A quiet line in which White contents himself with the advantage of two Bishops and gets some pressure on the Black centre: this line is also slightly in White's favour. Alekhine adopts the second system in this game.

5. Kt—B 3	P—Q 3
6. B—Q 2	Castles
7. P—Q R 3	B × Kt
8. B × B	R—K 1

An immediate Q—K 2 is better since it is not at all certain that K 1 is the right square for the Rook. Euwe-Alekhine (22nd match game, 1935) here continued 8. .... Q—K 2; 9. P—K 3, P—K 4; 10. P—Q 5, Kt—Kt 1; 11. B—Q 3, Q Kt—Q 2; 12. Kt—Kt 5, P—K Kt 3; 13. Kt—K 4, Kt × Kt; with an equal game.

9. R—Q 1	Q—K 2
10. P—K Kt 3 !	

The Bishop has no future on K 2 or Q 3—both for action against the Black's Queen side or for defence against a King's side Pawn advance it is better on Kt 2.

10.	P—K 4
11. P—Q 5	

Closing the centre. Normally in the Nimzowitsch Defence it is to Black's advantage to have the pressure removed from the centre in this way: in the blocked position that results his Knights can often operate more effectively than White's Bishops, and he has a powerful counter-attack available in an early P—K B 4. Here, however, there are two important differences from the "normal" line. (1) White has fianchettoed his K Bishop and (as has been found in the King's Indian Defence) the fianchetto formation is by far the best against the advance of the K side Pawns. (2) Black's K R is misplaced on K 1. These differences are sufficient to give White the better game.

11.	Kt—Kt 1
12. B—Kt 2	Q Kt—Q 2

It would be better to play at once 12. .... Kt—R 4; whereupon after 13. Kt—R 4, P—K Kt 3; 14. Castles, P—K B 4; 15. P—K 3 a similar position to that in the game would be obtained but Black would have avoided the exchange of his second Bishop. Notice in this variation that the Black Rook would be far better on K B 1.

13. Castles	Kt—B 1
14. Kt—R 4	Kt—R 4
15. Kt—B 5	B × Kt

If 15. .... Q—B 3; 16. P—K 4, P—K Kt 3; 17. Kt—K 3 threatening P—B 4. If 15. .... Q—Q 1; 16. P—K 4, P—K Kt 3; 17. Kt—K 3, Kt—Kt 2; 18. P—B 4. In either case White has much the better game.

16. Q × B	P—K Kt 3
17. Q—B 2	P—B 4
18. P—K 3	P—K 5

Position after Black's 18th move

Played to prevent the advance of the K B P; but it does not succeed in doing this, and merely results in the position being broken up whereupon the two Bishops at once make themselves felt.   It is difficult to see a satisfactory line for Black, however: if 18. ....Kt—Q 2; 19. P—B 4, P—K 5; 20. P—Q Kt 4, P—Kt 3; 21. P—Q R 4 and White will ultimately break through on the Queen's side.   Best is probably 18. ....Kt—Q 2; 19. P—B 4, P—Kt 3; 20. Q R—K 1, K Kt—B 3; but even in this case White retains the advantage by 21. P—Q Kt 4. Sooner or later the position will become open and when it does the Bishops will be much stronger than the Knights.

19. P—B 3 !

A remarkable Pawn sacrifice which most players would not even consider.   Such moves are very typical of Alekhine and occur again and again in his games.

19. ......   P × P
20. B × P   Kt—B 3

Since Black is subjected to a very severe attack in any case he might as well accept the Pawn and have some compensation for his bad position.   The best line is 20. .... Q × P ch; 21. K—Kt 2, Kt—Kt 2; 22. Q R—K 1, Q—Kt 4 ! (22. .... Q—R 3; 23. B—Q 2, P—K Kt 4; 24. P—K R 4 and 22. ....Q—B 4; 23. B × Kt, K × B; 24: P—K Kt 4 !, P—B 5 !; 25. B—K 4, P—K Kt 4; 26. P—K R 4, Kt—Kt 3; 27. B × Kt, P × B; 28. Q—B 3 ch, K—Kt 1; 29. Q—B 6 ! are both in White's favour); 23. P—K R 4, Q—Q 1; 24. P—R 5, R × R; 25. R × R, P × P !; 26. B × Kt, K × B; 27. Q × P, Q—B 3 !; 28. Q × Q ch, K × Q; 29. B × P and White has the better of the end-game, but it is doubtful whether he can win.   The diagrammed position is extremely difficult to analyse and my analysis is quite likely to be faulty; however that may be, in practical play all the chances are on White's side, Black's defence being difficult and a single mistake fatal.

21. B—Q 4   Kt (1)—Q 2
22. P—Q Kt 4   Kt—K 5 ?

22. ....Kt—K 4; is better, but after 23. B—K Kt 2 White retains the upper hand since Black will not be able to stop him from breaking up the position on one wing or the other, and after the position has been broken up the Bishops will be much better than the Knights, e.g. 22. ....Kt—K 4; 23. B—K Kt 2, Kt (4)—Kt 5; 24. Q R—K 1, Kt—K 5; 25. R—B 4 (threat B × Kt), Kt (Kt 5)—B 3; 26. P—Kt 4 !, P × P; 27. Q R—K B 1 winning a piece.

23. P—Kt 4 !   P × P

If 23. ....Kt (2)—B 3; 24. P × P, P × P; 25. B × Kt and wins.

24. B × Kt P

Position after White's 24th move

24. ...... Q—Kt 4

If 24. .... Kt—B 1; 25. R × Kt
ch !, Q × R; 26. R—K B 1, Q—R 3;
27. R—B 4, Kt—Kt 4; 28. P—
K R 4 !, Kt—B 2; 29. B—K 6 !,
R × B ! (29. .... R—K 2 ?;
30. R × Kt, R × R; 31. Q—K B 2,
R—K B 1; 32. Q—B 6); 30. P × R,
Kt—K 4; 31. Q—K 4, R—K B 1
(31. .... R—K 1; 32. B × Kt,
R × P ?; 33. Q—Q 5 ! or 31. ....
Q—Kt 2 ?; 32. R—B 7 !); 32.
P—K 7 and wins.

25. Q—Kt 2 Kt—B 1

If 25. .... Kt—K 4; 26. R—B 4 !,
Kt × B (26. .... Kt—B 3 ? ; 27.
B—K 6 ch); 27. R × Kt (Kt 4),
Q—B 4; 28. R—K B 1 and wins a
piece.

26. R—B 4 P—K R 4
27. P—K R 4 ! Q—R 3
28. B—R 3 Resigns

The Knight is lost. A very complicated game, especially for the
annotator.

32

PRAGUE 1942

Black: K. JUNGE

Catalan

1. P—Q 4   P—Q 4
2. P—Q B 4   P—K 3
3. Kt—K B 3   Kt—K B 3
4. P—K Kt 3   P × P
5. Q—R 4 ch   Q Kt—Q 2

Compare the opening of Game
No. 22, between the same players
with colours reversed. Alekhine on
that occasion played B—Q 2—B 2;
the more usual plan, adopted here
by Junge, of Kt—Q 2, aims at an
early advance of the Q side Pawns
combined with B—Q Kt 2. The
two lines are of about equal merit,
and either should give equality with
careful play by Black.

6. B—Kt 2   P—Q R 3
7. Q × B P   P—Q Kt 4
8. Q—B 6

The immediate Q—B 2 is rather
more usual, but White has in view
a continuation for which he wishes
to drive the Rook off the Rook file.

8. ......   R—Q Kt 1

8. .... R—R 2; is slightly better
as the Rook has little future on the
Knight file, and from R 2 it can later
play across to B 2 or Q 2 if necessary.
However, the text-move is perfectly
sound.

9. Castles   B—Kt 2
10. Q—B 2   P—B 4
11. P—Q R 4 !

Position after White's 11th move

Position after Black's 17th move

A far-sighted positional Pawn sacrifice which Black should decline by 11. ....P—Kt 5; which would maintain equality. After accepting the sacrifice the best Black can hope for is to avoid disaster if he defends with absolute accuracy.

11.	B × Kt
12. B × B	P × Q P
13. P × P	P × P
14. R—Q 1	Q—Kt 3

Not 14. ....B—B 4; 15. B—B 4, P—K 4 (15. ....R—Q B 1; 16. B—Kt 7, P—Q 6; 17. Q × P, B × P ch; 18. K—B 1 ! and wins); 16. B × P, Kt × B; 17. Q × B, Kt × B ch; 18. P × Kt, Q—K 2; 19. Q × P or Q × Q ch and White should win.

| 15. Kt—Q 2 | P—K 4 |
| 16. Kt—Kt 3 | Kt—B 4 ? |

Overlooking White's forthcoming sacrifice. The best line was 16. .... B—K 2; 17. P—K 3, P × P; 18. B × P, Q—K 3; White has adequate positional compensation for his Pawn, but nothing immediately decisive.

| 17. Kt × Kt | B × Kt |

If 17. ....Q × Kt; 18. B—B 6 ch, Kt—Q 2 (18. ....K—Q 1; 19. Q × Q, B × Q; 20. B × P !); 19. Q × Q, B × Q; 20. R—R 5 regaining the Pawn with advantage.

18. R—R 6 ! !

A magnificent and most unexpected sacrifice which is perfectly correct.

| 18. ...... | Q × R |
| 19. Q × B | Q—K 3 |

If 19. ....Kt—Q 2; 20. B—B 6, P—B 3; 21. Q—Q 6 simultaneously threatening Q × Kt ch, B × Kt ch, and Q—K 6 ch !

20. B—B 6 ch   Kt—Q 2

If 20. ....K—Q 1; 21. B—Q 2, P—Kt 5; 22. R—R 1 !, and wins: for if 22. ....R—Q B 1; 23. Q—Kt 6 ch, K—K 2; 24. B × P ch and if 22. ....Kt—Q 2; 23. B × Kt, Q × B; 24. R—R 7.

21. B × Kt ch   K × B

If 21. ....Q × B; 22. Q × K P ch wins the Rook on Q Kt 1.

22. Q—R 7 ch   K—B 3

If 22. ....K—B 1; 23. B—Q 2 followed by R—Q B 1 is immediately decisive.

| 23. B—Q 2 | K R—Q B 1 |
| 24. P—K 4 | Q—Kt 6 |

White threatened 25. R—B 1 ch, K—Q 3; 26. B—Kt 4 ch.

25. R—R 1	P—Kt 5
26. R—R 6 ch	K—Kt 4
27. R—R 5 ch	K—B 3
28. Q—B 5 ch	K—Q 2
29. R—R 7 ch	Resigns

33

WARSAW 1943

(Exhibition Game)

Black: E. D. BOGOLJUBOW

Catalan

1. P—Q 4	P—Q 4
2. P—Q B 4	P—K 3
3. Kt—K B 3	Kt—K B 3
4. P—K Kt 3	P × P

Against the rather slow Catalan system this move is quite satisfactory for Black, provided that he can solve the problem of the development of his Q B. The normal drawback to an early P × P —that White can retake with the K B, gaining time, and follow up with a strong central advance—does not apply here; on the other hand Black is subjected to pressure on the long diagonal, but he should with correct play neutralise this and obtain equality. See Games Nos. 32 and 26 (v. Junge and Rabar respectively) for further comment on the Catalan.

| 5. Q—R 4 ch | Q—Q 2 |

Although Black will force the exchange of Queens by this manœuvre he remains with the problem of the development of his Q B unsolved and this ultimately costs him the game. Either 5. .... Q Kt—Q 2 (Alekhine-Junge, Game No. 32); or 5. ....B—Q 2 (Junge-Alekhine, Game No. 22); is better. An unfair advantage of being Alekhine is that opponents will play inferior moves in an attempt to simplify and avoid catastrophe—thus in fact precipitating it.

6. Q × B P	Q—B 3
7. Q Kt—Q 2	Q × Q
8. Kt × Q	B—Kt 5 ch
9. B—Q 2	B × B
10. Q Kt × B	

If 10. K Kt × B, Kt—B 3; 11. Kt—B 3, Kt—Q Kt 5 !; and Black has good counter chances. After the text-move White has three advantages: (1) the open Q B file; (2) the diagonal K R 1—Q R 8; (3) the weakness of the opposing Bishop. The pressure against the Queen's side Pawns arising from (1) and (2) prevents P—Q Kt 3 and P—Q B 4, which would be the only satisfactory way of solving Black's Q side difficulties: thus Black is condemned to a cramped and difficult defence. Bogoljubow is too impatient to undertake this and attempts an over venturesome solution—it will be seen with what result.

10.	Kt—B 3
11. B—Kt 2	B—Q 2
12. Castles K R	Castles Q R

This is the too venturesome solution. The correct method of play was Castles K R followed by K R—Q 1, Q R—B 1 and B—K 1, after which Black's position, though difficult, should be tenable. The object of castling Q R is to support the Q side Pawns with the King, but it has two serious drawbacks: (1) even with the reduced material White has good prospects of a direct attack on the King; (2) Black cannot easily get his Bishop out of the way of his Rooks and unless therefore he can force P—K 4 (which proves impossible) he will be unable to disentangle his pieces.

13. Q R—B 1   K R—K 1
14. Kt—B 4

Preventing P—K 4 and threatening 15. Kt (B 3)—K 5 !, R—B 1 (15. .... Kt × Kt ?; 16. P × Kt, Kt moves; 17. Kt—Q 6 ch or 15. .... Kt × Q P ?; 16. Kt—Q 6 ch); 16. Kt × Kt, B × Kt; 17. B × B, P × B; 18. P—K 3 followed by Kt—K 5 or R 5 winning the Pawn on Q B 3.

14. ......   R—K 2
15. P—Q R 3 !

The beginning of the decisive Q side advance.

15. ......   B—K 1
16. K R—Q 1   Kt—Q 4
17. P—Q Kt 4   Kt—Kt 3

17. .... P—Q R 3; is better but this leaves a bad weakness on Black's Q B 4 on which square White can later establish a Knight. I believe the position to be already lost.

18. P—Kt 5 !   Kt—Kt 1

If 18. .... Kt × Kt; 19. P × Kt, Kt × P; 20. P × P ch, K × P; 21. Kt—K 5 ch, K—B 1 ; 22. Kt—B 6, B × Kt; 23. B × B, R—Q 3; 24. R—B 3 followed by R—R 1 winning the Knight.

19. Kt × Kt ch   R P × Kt
20. P—Q R 4   P—K B 3
21. B—R 3   B—Q 2

Now at last it looks as if Black will be able to free himself by

P—K 4, but—"when one sups with the devil, one needs a long spoon ! "

Position after Black's 21st move

22. Kt—Q 2 ! !

A devastating surprise threatening Kt—B 4 followed by Kt—Q 6 or Kt × P mate—and if 22. .... P—K 4; 23. Kt—B 4, B × B; then 24. Kt × P is still mate.

22. ......   R—B 1
23. B—Kt 2 !

Preventing Black from escaping by K—Q 1 and threatening to win one of the Q Kt P's by Kt—B 4.

23. ......   P—B 3
24. Kt—B 4   K—B 2
25. P—K 4   P × P

This loses quickly but Black is defenceless against the threat of 26. P—Q 5, K P × P; 27. P × P, P × Q P (otherwise 28. P—Q 6); 28. B × P followed by Kt—R 5 ch and Kt × Kt P ch.

26. P × P   B × P

Hoping after 27. Kt—R 3 ch, B—B 3; 28. P—Q 5, R—Q 2; to have some slight chance with the two passed Queen's side Pawns. White, however, plays so as to force the exchange of Pawns in the centre first which allows his Bishop to come into the attack with decisive effect.

27. P—Q 5 !	P × P
28. Kt—R 3 ch	B—B 3
29. P × P	R—Q 2
30. Kt—Kt 5 ch	K—Q 1
31. P × B	P × P
32. Kt—Q 4	Resigns

Black loses the Q B P (since he must protect himself against Kt—K 6 ch) and is therefore quite lost. A masterly game, strategically and tactically.

34

PRAGUE 1943

White: F. SAEMISCH

Ruy Lopez

1. P—K 4	P—K 4
2. Kt—K B 3	Kt—Q B 3
3. B—Kt 5	P—Q R 3
4. B—R 4	Kt—B 3
5. Castles	P—Q 3

A rather unusual, but quite playable, combination of Steinitz and Morphy defence.

6. R—K 1

This allows Black fairly easy equality. The best line is 6. B × Kt ch, P × B; 7. P—Q 4, Kt—Q 2; 8. P—Q Kt 3, B—K 2; 9. B—Kt 2, P—B 3; 10. P—B 4 with slight advantage to White.

| 6. ...... | P—Q Kt 4 |
| 7. B—Kt 3 | Kt—Q R 4 |

Having played P—Q 3 earlier than usual (instead of 5. .... B—K 2), Black is able to play Kt—R 4 before White can get in P—B 3 and is thus able to eliminate the K B. Since White failed to exploit the transposition of moves Black has taken advantage of it himself as not uncommonly happens in opening play.

| 8. P—Q 4 | Kt × B |
| 9. R P × Kt | Kt—Q 2 |

9. ....B—Kt 2; is preferable. If 10. P × P, Kt × P; 11. P × P, B × P; 12. Kt—B 3, Castles !; and White cannot win a piece either (*a*) by 13. Kt × Kt, B × Kt; 14. R × B ? ?, B × P ch; winning the Queen, or (*b*) by 13. Kt × Kt, B × Kt; 14. B—Kt 5 ?, B × Kt; and Black wins the piece, not White.

10. P × P ?

This results in a liquidation of the position leaving Black with the better end-game. The correct line is 10. B—Q 2 ! followed by 11. B—R 5 with considerable pressure on Black's Queen's side (as played in the game Junge-Keres, Salzburg 1943). It is most interesting to see how Alekhine (somewhat helped, it must be admitted, by Saemisch) transforms his small advantage into a win, the game being finished only 15 moves after the Queen exchange.

10.	Kt × P
11. Kt × Kt	P × Kt
12. Q × Q ch	K × Q
13. B—K 3	B—Kt 2

Position after Black's 13th move

It is difficult to believe that White will have lost in another 14 moves !

14. Kt—Q 2 ?

The natural move 14. Kt—B 3 is better from every point of view. If in reply 14. ....B—Kt 5; 15. K R—Q 1 ch followed by Kt—Q 5.

14. ......   B—Q 3
15. P—K B 3   K—K 2
16. B—B 2   K—K 3 !
17. Kt—B 1

Hoping for time to play Kt—K 3, P—Q B 4 and Kt—Q 5, but before he can execute this manœuvre Black undermines Q 5 by forcing the exchange of White's K P.

17. ......   P—Kt 3
18. P—B 3

If 18. Kt—K 3, P—K B 4; 19. P × P, P × P; with advantage to Black who has strong central Pawns and open lines for his Rooks and Bishops. White abandons his plan of occupying Q 5, therefore, and plays to force P—Q Kt 4 and then B—B 5, exchanging off one of Black's objectionable Bishops.

18. ......   P—Q R 4

Delaying White's P—Q Kt 4.

19. R—R 2 ?

This merely puts the Rook out of play, since Black easily deals with the threat of 20. K R—R 1 winning the Q R P. White should have played at once Kt—K 3—B 2 and P—Q Kt 4.

19. ......   R—R 3

To meet 20. K R—R 1 with 20. ....K R—R 1. The pair of moves 19. R—R 2, R—R 3; by no means cancel each other out, however,

since White's Rook has no future on R 2 whereas Black has an open 3rd rank which he can use to bring his Rook to the centre without loss of time.

20. Kt—K 3   P—K B 4
21. P × P ch   P × P
22. Kt—B 2   K—B 2

White threatened 23. Kt—Q 4 ch.

23. P—Q Kt 4   P—R 5
24. B—B 5

White has carried out his plan of exchanging Bishops but only at the cost of disorganising his position— his Knight is badly placed and his Rook worse. He would have done rather better to have played 24. Kt—R 3 threatening the Kt P, but after 24. ....B—Q 4; 25. R—R 1, P—B 3; 26. B—B 5, B—B 2; he still has a very bad game.

24. ......   R—K Kt 1
25. K—B 2

If 25. K—B 1, Black will later gain a tempo after ....B—Q 4 by playing ....B—B 5 check.

Position after White's 25th move

25. ......   R—B 3 !

An excellent move, forcing White either to abandon the idea of exchanging Bishops or else to allow Black a dominating position in the centre.

26. B × B

26. B—K 3, P—B 5; 27. B—Q 2, R—R 3; would be rather better for White but he will hardly save the game in any case.

26. ......   R × B
27. R—K 2 ? ?

A blunder, losing at once, but after 27. P—K Kt 3 (not 27. R × P ?, R—Q 7 ch; 28. R—K 2, R × P ch ! winning a piece), B—Q 4; 28. R—R 1, B—B 5; 29. Q R—Q 1, K R—Q 1; 30. R × R, R × R; 31. R—Q B 1 (31. K—K 3, R—Q 6 ch;), R—Q 7 ch; 32. K—Kt 1, B—Kt 6; Black wins easily.

27. ......   B—Q 4

Resigns. If 28. R—R 1, B—B 5; winning the exchange after which the ending is quite hopeless. Seldom can a Rook have had a more ignoble career than the White Rook on R 2.

35

PRAGUE 1943

Black: Dr M. Bartosek

French Defence

1. P—K 4   P—K 3
2. P—Q 4   P—Q 4
3. Kt—Q 2

See Game No. 7, *v*. Capablanca, for general remarks on this variation.

3. ......   P—Q B 4

4. K Kt—B 3   Q Kt—B 3
5. B—Kt 5

Keeping up the tension: White's idea is to castle as soon as possible and then to exploit the King's file (opening this by an exchange of Pawns). If 5. K P × P, K P × P; 6. B—Kt 5, Q—K 2 ch; 7. B—K 2, Q—B 2; with equality — White therefore delays the exchange until after castling.

5. ......   B—Q 2

Black in turn, however, could have exploited White's change in order of the moves by 5. .... P—Q R 3 !; 6. B × Kt ch, P × B; and now if 7. K P × P ?, P (B 3) × P !; with an excellent game or 7. Castles, Kt—B 3; with equal chances. After the text-move he gets into difficulties almost at once.

6. K P × P   K P × P

Not 6. .... Kt × P ?; 7. Kt × Kt, P × Kt; 8. P × P !, B × B; 9. Q—R 5 with a winning game.

7. Castles   Kt × Q P

If 7. .... Kt—B 3; 8. R—K 1 ch, B—K 3 (8. .... B—K 2; 9. P × P or 9. Q—K 2); 9. P × P, B × P; 10. Kt—Kt 3, B—Kt 3 (10. .... B—Q 3; 11. Kt—Q 4, Q—Q 2; 12. Kt—Kt 5); 11. Q Kt—Q 4, Q—Q 3; 12. Kt—B 5, Q—B 1; 13. Kt (3)—Q 4, Castles; 14. B × Kt !, P × B; 15. Q—Q 3, Q B × Kt !; 16. Q—R 6 ch, K—Kt 1; 17. B—B 4 ch, K—R 1; 18. Kt × B with better chances for White. Black's difficulty is that he cannot get time to castle K R, and when he castles Q R he is exposed to a dangerous attack.

8. Kt × Kt   P × Kt
9. Q—K 2 ch   B—K 2
10. Kt—B 3   B × B
11. Q × B ch   Q—Q 2
12. Q—K 2   Castles

If 12. . . . .Kt—B 3; 13. R—K 1 tieing the Black King to the defence of the Bishop.

13. B—B 4

Forcing off one of Black's best defensive pieces, White now remains with two advantages: (1) an unassailable post on Q 4 in front of the weak Q P; (2) good attacking chances on the Q side. All Black has to set against this is his chance of gaining control of the K file plus a slight advantage in space through having a central Pawn.

13.	B—Q 3
14. B × B	Q × B
15. Kt × P	Kt—B 3
16. Q—B 3	

16. Kt—B 5, Q—B 5; would be premature (or if 16. Kt—Kt 5, Q—Kt 3;). The text-move threatens Kt—B 5 followed by the capture of the Kt P.

| 16. . . . . . . | Q—Kt 3 |
| 17. K R—Q 1 | K R—K 1 |

Here or later . . . . Q × P; is quickly fatal, e.g. 17. . . . . Q × P; 18. Q R—Kt 1, Q × R P; 19. R—R 1, Q—B 5; 20. R × P, K—Kt 1; 21. Q—R 3 with a winning attack.

| 18. P—Q R 4 | R—K 5 |
| 19. P—R 5 | Q—B 4 |

Better 19. . . . . Q—B 2; at once. On B 4 the Queen is misplaced and Black loses further time. It is probable that the game cannot be saved after the text-move.

| 20. P—B 3 | Q R—K 1 |

Again 20. . . . . Q—B 2; threatening Q—B 5 or Kt—Kt 5—K 4 would be a better chance. The Rook is needed on Q 1 to hold Q 3.

21. P—R 3 !
G

Preventing Kt—Kt 5 and avoiding any tiresome threats of back row mates later on. A typically well-timed move.

21.	Q—B 2
22. P—R 6	P—Q Kt 3
23. P—B 4 !	

Position after White's 23rd move

22. Kt—Kt 5, Q—B 4 !; would be premature. The text threatens P × P followed by Q R—B 1 and if 23. . . . .P × P ?; 24. Kt—Kt 5 and 25. Kt—Q 6 ch wins the exchange.

| 23. . . . . . . | Q—B 4 |
| 24. Kt—B 5 | |

Threatening Kt × P followed by Q × Kt.

| 24. . . . . . . | Q—Kt 5 |
| 25. P × P | |

Better than 25. . . . .Kt × P; 26. R—K 8 ch, though this would also win for White.

25.	R—K B 5
26. Q—Q 3	R—K 4
27. Q R—B 1 ch	K—Q 2

If 27. . . . .K—Kt 1; 28. P—Q 6, R (either) × Kt; 29. P—Q 7 and wins.

28. Kt—K 3   Kt—K 5

Black is apparently getting up quite a formidable counter-attack—but only apparently !

29. Kt—Kt 4 !   R—K 1
30. P—K Kt 3

Decisive. Not, however, 30. R—B 4 ? immediately, because of 30. Kt × P !; 31. Kt × Kt, Q × R; or 31. R × Q, Kt × Q.

30. ......   Kt—B 4

If 30. .... R—B 4; 31. R—B 4 wins a piece.

31. R × Kt   R—K 8 ch
32. R × R   Q × R ch
33. K—Kt 2   R × Kt

34. Q—B 5 ch and mates in a few moves.

36

SALZBURG 1943

Black: P. SCHMIDT

Ruy Lopez (Morphy Defence)

1. P—K 4   P—K 4
2. Kt—K B 3   Kt—Q B 3
3. B—Kt 5   P—Q R 3
4. B—R 4   Kt—B 3
5. Castles   B—K 2
6. Kt—B 3

See Game No. 24, Alekhine-Barcza for a general discussion of this variation. 6. R—K 1 or 6. Q—K 2 are usually played here.

6. ......   P—Q Kt 4
7. B—Kt 3   P—Q 3
8. Kt—Q 5   B—K 3

Here 8. .... Kt—Q R 4; is also good, but the text is quite satisfactory. Barcza played the inferior move 8. .... B—Kt 5.

9. R—K 1   Kt—Q R 4
10. Kt × B   Q × Kt
11. P—Q 4   Kt × B
12. R P × Kt   Kt—Q 2

Better 12. .... B—Kt 5; 13. P—B 3, P—B 4 with equality. In most positions in the opening and early middle game an attack in (or on) the centre, if at all feasible, is the best policy. As the result of the cramped and artificial text-move Black gets into some difficulties.

13. P—K R 3

Threatening 14. P—Q 5, an immediate (and tiresome) tactical consequence of Kt—Q 2.

13. ......   P—K B 3
14. Kt—R 4   P × P
15. Kt—B 5   Q—B 2
16. Q—Kt 4 ?

A tactical error, losing two moves and giving Black an opportunity of equalising. The correct line was 16. Q × P, Castles; 17. P—Q Kt 4 ! with advantage since White is very well centralised and the Black Queen's side Pawns are under considerable pressure which cannot easily be relieved.

16. ......   Kt—K 4 !
17. Q—Q 1

17. Kt × P ch, K—Q 2; 18. Q × B ch, Q × Q; 19. Kt × Q, K × Kt; leaves Black with good chances for the ending.

17. ......   B × Kt
18. P × B   Castles K R
19. Q × P   K R—K 1 ?

Missing his chance. 19. .... K R—Q 1 !; is correct followed by

P—Q B 4 and P—Q 4 with complete equality. If 20. P—K B 4, P—B 4; 21. Q—K 4 (21. Q any other, Kt—B 3;), P—Q 4; 22. Q—K 3, Kt—Q 2; 23. Q—K 6, R—K 1 and if 20. P—Q Kt 4, Q—B 5; 21. Q × Q ch, Kt × Q; 22. P—Q Kt 3 (22. R—K 7, P—B 4; 23. P—Q Kt 3, Kt—Kt 3 followed by Kt—Q 4), Kt—Kt 3; followed by . . . . P—B 4 since if 23. B—K 3, Kt—Q 4.

20. B—K 3   Kt—B 3
21. Q—B 3   Q—Q 2
22. P—Q Kt 4 !

Position after White's 22nd move

White has seen his way through the complicated play that follows this move: if Black now plays quietly (instead of aggressively as in the text) White will have a winning game because of his pressure on the Queen's side.

22. . . . . . .   R—K 5
23. B—Q 2   R—Q B 5

If 23. . . . . R × P; 24. P—Q Kt 3 !; R—K R 4 (what else ?); 25. P—K Kt 4 !, Kt—K 4; 26. Q—Kt 3 (threat 27. R × Kt, P × R; 28. Q × R or 27. P—B 4), P—Kt 4; 27. P—K B 4, Kt—B 2; 28. R—K 6 with an overwhelming game.

24. Q—B 3   P—Q 4

If 24. . . . . R × B P; 25. B—B 3 followed by Q—Q 3 winning the exchange.

25. P—Q Kt 3   R—K 5

If 25. . . . . R × B P; 26. Q—Q 3, R × B; 27. Q × R, Q × P; 28. Q R—B 1, Q—Q 2; 29. Q—B 3, Kt moves; 30. Q × P with a winning ending.

26. R × R   P × R
27. Q × P   R—K 1

27. . . . . Q × B; 28. Q × Kt leaves White with a winning Q and R end-game.

28. Q—Q 3   Q × Q
29. P × Q   R—K 7

Position after Black's 29th move

At first sight one would think that Black had equalised in spite of having lost a Pawn since White's Pawns are broken up and the Black Rook is on the seventh. Three factors combine to give White a marked advantage, however: (1) the Bishop is a better piece than the Knight; (2) the White Queen's side Pawns fix the Black Pawns and the latter are very vulnerable; (3) Black cannot maintain his Rook on K 7. It is very instructive to see the skill with which Alekhine exploits these advantages, and the tenacity with which Schmidt defends — seizing every opportunity of forcing off Pawns.

30. R—Q 1	Kt—Q 5
31. K—B 1	R—K 4
32. P—Kt 4	Kt × Kt P
33. B—B 4	R—K 2
34. R—Kt 1	Kt—Q 5
35. R—B 1 !	

A subtle finesse, the reason for which becomes clear on Black's 36th move.

| 35. ...... | P—B 3 |
| 36. R—R 1 | R—R 2 |

Not 36. .... Kt—B 7; 37. R × P, Kt × P; 38. R—R 8 ch, K—B 2; 39. B—Q 6, Kt × P; 40. B × R, K × B; 41. R—R 7 ch, K—B 1; 42. K—K 2 and White has a winning ending. Note that if 35. R—R 1 immediately (instead of R—B 1) this line cannot be played by White since the Black Q B P is on B 2 and B—Q 6 is therefore not feasible.

| 37. B—K 3 | R—Q 2 |

If 37. .... Kt—B 7; 38. B × R, Kt × R; 39. K—K 2, Kt—Kt 6 (39. .... Kt—B 7; 40. B—B 5, etc.); 40. B—Kt 6, P—B 4; 41. K—Q 1 !, P—B 5; 42. P × P, P × P; 43. K—B 2, K—B 2; 44. B—K 3 (threat K—B 3, K × P winning Knight), P—Q R 4; 45. K—B 3, P × P ch; 46. K × Kt P, K—K 2; 47. K × P and White should win.

| 38. R × P | P—R 4 |

Best: it nearly always pays the weaker side to reduce the number of Pawns.

| 39. P × P | Kt × P |
| 40. K—K 2 | |

If 40. R × P ?, Kt × B ch; 41. P × Kt, R × P; 42. K—K 2, R—Q Kt 6; and Black may try to win.

| 40. ...... | Kt—Q 5 ch |
| 41. K—Q 2 | K—R 2 |

If 41. .... K—B 2; White will later play P—R 6 and force a passed Pawn.

| 42. R—R 8 | P—Kt 3 |

He cannot afford to have his King shut out of the game.

43. P × P ch	K × P
44. R—Kt 8 ch	K—B 4
45. R—K R 8	Kt—B 6 ch
46. K—B 3	Kt—K 4
47. B—Q 4	

Not 47. P—Q 4, Kt—B 5; and the Kt is very strongly posted.

| 47. ...... | P—B 4 ! |

Further reducing the material.

48. B × P	R × P ch
49. K—B 2	R—R 6
50. P—R 4	Kt—Q 6
51. K—Q 2	R—Kt 6
52. K—B 2	R—R 6
53. R—Q Kt 8	Kt × B P
54. R × P	

Not 54. B × Kt, R—R 7 ch; 55. K—Q 3, R × B and draws.

54.	Kt—K 5
55. B—Q 4 ch	K—Kt 5
56. R—Q 5	R—R 6
57. P—Kt 5	R × P

Even now, with R, Kt and P v. R, B and P it is very difficult for Black to draw. If he can sacrifice the Kt for the P White cannot win, but it is by no means easy to do this: here again we see the inferiority of the Kt to the B.

58. P—Kt 6	R—R 2
59. K—Q 3	R—K 2
60. R—Q R 5	Kt—Q 3
61. R—R 7 !	

Position after White's 61st move

61. ......   R—K 1 ?

After conducting a difficult ending very well, Black now makes a fatal error. The drawing line was 61. ....R—Q Kt 2 ! If 62. B—B 5, K—B 4 !; and White can make no further progress since 63. B × Kt, R × P; only gives a draw. If 62. R × R, Kt × R; 63. K—B 4, P—B 4; 64. K—Kt 5, P—B 5; 65. K—B 6 (65. K—R 6, Kt—Q 6 !; 66. B—B 5, P—B 6 ! and draws), Kt—R 4 ch; 66. K—B 7, P—B 6; and draws.

62. R—Q 7   Kt—B 4

If 62. .... Kt—Kt 4; 63. B—B 5! and the Kt is lost.

63. B—B 5	Kt—Kt 6
64. P—Kt 7	Kt—K 5
65. B—R 7	Resigns

A very interesting end-game, which Schmidt deserved to draw— but Alekhine deserved to win !

37

SALZBURG 1943

White: J. FOLTYS

Queen's Pawn (Nimzowitsch Defence)

1. P—Q 4	Kt—K B 3
2. P—Q B 4	P—K 3
3. Kt—Q B 3	B—Kt 5
4. Q—B 2	

See Game No. 12 (*v.* Enevoldsen) for general discussion of the opening.

4. ......   Castles

It is better to delay the move and play first P—Q 4, P—B 4 or Kt—B 3.

5. Kt—B 3

A tame move, failing to take advantage of Black's slight inaccuracy. After 5. B—Kt 5 !, P—K R 3; 6. B—R 4, Kt—B 3; 7. Kt—B 3. White would have a favourable form of the 4. .... Kt—B 3; line since Black (having castled) dare not play 7. ....P—K, Kt 4; 8. B—Kt 3, P—Kt 5; which would leave him too exposed.

5.	P—B 4
6. P × P	Kt—R 3
7. B—Q 2	

Now 7. B—Kt 5 is not so good because of 7. ....B × Kt ch; 8. P × B (8. Q × B, Kt—K 5;), Kt × P; followed by P—Q Kt 3 and B—Kt 2 with an excellent game for Black.

7. ......   B × P

Better than 7. ....Kt × P; 8. P—Q R 3, B × Kt ch; 9. B × B; Q Kt—K 5; 10. B × Kt, Kt × B; 11. P—K 4 and White has a slight advantage.

8. P—K 3   P—Q Kt 3
9. B—K 2   B—Kt 2
10. Castles K R

He should play 10. P—Q R 3 (to prevent Kt—Q Kt 5) and 11. P—Q Kt 4 with about equal chances. Now Black gets the better game.

10. ......   Kt—Q Kt 5
11. Q—Kt 1   P—Q R 4

Effectively holding White up on the Q side and remaining with the better K side prospects.

12. R—Q 1   Q—Kt 1 !

Much the best square for the Queen. K 2 is left open for the Bishop, the Queen is immune from attack, K 4 is again protected so that White cannot play P—K 4—K 5 and in some cases Black has threats against K R 7. In all openings in which the Q B P is moved early on, Q Kt 1 is liable to be a very good square for the Queen.

13. P—Q R 3   Kt—B 3
14. Kt—K Kt 5

Best. Black threatened 14. .... Kt—K 4; followed by K Kt—Kt 5 or if 15. Kt × Kt, Q × Kt; with good attacking chances in either case.

14. ......   Kt—K 4
15. Q Kt—K 4   Kt × Kt
16. Kt × Kt   B—K 2
17. B—Q B 3   P—K B 4
18. Kt—Kt 3   P—Q 3
19. Kt—R 5

An unfortunate sortie: it would be much better to play 19. P—Kt 3 followed by Q—Kt 2 with pressure on the long diagonal—the text-move merely results in loss of time.

19. ......   R—B 2
20. Q—B 2

Here again 20. P—Q Kt 3 should be played.

20. ......   Q—B 2
21. Kt—B 4   Q—B 3
22. B—B 1

Not 22. P—B 3, Kt × P; threatening 23. ....Kt × K P.

22. ......   R—B 3
23. Q—K 2

Black threatened 23. ....R—R 3; and 24. ....Kt—B 6 ch (not 23. ....Kt—B 6 ch; 24. K—R 1 !, R—R 3; 25. P × Kt).

23. ......   R—R 3
24. Q R—B 1

Black was threatening 24. .... P—K Kt 4; 25. Kt—Q 3 (25. Kt—R 3 ?, R × Kt;), Kt × P. Now this is not playable because of 26. P—Q Kt 3 winning a piece.

24. ......   P—R 5

Preventing P—Q Kt 3 and threatening to win the Q B P by B—R 3 and R—B 1—naturally White wants to avoid B × Kt at all costs because after ....P × B followed by B—Q 3 and the advance of the K side Pawns, Black's attack would be irresistible.

25. P—B 3   R—B 1

Not 25. ....P—K Kt 4; 26. Kt—Q 3, Kt × P ?; 27. Kt—Kt 4 and White wins a piece.

26. Kt—Q 3

Otherwise 26. ....B—R 3; will force 27. B × Kt.

26. ......   Kt × Q B P
27. Kt—Kt 4   Q—K 1
28. B × P   K × B
29. R × Kt   P—Q 4

30. R × R   Q × R
31. R—Q 2

White has regained his Pawn but Black with two Bishops and the attack has a clear advantage.

31. ......   Q—B 2
32. P—B 4

32. P—K Kt 3 is a little better but even so his position is very bad.

32. ......   B—B 4
33. K—R 1

33. ....Q × P was threatened.

Position after White's 33rd move

33. ......   P—K 4 ! ?

Alekhine had one minute left for his last eight moves so it is perhaps not surprising that he missed Foltys' ingenious resource against the text-move. The correct line was 33. ....Q—K 2 !; 34. Kt—Q 3 (otherwise White just loses a Pawn by 34. ....B × Kt), Q—R 5; 35. P—Kt 3, P—Q 5 ch ! (35. .... Q × P; 36. Kt × B, P × Kt; 37. Q— Kt 5); 36. K—Kt 1, P × P ! !; and wins for if A. 37. Kt × B, Q × Kt P ch !; 38. B—Kt 2, Q × P ch; 39. K—B 1, Q—R 8 ch; 40. B × Q,

R × B mate. B. 37. P × Q, R—Kt 3 ch; 38. B—Kt 2, P × R ch; 39. Kt × B, R × B ch; 40. Q × R ch, B × Q; and wins.

34. Kt × P

The only move. If 34. P × P, Q × P; 35. P—R 3, B × P; 36. Kt—B 2, P—Q 5; 37. Kt × B, R × P ch; 38. K—Kt 1, Q—R 7 ch; 39. K—B 2, P × Kt ch and wins easily.

34. ......   Q—Q 1

34. ....Q—B 2; is better, maintaining a strong attack for the Pawn but Black must have thought the text decisive.

35. Kt—B 6 !

A truly remarkable move !

35. ......   Q × Kt
36. R—Q 7 ch   K—Kt 3
37. R × B   P × P

Black is now in some danger and has to play carefully to save the game.

38. Q—B 3

38. P × P ? ?, R × P ch; 39. K × R, Q—R 5 mate.

38. ......   B × P

38. ....P × P ? ?; 39. Q—Kt 3 ch, Q—Kt 4 (39. ....K—R 4; 40. B—K 2 ch); 40. R—Kt 7 ch and wins.

39. P—R 3

If 39. R—Q B 7, Q—R 5; 40. R—B 6 ch, K—Kt 4; and the Black King is safe.

39. ......   Q × P
40. Q—Q 5

Position after White's 40th move

Now it is Black's turn to save an apparently lost position.

40. ......   Q—Kt 6 !
41. Q—Q 7   Q—Kt 1
42. B—Q 3   K—Kt 4 !
43. Q × P ch   K—R 5

Safe at last and quite ready to participate in a mating attack if White will allow 44. .... Q—Kt 6 !

44. R × R P !

A very discreet move.

44. ......   R × R
45. Q × R ch   Q × Q
46. B × Q   B—B 4

Draw agreed. After 47. B—B 2, B × P (47. .... P—Kt 4; 48. B—Q 3); 48. B × P neither side has the slightest chance of winning. A most exciting game: Alekhine had the better of it on the whole, but Foltys' 35th move earned him the draw.

38

GIJON 1944

White: A. MEDINA

Giuoco Piano

1. P—K 4   P—K 4
2. Kt—K B 3   Kt—Q B 3
3. B—B 4   B—B 4
4. P—B 3   B—Kt 3

This, with 5. .... Q—K 2; is one of the best defences to the Giuoco Piano if Black is the stronger player and must play to win. Black sets up a somewhat cramped but firm position in the centre, intending later on to counter attack with P—K B 4. White must try to use his advantage in space to constrict Black and reduce him to immobility: this is a most difficult type of game for both sides and therefore an excellent line for Black to adopt against a weaker opponent.

5. P—Q 4   Q—K 2
6. P—Q 5

Premature. In such positions it is nearly always best to keep the centre fluid as long as possible—as soon as White commits himself (either by P × P or P—Q 5) most of the pressure on the Black centre disappears. 6. Castles, Kt—B 3; 7. R—K 1, P—Q 3; 8. P—K R 3, (typical restraining move in such a position), Castles; 9. P—Q R 4, P—Q R 3; 10. P—Q Kt 4 followed by B—R 3 with pressure on K P and Q P is White's correct method of play.

6. ......   Kt—Q 1
7. P—Q 6

The idea behind White's 6th move; he hopes that the backward doubled Pawns will seriously retard Black's development and that he will be able permanently to prevent P—Q 4, either recovering the sacrificed Pawn or rendering it useless. However, it is an error of judgment on White's part, since the extra central Pawn allows Black to set up a very solid position against which White can do nothing while Black gradually extricates himself.

7.	P × P
8. Kt—R 3	Kt—K B 3
9. Q—Q 3	

Not 9. Kt—Q Kt 5 ?, Kt × P !; and not 9. B—K Kt 5 ?, B × P ch !;

| 9. ...... | P—Q R 3 |

Now this is necessary to prevent Kt—Q Kt 5.

| 10. B—K Kt 5 | P—R 3 |
| 11. B × Kt | |

If 11. B—R 4, Kt—K 3; 12. B—K Kt 3, Kt—R 4; 13. Castles K R, K Kt—B 5; 14. Q—Q 2, Castles; followed later by P—B 4 with an excellent game. White's exchange is made partly to prevent this line and partly in accordance with his general plan of keeping complete control over his Q 5.

11.	Q × B
12. R—Q 1	B—B 2
13. B—Q 5	Kt—K 3
14. P—K Kt 3	

Creating a tiresome weakness in his position. It would be better to play 14. Castles, Kt—B 5; 15. Q—Q 2, R—Q Kt 1; 16. Kt—B 2, Kt × B; 17. Q × Kt, P—Q Kt 4; 18. Kt—K 3, B—Kt 2; 19. Q—Q 3 followed by Kt—Q 5 and White can still hold the position.

| 14. ...... | R—Q Kt 1 |
| 15. Kt—B 4 ? | |

Threatening 16. B × Kt, B P × B; 17. Kt × P ch, B × Kt; 18. Q × B, Q × Kt; 19. Q × R, Q × R ch; 20. K—Q 2 ! etc. However, as will be seen, it would be better to play the quieter move Kt—B 2.

| 15. ...... | Castles |

Developing and meeting the threat to the Q P incidentally, White would give a good deal to have his Pawn back on K Kt 2 !

| 16. K—K 2 | |

Illogical play: having created a serious King's side weakness to keep the Black Knight from establishing itself on K B 5 he allows it to settle on the almost equally strong square Q B 4. The best line is 16. P—Q Kt 4, P—Q Kt 4; 17. Kt—R 3 followed by Kt—B 2, K—K 2 and Kt—K 3. Note that had White played 15. Kt—B 2 instead of Kt—B 4 then he could have played simply 17. P—Q Kt 4, P—Q Kt 4; 18. K—K 2 followed by Kt—K 3 saving two moves.

16.	P—Q Kt 4
17. Kt—K 3	P—Kt 5 !
18. P—B 4	P—Kt 6 !

This charge by the Kt P is typical Alekhine and gives Black a permanent hold on his Q B 4.

| 19. P—Q R 3 | |

If 19. P × P, Kt—B 4; 20. Q moves, R × P; and if 19. B × Kt, B P × B; threatening Q × Kt ch (the Kt P is again wanted on Kt 2 !).

| 19. ...... | Kt—B 4 |
| 20. Q—Q 2 | |

20. Q—Kt 1 is better, keeping up the protection of the K P, e.g. 20. Q—Kt 1, B—Kt 2; 21. B × B, R × B; 22. Kt—Q 5, Q—K 3;

23. Kt—R 4, P—Kt 3; 24. Kt—B 5 !, B—Q 1 ! (24. ....P × Kt ?; 25. P × P winning Queen); 25. K Kt—K 3, P—B 4; 26. P × P, P × P; 27. P—Kt 4 !, a highly critical position with chances for both sides.

20.	......	B—Kt 2
21.	B × B	R × B
22.	Kt—Q 5	Q—K 3
23.	Q—K 3	B—Q 1
24.	Kt—Q 2	P—B 4
25.	P—B 3	

As White will have to exchange Pawns anyway, he would do better to do so at once.

25. ......   B—Kt 4 !

Position after Black's 25th move

26. P × P

Forced. If 26. P—B 4, B P × P !; 27. P × B, Q—Kt 5 ch; 28. K—K 1, Kt—Q 6 ch winning the Queen with mate to follow. If 26. P—B 4, B P × P; 27. Kt × P, P × P; 28. Kt × Kt (28. P × P, Kt × Kt; 29. P × B, Q—Kt 5 ch; 30. K—K 1, Q—R 5 ch; 31. K—K 2, R—B 7 ch; 32. K—Q 3, Kt—B 4 ch; 33. K—B 3, Kt—R 5 ch and mate in 2), P × Q; 29. Kt × Q, R—B 7 ch; 30. K—Q 3, P × Kt; 31. Kt × P,

R × Kt P; winning. Finally, if 26. Q—Kt 1, P × P; 27. Kt × P, Kt × Kt; 28. P × Kt, Q—Kt 5 ch; and wins.

26. ......   Q × P
27. Kt—K 4

If 27. Q—B 3, Kt—R 5; 28. Q—B 1 (28. Q—R 5, Kt × P;), P—K 5; 29. K R—B 1 (29. P × P, Q—B 7 ch; 30. K—Q 3, R—B 6 ch !;), P × P ch; 30. R × P (30. K—B 2, Q—R 6), Q × R ch ! If 27. Q—Kt 1, Q—Q 6 ch; 28. K—K 1, B × Kt ch; 29. R × B, Q × Q B P. If 27. Q—B 2, Kt—Q 6; 28. Q moves, Kt × P. In every case Black wins easily.

27. ......   Kt—K 3 !

If 27. ....B × Q; 28. Kt—K 7 ch, K—R 2; 29. Kt × Q, R × Kt; 30. K × B. If 27. ....Kt × Kt; 28. Q × Kt. The text threatens 28. ....Kt—Q 5 ch, followed by the capture of the K B P.

28. Kt × B

There is nothing better.

28.	......	Q—B 7 ch !
29.	R—Q 2	Q × P ch
30.	Q—Q 3	Q × Q ch
31.	R × Q	P × Kt

Reaching an end-game in which the long-blockaded Q P's—now both passed !—will decide the issue.

32.	R—Q B 1	Kt—Q 5 ch
33.	K—B 2	R—Kt 4
34.	Kt—B 7	

34. Kt—B 3 is the alternative but the position is quite lost after 34. ....R—B 4; 35. K—Kt 2, Kt—Q 7; 36. Q R—Q 1, Kt × Kt 37. P × Kt, R—Q Kt 1.

34. ......   R—B 4

Position after Black's 34th move

At last liquidating the doubled Pawns: challenging like this in such a way that an exchange removes the weakness is a typical method of handling doubled Pawns.

35. R × R

If 35. R (3)—B 3, R × P ch !; 36. R × R, R × R; 37. R—B 3, R × R; 38. P × R, P—Kt 7; and wins.

35. ...... P × R
36. Kt × P P—Q 3

Better than 36. ....P—K 5; 37. R—K 3, R × P ch; 38. R × R, P × R; 39. Kt × P.

37. K—Kt 2 R—Q B 1
38. P—Q R 4 R—R 1

A still simpler win is 38. .... R—B 3; 39. Kt—Kt 8, R—Kt 3; 40. Kt—Q 7, R—Kt 2; and the Knight is trapped.

39. Kt—B 7 R × P
40. Kt—K 8 R—R 3
41. Resigns

The time scramble being over, White has time to look round and see the hopelessness of his position ! Black clearly wins the ending with great ease.

39

MADRID 1945

Black: F. J. PÉREZ

Ruy Lopez (Steinitz Defence Deferred)

1. P—K 4   P—K 4
2. Kt—K B 3   Kt—Q B 3
3. B—Kt 5   P—Q R 3
4. B—R 4   P—Q 3

An excellent defence if Black is content to draw, since it is harder for White to build up an attack against it than against the Morphy defence. Its chief drawback is that it gives Black few winning chances.

5. P—B 4

5. P—Q 4, 5. B × Kt ch and 5. P—B 3 are the alternatives, none of which give more than equality.

5. ......   B—Q 2

This is too quiet. White's idea in playing 5. P—B 4 is to play P—Q 4 later with a strong grip on the centre; in order to counter this Black should play 5. ....B—Kt 5 !; 6. P—K R 3, B × Kt; 7. Q × B, Kt—B 3; 8. Kt—B 3, Kt—Q 2 ! (threat 9. ....Kt—Q 5); 10. B × Kt, P × B; with an equal game.

6. Kt—B 3

Rather better than the immediate P—Q 4 which allows too much simplification, e.g. 6. P—Q 4, P × P; 7. Kt × P, Kt × Kt; 8. B × B ch, Q × B; 9. Q × Kt, Kt—K 2; and although White has an advantage of the space the exchange of minor pieces make it hard for him to exploit it successfully.

| 6. ...... | P—K Kt 3 |
| 7. P—Q 4 | B—Kt 2 |

Now 7. ....P × P; 8. Kt × P does not give the simplification Black desires since if 8. ....Kt × Kt; 9. Q × Kt, P—B 3 (9. ....Q or Kt—B 3; 10. B × B ch with advantage); 10. B—Kt 3 with the better game.

8. B—K Kt 5

A finesse to induce P—B 3 and thus prevent Kt—B 3, but hardly as good as the immediate 8. B—K 3.

| 8. ...... | P—B 3 |

If 8. ....Kt—B 3 ?; 9. B × Q Kt, B × B; 10. P × P, P × P; 11. Q × Q ch, R × Q; 12. Kt × P, and if 8. .... K Kt—K 2; 9. Kt—Q 5 threatening 10. B × Q Kt. Black could (and should), however, play 8. ....B— B 3 !; 9. B—K 3, P × P; 10. Kt × P, Kt × Kt; 11. B × Kt, B × K B; 12. Q × B ch, Q—Q 2; and the exchanges have greatly reduced the pressure on his position. Note that this variation would have been much less effective after 8. B—K 3 since the Black Bishop would then have been on Kt 2 unprotected. The text-move is not definitely bad but leads to a much more difficult type of game.

| 9. B—K 3 | K Kt—K 2 ? |

Wrong. This square should be kept for the Q Kt and Black should play the K Kt to R 3 and thence to B 2 with a solid, if cramped, position.

10. P—Q 5 !

Taking immediate advantage of Black's error. Now the Black Knight has no good square.

| 10. ...... | Kt—Q Kt 1 |
| 11. P—B 5 ! | |

Very strong, putting pressure on the Q P and making it very difficult for Black to free his Queen's side.

| 11. ...... | Castles |
| 12. Castles | P—R 3 |

An unsavoury move but a necessary preliminary to P—B 4 (12. ....P—B 4 ?; 13. Kt—K Kt 5, etc.) and P—B 4 must be played as it is Black's only way of getting any counter chances.

| ·13. Kt—Q 2 | P—B 4 |
| 14. K P × P | Kt P × P |

Better 14. ....Kt × P; 15. B × B, Kt × B; and although White has an advantage because of his hold on K 4 and the weak Black Pawn on Q 3, the advantage is less than in the actual game.

| 15. P—B 3 | B × B |
| 16. Q × B | P × P ? |

A mistake after which the game is lost. However, in any case after 16. ....Kt—Q 2; 17. P × P, P × P; 18. Kt—B 4 White has a marked positional advantage.

Position after Black's 16th move

17. Q—Kt 3 !

Threatening P—Q 6 ch and thus winning the Q Kt P after which Black's Pawn position is completely shattered.

17.	R—B 2
18. Q × P	Kt—Q 2
19. Kt—B 4	R—B 3

Threatening 20. . . . .R—Kt 1; 21. Q—R 7, Kt—Q B 1 winning the Queen.

| 20. Q—Kt 3 | R—Kt 1 |
| 21. Q—R 3 | P—B 5 |

Black must try for a King's side attack since he is clearly lost on the Queen's wing. However, since he is bound to give up K 4 to White and since his Bishop is inactive he can have little hope of the attack succeeding.

22. B × Q B P	Kt—B 4
23. Kt—K 4	R—K Kt 3
24. B—R 7	R—Q Kt 4
25. P—Q 6	Q—R 1
26. B—B 2	

Of course not 26. Q × P ?, R—Kt 2; and White loses a piece.

| 26. . . . . . . | P × P |
| 27. Q R—Q 1 ! | Kt—B 3 |

If 27. . . . .P—Q 4; 28. Kt—B 3, R moves; 29. Kt × Q P.

| 28. Kt (K 4) × P | B—B 1 |
| 29. Q—Q 3 | P—K 5 |

Forced; otherwise Black loses at least the exchange.

| 30. Kt × P | Kt—Q 4 |

This loses another Pawn but the position is quite lost anyway.

| 31. P—Q R 4 | Kt—Kt 5 |

The only way to avoid the immediate loss of a piece.

| 32. Q—Q 2 | R—Kt 2 |
| 33. Q × P | R—K B 2 |

Or 33. . . . .Kt—K 2; 34. Kt—K 5, R—Kt 2 (the only square for the Rook); 35. Kt—B 6 ch, K—R 1; 36. Q × P ch and mate next move. Black might as well have resigned here.

| 34. Kt—K 5 | Kt—Q 4 |
| 35. Q—Q 2 | Resigns |

White is already 3 Pawns up and will also in addition win at least the exchange. A forceful and accurate game by Alekhine, who exploited Black's mistakes in the opening in exemplary style.

40

ALMERIA 1945

Black: LOPEZ JULIO

French Defence

1. P—K 4	P—K 3
2. P—Q 4	P—Q 4
3. Kt—Q 2	

See the games v. Capablanca (No. 7) and Bartosek (No. 35) for other examples of 3. Kt—Q 2.

| 3. . . . . . . | P × P |

This exchange gives Black a lifeless game with few counter chances. It does, however, reduce the tension and although White has a clear advantage in position (because of his control of the centre), it is harder for him to get an attack than in the more critical variations arising from . . . .P—Q B 4 or . . . .Kt—K B 3. It is therefore very understandable that Black should choose it against Alekhine !

| 4. Kt × P | Kt—Q 2 |

4. ....Kt—B 3; 5. Kt × Kt ch, Q × Kt; 6. Kt—B 3 threatening B—Kt 5 is very good for White.

| 5. Kt—K B 3 | K Kt—B 3 |
| 6. B—Q 3 | B—K 2 |

6. ....P—B 4; is slightly preferable, e.g. 7. Kt × Kt ch, Kt × Kt; 8. P × P, B × P; and although White with three Pawns to two on the Q side and the freer game has some advantage, there is nothing seriously wrong with Black's game.

7. Castles	Castles
8. P—B 3	P—Q Kt 3
9. Q—K 2	B—Kt 2
10. R—Q 1	R—K 1
11. Kt—K 5	P—K R 3 ?

Here Black should simplify by 11. ....K Kt × Kt; 12. B × Kt, B × B; 13. Q × B, Kt × Kt; 14. Q × Kt, B—Q 3.

This leaves White rather the better end-game because of Black's weakness on the White squares, but the game should be a draw. The text-move not only fails to take advantage of this opportunity but creates a weakness on the K side which White quickly exploits.

12. B—K B 4

Now if 12. ....K Kt × Kt; 13. B × Kt, B × B; 14. Q × B, Kt × Kt; 15. P × Kt !, Q—B 1; 16. R—Q 3; with a very strong attack—or if here 14. ....Kt—B 3; 15. Q—B 3 again with a very promising game. Black has missed his chance.

| 12. ...... | Kt—Q 4 |

Nevertheless the line given in the last note (with 14. ....Kt—B 3;) would be better than this. In a cramped position it almost always

pays to exchange. Black was probably reckoning on being able to meet 13. B—Kt 3 with P—B 4.

13. B—Kt 3 !   Q—B 1

If 13. ....P—K B 4; 14. Kt—Q 2, P—B 5; 15. Q—K 4 !, Kt × Kt; 16. P × Kt, P × B; 17. Q—R 7 ch, K—B 1; 18. B—Kt 6 and White wins. Or, here, if 15. ....Q Kt—B 3; 16. Q—Kt 6, R—K B 1; 17. B—R 4, Q—K 1; 18. Kt—K 4, Q × Q; 19. Kt × Q, K R—K 1; 20. P—B 4 ! winning at least a Pawn, since if 20. ....Kt × Kt ?; 21. B × Kt ! and the Kt on Q 4 is pinned and if 20. ....Kt—Q Kt 5; 21. Kt × B ch, etc.

14. Q—R 5   R—B 1

If 14. ....Kt × Kt; 15. P × Kt followed by P—Q B 4 later, driving away the Kt and remaining with a winning attack.

15. Kt—Kt 4 !

Position after White's 15th move

15. ......   P—K B 4

Fatal, but there is nothing good. White threatens Kt × P ch and there is nothing Black can do, e.g. 15. ....Kt (2)—B 3; 16. Kt × P ch,

P × Kt (16. .... K—R 1; 17.
Kt × P dble ch. K—Kt 1; 18.
Kt (4)—Kt 5 ! and wins at once);
17. Kt × Kt ch, Kt × Kt; 18. Q × P,
Kt—K 5 (18. ....B—K 5; 19.
B—K 5, B × B; 20. R × B); 19. B—
K 5, P—K B 3; 20. Q—Kt 6 ch,
K—R 1; 21. Q B—B 4 !, regaining
the piece and coming out two Pawns
up.

16. Kt × P ch	P × Kt
17. Q—Kt 6 ch	K—R 1
18. Q × P ch	K—Kt 1
19. Q × P ch	K—R 1
20. Q—R 6 ch	K—Kt 1
21. Q—Kt 6 ch	K—R 1
22. B—K 5 ch !	Kt × B

Not 22. ....Kt or B—B 3; 23.
Kt—Kt 5 followed by mate.

| 23. P × Kt | Q—K 1 |

Not 23. ....P × Kt; 24. B × P
and mate in a few moves is unavoidable.

24. Q—R 6 ch	K—Kt 1
25. Kt—Kt 5	B × Kt
26. Q × B ch	K—R 1
27. B × P	Q—B 2

27. ....R × B; 28. Q × R is of
course quite hopeless for Black,
White having R and 4 P's for B and
Kt besides retaining all his attack.

| 28. Q—R 6 ch | K—Kt 1 |
| 29. B—K 6 | Kt—K 2 |

29. ....Resigns; is better.

| 30. R—Q 3 | Kt—B 4 |

White announced mate in 4.

41

ALMERIA 1945

White: F. MARTINEZ

*Queen's Pawn, Queen's Indian
Defence*

| 1. P—Q 4 | Kt—K B 3 |
| 2. Kt—K B 3 | P—Q Kt 3 |

An excellent system against
2. Kt—K B 3. Against 2. P—Q B 4
the immediate P—Q Kt 3 is not
good because of 3. P—B 3 !, B—Kt 2;
4.P—K 4 with a tremendous position
in the centre.

3. P—B 4

Bad timing. The best antidote
to the Queen's side fianchetto is
counter fianchetto on K Kt 2—the
K B is then usually rather better
than the opposing Q B as it gets the
protection of the castled King while
the B on Q Kt 2 is loose. White
should play immediately 3. P—
K Kt 3 to meet B—Kt 2 with
B—Kt 2.

| 3. ...... | B—Kt 2 |
| 4. Q Kt—Q 2 | |

A consequence of his faulty 3rd
move. If 4. P—K Kt 3, B × Kt;
5. P × B, P—Q 4; and White is left
with an inferior Pawn formation.
He has therefore first to protect his
K Kt if he wants to play P—K Kt 3.
Q 2 is, however, an unnatural square
for the Q Kt in this variation and it
would be better to abandon the
whole idea of P—K Kt 3 and to play
Kt—B 3, P—K 3 and B—Q 3.

| 4. ...... | P—K 3 |
| 5. P—K Kt 3 | P—B 4 ! |

Taking immediate advantage of White's uncomfortable position by threatening to win the Q P. 6. B—Kt 2 is of course useless since after 6. ....P × P; the Knight can still not retake.

6. P—K 3 ?

This leads to trouble straight away as White gets saddled with an isolated Q P without compensation. The best line would be 6. P × P, B × P; 7. B—Kt 2, Kt—B 3; 8. Castles (8. Kt—K 5, Q—B 2;), P—Q 4; with approximate equality.

6. ......   P × P
7. P × P   Kt—B 3
8. Kt—Kt 3   P—Q 4

Note the precision of Black's play. If 7. ....P—Q 4 ?; 8. B—Kt 2, Kt—B 3; 9. Castles and White's position is much less serious: the whole opening is an object lesson in the importance of timing.

9. P × P   Q × P
10. B—Kt 2   B—Kt 5 ch

Position after Black's 10th move

The opening is over and Black is left with a winning game. He has an ideal development for all his pieces whereas White has two fewer pieces in play, a displaced Knight

and a weak Pawn on Q 4. A remarkable result after 10 moves in a Queen's Pawn.

11. B—Q 2   Q—K 5 ch

11. ....B—R 3; is met by 12. Kt—R 4

12. Q—K 2   B × B ch
13. K × B

Although both Knights and the Queen guard Q 2, this is forced. If 13. Q Kt × B, Q × Q ch; 14. K × Q, Kt × P ch; 15. Kt × Kt. B × B; winning a Pawn.

13. ......   Castles K R
14. Kt—R 4

If 14. Q × Q, Kt × Q ch; 15. K—K 3, Kt—Q 3 !; 16. Q R—B 1, Kt—B 4 ch; 17. K—Q 3, Q R—Q 1; and wins the Q P.

14. ......   Q × Q ch
15. K × Q   Q R—Q 1
16. Q R—Q 1   B—R 3 ch
17. K—K 3

If 17. K—K 1, Kt—Q Kt 5; 18. Kt—B 1, Kt—B 7 ch; 19. K—Q 2, Kt × P; winning.

17. ......   Kt—Q Kt 5
18. P—B 4

Black threatened 18. ....Kt—B 7 ch; 19. K—B 4 (19. K—B 3, P—K Kt 4 !; or 19. K—Q 2, Kt × P;), P—R 3; 20. Kt—B 3, P—Kt 4 ch; 21. K—K 5, Kt—Kt 5 ch; 22. K—K 4, P—B 4 mate.

18. ......   Kt—B 7 ch
19. K—B 2

If 19. K—B 3, P—K R 3; and the threat of P—K Kt 4 forces 20. K—B 2

19. ......   Kt—Kt 5 ch
20. K—B 3

20. K—Kt 1 is better, but after 20. ....B—B 5; 21. Kt—B 3, Kt—Kt 5; Black wins at least a Pawn.

20. ......   Kt (7)—K 6

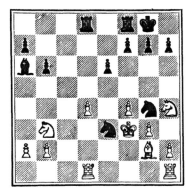

Position after Black's 20th move

21. Q R—K Kt 1

A pathetic state of affairs ! The text is forced as against other R moves 21. ....B—Kt 2 ch; wins a piece.

21. ......   R—Q B 1
22. P—K R 3   B—Kt 2 ch
23. K—K 2   R—B 7 ch
24. K—K 1

If 24. Kt—Q 2, B—R 3 ch; 25. K—B 3 (25. K—K 1, R—B 8 mate), R × Kt; 26. P × Kt, Kt × B; 27. Kt × Kt, B—Kt 2 ch winning a piece. If 24. K—Q 3, B—R 3 ch; 25. K—K 4, P—B 4 ch; 26. K—B 3, B—K 7 mate.

24. ......   Kt—B 7
25. Kt—Q 2

25. ....Kt—Q 6 mate was threatened.

25. ......   Kt × B ch

Humdrum, but very effective.

H

26. R × Kt

If 26. K × Kt, R × Kt ch; 27. K—B 1, B—R 3 mate. If 26. Kt × Kt, Kt × R; winning as in the game.

26. ......   Kt × R
27. Resigns

An instructive game, White's inaccurate opening play being severely punished. In this, as in many other games, Alekhine shows his ability to work up a violent attack after the exchange of Queens —a point which might be noted with advantage by that (too numerous) class of players who think the game automatically becomes "dull" when the Queens go.

42

MELILLA 1945

Black: J. M. FUENTES

Evans Gambit Declined

1. P—K 4   P—K 4
2. Kt—K B 3   Kt—Q B 3
3. B—B 4   B—B 4
4. P—Q Kt 4   B—Kt 3

The gambit can safely be accepted —there are a number of sound defences—but it is necessary to know the variations thoroughly. Declining the gambit leads usually to a rather dull game in which it is difficult for White to get much attack.

5. P—Q R 4   P—Q R 3
6. Kt—B 3

A recent innovation. The older line is 6. B—Kt 2, P—Q 3; 7. P—Kt 5, P × P; 8. P × P, R × R; 9. B × R, Kt—Q 5 with an equal game.

6. ......   Kt—B 3
7. Kt—Q 5   Kt × Kt

If 7. ....K Kt × P; 8. Castles and White gets a strong attack, *e.g.* 8. ....Castles; 9. P—Q 3, Kt—B 3 (9. ....Kt—Q 3; 10. B—K Kt 5, Q—K 1; 11. P—R 5, B—R 2; 12. Kt × B P and wins); 10. B—K Kt 5, P—Q 3; 11. Kt—Q 2, B—K 3; 12. Kt × Kt ch, P × Kt; 13. B—R 6, R—K 1; 14. B × B, P × B; 15. Q—Kt 4 ch, K—B 2; 16. Q—Kt 7 mate. If 7. ....P—Q 3; 8. Kt × B, P × Kt; 9. P—Q 3, B—Kt 5; 10. P—B 3 and White has a slight advantage.

8. P × Kt   Kt—Q 5

The best line is 8. ....P—K 5 !; 9. P × Kt, Castles ! (9. .... P × Kt ?; 10. Q × P, Q—K 2 ch; 11. K—Q 1, Q P × P; 12. B—Kt 2 with advantage); 10. Castles!, P × Kt; 11. Q × P, Q P × P; with equal chances. After the text-move White gets the better game through his preponderance of Q side Pawns.

9. Castles   P—Q 3

9. ....Kt × Kt ch; 10. Q × Kt, P—Q 3; is better as Black can then hold up White's P—Q 4.

10. Kt × Kt	B × Kt
11. P—B 3	B—R 2
12. P—Q 4	Q—R 5
13. B—Q 3	Castles
14. P × P	P × P
15. Q—K 2	R—K 1
16. B—K 3	B—Kt 5

Best. The trouble about Black's game if he does not play B—Kt 5 is that sooner or later he will have to play B × B (in order to develop his Q R) and White will recapture with the Pawn. After this Black can do little with his K side majority and White can advance on the Q side while maintaining attacking chances on the open K B file.

17. P—B 3   B × B ch
18. Q × B   B—R 4 ?

This is quite wrong as Alekhine at once demonstrates. 18. ....B—Q 2 ! is necessary and although White has the advantage the game is by no means won.

Position after Black's 18th move

19. Q—K 4 !

Forcing the Queens off and leaving Black with a very unfavourable ending since White can immediately advance on the Q side and the Black Bishop is misplaced.

19. ......   Q × Q
20. P × Q   P—Q R 4
21. Q R—Kt 1   P—Q B 3 ?

21. ....P—Q Kt 3; is better but the position is lost, *e.g.* 21. .... P—Q Kt 3; 22. B—Kt 5, R—K 2 (22. ....R—Q 1; 23. R—B 5); 23. B—B 6, R—R 2 (23. .... R—Q 1; 24. P × P, P × P; 25. R—Kt 7 followed by R—R 7 later);

24. P × P, R × P; 25. P—Q 6,
P × P; 26. R × P, P—R 3; 27.
B—Kt 5, R—K 3; 28. B—Q 7,
R—K 2 (28. ....R—Kt 3 ?;
29. B—B 5); 29. R × P winning a
Pawn.

22. Kt P × P   P × P

If 22. ....R × P; 23. R × P,
P × P; 24. B—Kt 5 !, R—Q 1;
25. P × P and White wins.

23. R × Kt P   P × P

Relying no doubt on 24. B × P,
R × P; and Black has good chances.

24. B—B 4 !   R—K B 1

If 24. .... R × P; 25. R (1) × P !,
B × R; 26. B × B ch, K—B 1;
27. B × R, K × B; 28. R × P, R × P;
29. K—B 2; and White wins the
ending easily.

25. P—R 6   Q R—B 1
26. B—Q 5   B—K 7

Desperation. 26. ....R × P; was
a little better but after 27. P—R 7,
R (6)—B 1; 28. R (1)—Kt 1,
R—R 1; 29. R × P !, B × R; 30.
B × R, Black has no defence against
the threat of R—Kt 8.

27. R (1) × P   R × R
28. R × R   Resigns

28. .... K—R 1; 29. P—R 7 and
wins.

INDEX OF OPENINGS

INDEX OF OPPONENTS

INDEX OF OPENINGS

NOTE: *The Numbers in heavy type denote the games in which Alekhine had White*

INDEX OF OPPONENTS

NOTE: *The Numbers in heavy type denote the games in which Alekhine had White*

ALL THE GAMES TRANSLATED INTO ALGEBRAIC FIGURINE PGN NOTATION: The following is every game in this book, but in Algebraic Notation with the concluding diagram at the end. These games have all been translated and converted into Figurine Notation by Sam Sloan.

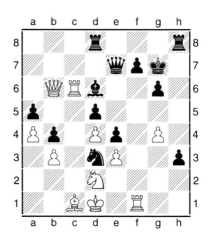

[Site "Carrasco"]
[Date "1938"]
[Round "06"]
[White "Julio Cesar Balparda"]
[Black "Alexander Alekhine"]
[Result "0-1"]
[ECO "A47"]
1.d4 ♘f6 2.♘f3 b6 3.g3 ♗b7 4.♗g2 c5 5.c3 e6 6.O-O ♗e7 7.b3 O-O 8.♗b2 cxd4 9.cxd4 b5 10.♘bd2 ♛b6 11.e3 a5 12.a3 ♘c6 13.♘e5 d6 14.♘xc6 ♗xc6 15.♗xc6 ♛xc6 16.♖c1 ♛b7 17.♕f3 d5 18.♖c2 ♗d6 19.♖fc1 ♛e7 20.♕e2 ♖fb8 21.♘b1 h5 22.♖c6 h4 23.g4 ♘e4 24.f3 ♘g5 25.♔g2 b4 26.a4 e5 27.♘d2 ♖e8 28.♕b5 e4 29.f4 h3+ 30.♔g3 ♖ad8 31.♖f1 g6 32.♕b6 ♔g7 33.♗c1 ♘e6 34.♖g1 ♖h8 35.♔f2 ♘xf4 36.♔e1 ♘d3+ 37.♔d1 ♗xh2 38.♖f1 ♗d6 0-1

[Site "Margate"]
[Date "1938"]
[White "Alexander Alekhine"]
[Black "Eero Einar Book"]
[Result "1-0"]
[ECO "D26"]

1.d4 d5 2.c4 dxc4 3.♘f3 ♘f6 4.e3 e6 5.♗xc4 c5 6.O-O ♘c6 7.♕e2 a6 8.♘c3 b5 9.♗b3 b4 10.d5 ♘a5 11.♗a4+ ♗d7 12.dxe6 fxe6 13.♖d1 bxc3 14.♖xd7 ♘xd7 15.♘e5 ♖a7 16.bxc3 ♔e7 17.e4 ♘f6 18.♗g5 ♛c7 19.♗f4 ♛b6 20.♖d1 g6 21.♗g5 ♗g7 22.♘d7 ♖xd7 23.♖xd7+ ♔f8 24.♗xf6 ♗xf6 25.e5 1-0

118

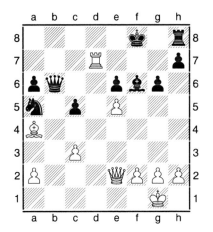

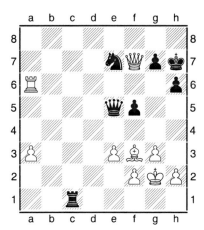

[Site "Margate"]
[Date "1938"]
[Round "03"]
[White "Alexander Alekhine"]
[Black "Harry Golombek"]
[Result "1–0"]
[ECO "E20"]

1.d4 ♘f6 2.c4 e6 3.♘c3 ♗b4
4.g3 d5 5.♗g2 O-O 6.♘f3 c5
7.cxd5 ♘xd5 8.♗d2 ♘c6
9.a3 ♘xc3 10.bxc3 ♗a5
11.O-O cxd4 12.cxd4 ♗xd2
13.♕xd2 ♕e7 14.♕b2 ♖d8
15.♖fc1 ♕d6 16.e3 ♖b8
17.♘g5 ♗d7 18.♕c2 f5
19.d5 ♘e7 20.dxe6 ♗xe6
21.♖d1 ♕e5 22.♗xb7 h6
23.♘xe6 ♕xe6 24.♕c7
♖xd1+ 25.♖xd1 ♖e8 26.♗f3
a6 27.♖d6 ♕e5 28.♕c4+
♔h7 29.♖xa6 ♖c8 30.♕f7
♖c1+ 31.♔g2 1–0

[Site "Plymouth"]
[Date "1938"]
[White "Alexander Alekhine"]
[Black "Ron Bruce"]
[Result "1–0"]
[ECO "♗10"]

1.e4 c6 2.♘c3 d5 3.♘f3
dxe4 4.♘xe4 ♗f5 5.♘g3 ♗g6
6.h4 h6 7.♘e5 ♗h7 8.♕h5
g6 9.♗c4 e6 10.♕e2 ♘f6
11.♘xf7 ♔xf7 12.♕xe6+ 1–0

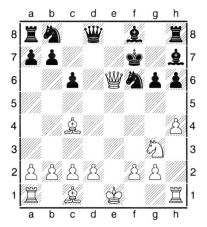

[Site "Madrid"]
[Date "1940"]
[White "Alekhine,Alexander"]
[Black "Navarro"]
[Result "1-0"]
[ECO "B10"]

1.e4 c6 2.♘c3 d5 3.♘f3
dxe4 4.♘xe4 ♗f5 5.♘g3 ♗g6
6.h4 h6 7.♘e5 ♘d7 8.♘xg6
fxg6 9.d4 e5 10.♕g4 ♕f6
11.♗e3 ♘e7 12.♘e4 1-0

h6 12.♗g3 h5 13.♘xd7 ♘xd7
14.gxh5 ♘f6 15.♗f3 ♗b4
16.♖c1 ♔f8 17.a3 ♗xc3
18.♖xc3 ♘e7 19.♕b3 ♖xc3
20.bxc3 ♕d7 21.♕b6 ♘c8
22.♕c5+ ♔g8 23.♖b1 b5
24.h6 gxh6 25.♗e5 ♔g7
26.a4 bxa4 27.c4 ♘e7
28.cxd5 ♘exd5 29.♔h1 ♖c8
30.♖g1+ ♔h7 31.♕a3 ♖g8
32.e4 ♖xg1+ 33.♔xg1 ♕b5
34.exd5 ♕b1+ 35.♔g2 ♕g6+
36.♔f1 ♕b1+ 37.♔g2 ♕g6+
38.♗g3 ♘xd5 39.♗xd5 exd5
40.♕xa4 h5 41.h4 1-0

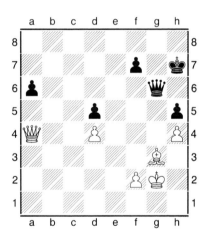

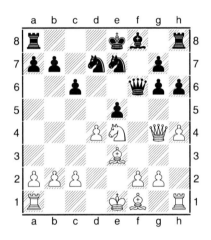

[Site "Amsterdam"]
[Date "1938"]
[Round "03"]
[White "Alexander Alekhine"]
[Black "Max Euwe"]
[Result "1-0"]
[ECO "D14"]

1.d4 d5 2.c4 c6 3.♘f3 ♘f6
4.cxd5 cxd5 5.♘c3 ♘c6
6.♗f4 ♗f5 7.e3 a6 8.♘e5 ♖c8
9.g4 ♗d7 10.♗g2 e6 11.O-O

[Site "AVRO"]
[Date "1938"]
[White "Alexander Alekhine"]
[Black "Salomon Flohr"]
[Result "1-0"]
[ECO "C84"]

1.e4 e5 2.♘f3 ♘c6 3.♗b5 a6
4.♗a4 ♘f6 5.O-O ♗e7 6.♖e1

120

b5 7.♗b3 d6 8.c3 ♘a5 9.♗c2
c5 10.d4 ♕c7 11.♘bd2 O-O
12.♘f1 ♗g4 13.dxe5 dxe5
14.♘e3 ♗e6 15.♕e2 ♖fe8
16.♘g5 c4 17.b4 cxb3
18.♘xe6 fxe6 19.axb3 b4
20.cxb4 ♗xb4 21.♗d2 ♗xd2
22.♕xd2 ♘c6 23.♕c3 ♕b6
24.♗d3 ♘d4 25.b4 ♖ec8
26.♘c4 ♖ab8 27.♖a5 ♕xb4
28.♕xb4 ♖xb4 29.♘xe5 ♘b3
30.♖xa6 ♘c5 31.♖c1 ♖bb8
32.♗c4 ♔h8 33.♘f7+ ♔g8
34.♘d6 ♖c7 35.♖aa1 ♔f8
36.e5 ♘g4 37.♖e1 g5
38.♖a3 ♘h6 39.♖f3+ ♔g7
40.♖g3 g4 41.h3 ♔h8
42.hxg4 1-0

[ECO "C05"]

1.e4 e6 2.d4 d5 3.♘d2 ♘f6
4.e5 ♘fd7 5.♗d3 c5 6.c3
♘c6 7.♘e2 ♕b6 8.♘f3 cxd4
9.cxd4 ♗b4+ 10.♔f1 ♗e7
11.a3 ♘f8 12.b4 ♗d7 13.♗e3
♘d8 14.♘c3 a5 15.♘a4 ♕a7
16.b5 b6 17.g3 f5 18.♔g2
♘f7 19.♕d2 h6 20.h4 ♘h7
21.h5 ♘fg5 22.♘h4 ♘e4
23.♕b2 ♔f7 24.f3 ♘eg5
25.g4 fxg4 26.♗g6+ ♔g8
27.f4 ♘f3 28.♗xh7+ ♖xh7
29.♘g6 ♗d8 30.♖ac1 ♗e8
31.♔g3 ♕f7 32.♔xg4 ♘h4
33.♘xh4 ♕xh5+ 34.♔g3 ♕f7
35.♘f3 1-0

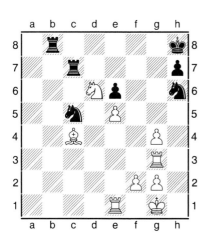

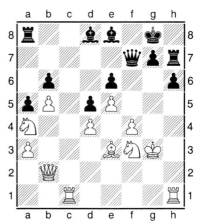

[Event "Amsterdam AVRO"]
[Date "1938"]
[White "Alexander Alekhine"]
[Black "Jose Raul
Capablanca"]
[Result "1-0"]

[Site "Caracas"]
[Date "1939"]
[White "Kausz"]
[Black "Alexander Alekhine"]
[Result "0-1"]
[ECO "A80"]

121

1.d4 f5 2.♘f3 ♘f6 3.c4 e6
4.♘c3 ♗b4 5.♗d2 O-O
6.♕c2 b6 7.g3 ♗b7 8.♗g2
♘e4 9.O-O ♘xd2 10.♘xd2
♗xg2 11.♔xg2 ♘c6 12.e3 e5
13.♘d5 exd4 14.e4 f4
15.♘f3 ♗d6 16.♕d2 ♕e8
17.♖ae1 ♕h5 18.♘h4 f3+
19.♔h1 ♖ae8 20.♘f5 ♕g4
21.b4 ♖xe4 22.♖xe4 ♕xe4
23.♘xd6 ♕e2 24.♕c1 cxd6
25.♘f4 ♖xf4 26.gxf4 ♘xb4
27.♔g1 ♘d3 28.♕d1 ♘xf4
0-1

♗e7 7.cxd5 ♘xd5 8.♗b5+
♗d7 9.♗xd7+ ♘xd7 10.♘xd5
exd5 11.♕b3 ♘b6 12.O-O
O-O 13.♗f4 ♗d6 14.♗xd6
♕xd6 15.♖fe1 ♖ac8 16.♖ac1
h6 17.♘e5 ♖c7 18.g3 ♖fc8
19.♖xc7 ♖xc7 20.♕b5 ♘d7
21.♘xd7 ♖xd7 22.♖e8+ ♔h7
23.h4 a6 24.♕e2 ♖d8
25.♖e7 ♖d7 26.♖e5 g6 27.h5
♕f6 28.♕d3 ♖d6 29.♕b3
♖b6 30.hxg6+ ♕xg6
31.♕xd5 ♖xb2 32.♖f5 ♖b5
33.♖xf7+ ♔g8 34.♖f6+ ♖xd5
35.♖xg6+ ♔h7 36.♖b6 ♖xd4
37.♖xb7+ ♔g8 38.♖b6 ♖a4
39.♖xh6 ♖xa2 40.♔g2 a5
41.♖a6 a4 42.♖a7 a3 43.g4
♖a1 44.♔g3 ♖g1+ 45.♔f4
♖a1 46.g5 ♔f8 47.♔f5 1-0

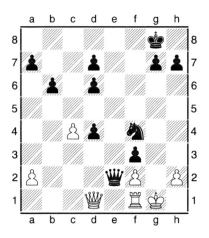

[Site "Buenos Aires"]
[Date "1939"]
[White "Alexander Alekhine"]
[Black "Erich Eliskases"]
[Result "1-0"]
[ECO "B14"]

1.e4 c6 2.d4 d5 3.exd5 cxd5
4.c4 ♘f6 5.♘c3 e6 6.♘f3

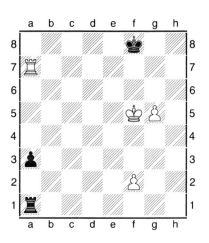

[Site "Buenos Aires"]
[Date "1939"]
[White "Alexander Alekhine"]
[Black "Alexandar Tsvetkov"]
[Result "1-0"]
[ECO "♗50"]

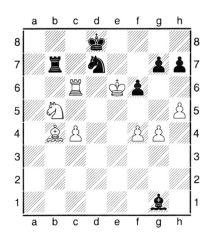

1.e4 c5 2.♘f3 d6 3.c3 ♘f6
4.e5 dxe5 5.♘xe5 ♘c6
6.♘xc6 bxc6 7.♗c4 ♗f5 8.d3
e6 9.♕f3 ♕d7 10.h3 ♗e7
11.♘d2 ♖d8 12.O-O ♗xd3
13.♗xd3 ♕xd3 14.♕xc6+
♕d7 15.♕a6 O-O 16.♘c4
♕c7 17.♕a5 ♕xa5 18.♘xa5
♖d6 19.♗e3 ♖a6 20.♘b3
♖c8 21.c4 ♔f8 22.♖fd1 ♖d6
23.♖xd6 ♗xd6 24.♖d1 ♔e7
25.♘a5 ♗e5 26.♖d3 ♖c7
27.♖b3 ♘d7 28.f4 ♗d6
29.♔f2 ♘b6 30.♔f3 ♔d7
31.♖d3 ♔e7 32.g4 f6 33.h4
♘a4 34.♖b3 ♘b6 35.♖b5
♔d7 36.h5 ♔e7 37.a3 ♔d7
38.♔e4 ♔e7 39.♔d3 ♔d7
40.♘b3 ♘a4 41.♘d2 ♔c6
42.b3 ♘b6 43.♘e4 ♘d7
44.♖a5 ♗e7 45.♘c3 ♖b7
46.♘b5 ♔b6 47.b4 a6
48.♘c3 ♔c7 49.♖xa6 cxb4
50.♘b5+ ♔d8 51.axb4 ♗xb4
52.♖xe6 ♗c5 53.♗d2 ♘f8
54.♖c6 ♘d7 55.♔e4 ♔e7
56.♔d5 ♗g1 57.♗b4+ ♔d8
58.♔e6 1-0

[Site "Buenos Aires"]
[Date "1939"]
[White "Moshe Czerniak"]
[Black "Alexander Alekhine"]
[Result "0-1"]
[ECO "A22"]

1.c4 ♘f6 2.♘c3 e5 3.g3 d5
4.cxd5 ♘xd5 5.♗g2 ♘b6
6.♘f3 ♘c6 7.O-O ♗e7 8.d3
O-O 9.♗e3 f5 10.♘a4 f4
11.♗c5 ♗g4 12.♖c1 ♗d6
13.♖e1 ♕e7 14.♘d2 ♖h8
15.♘e4 ♗xc5 16.♘axc5 ♘d4
17.♘b3 c6 18.♘xd4 exd4
19.♕d2 ♘d5 20.♖c4 ♕e5
21.b4 ♖ad8 22.♕b2 ♘b6
23.♖c5 ♖d5 24.♕a3 ♘d7
25.♖xd5 cxd5 26.♘c5 f3
27.h3 fxg2 28.hxg4 ♘f6
29.b5 ♕e7 30.♕b4 ♘d7
31.♕xd4 ♘xc5 32.♕xd5 ♖d8
33.♕f3 ♖xd3 34.exd3 ♕xe1+
35.♔xg2 ♕e7 36.d4 ♘e4
37.♕e3 ♕e8 38.f3 ♘f6

123

39.♕e5 ♔g8 40.g5 ♕xe5
41.dxe5 ♘d5 42.f4 ♘c3
43.♔f3 ♘xa2 44.f5 ♘c3
45.b6 a5 46.♔e3 ♘d5+
47.♔d4 ♘xb6 48.e6 a4 49.f6
gxf6 50.gxf6 a3 0-1

26.h5 ♕b6 27.♔h2 ♖fa8
28.♖b2 c6 29.f4 exf4 30.♖xf4
♖a1 31.dxc6 ♘xc6 32.♘d5
♕d8 33.♗e3 ♕h4+ 34.♗h3
♘e5 35.♗xc5 dxc5 36.♕f2
♖h1+ 37.♔xh1 ♕xh3+ 0-1

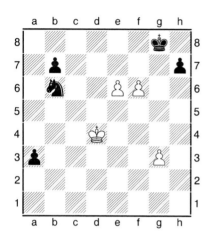

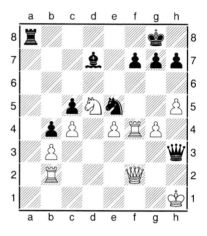

[Site "Buenos Aires"]
[Date "1939"]
[White "Jens Enevoldsen"]
[Black "Alexander Alekhine"]
[Result "0-1"]
[ECO "E33"]

1.d4 ♘f6 2.c4 e6 3.♘c3 ♗b4
4.♕c2 ♘c6 5.♘f3 d6 6.♗d2
e5 7.d5 ♗xc3 8.♗xc3 ♘e7
9.♘h4 ♕d7 10.g3 ♕g4
11.♕b3 ♘g6 12.f3 ♕d7
13.♘g2 O-O 14.e4 ♕d8
15.♘e3 ♘d7 16.♕c2 a5
17.♗g2 ♘c5 18.O-O ♗d7
19.b3 b5 20.♖ad1 b4 21.♗d2
♕b8 22.♖b1 a4 23.h4 ♘e7
24.g4 axb3 25.axb3 ♖a3

[Site "Montevideo"]
[Date "1939"]
[Round "01"]
[White "Alexander Alekhine"]
[Black "Harry Golombek"]
[Result "1-0"]
[ECO "♗72"]

1.e4 c5 2.♘f3 d6 3.d4 cxd4
4.♘xd4 ♘f6 5.♘c3 g6 6.♗e2
♗g7 7.♘b3 ♘c6 8.O-O O-O
9.♔h1 a5 10.a4 ♗e6 11.f4
♕c8 12.♗e3 ♗g4 13.♗g1
♖d8 14.♘d5 ♗xe2 15.♕xe2
♘xd5 16.exd5 ♘b4 17.c4
♕c7 18.♘d4 ♖dc8 19.b3
♘a6 20.♖ae1 ♖e8 21.f5 ♘c5
22.♕f3 ♖f8 23.♘b5 ♕d7

124

24.♗xc5 dxc5 25.♕e3 ♖fe8
26.♕xc5 gxf5 27.♕c7 ♖ad8
28.♕xa5 e5 29.♕c7 ♕xc7
30.♘xc7 ♖e7 31.♘b5 e4
32.♖xf5 e3 33.♖e2 ♖e4
34.g3 ♗h6 35.♔g2 1-0

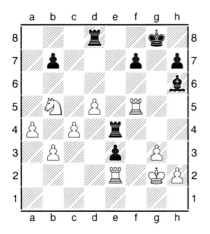

[Site "Rio de Janeiro"]
[Date "1939"]
[White "Alekhine/Cruz W"]
[Black "Silva Rocha
A/Charli"]
[Result "1-0"]
[ECO "D37"]

1.d4 ♘f6 2.c4 e6 3.♘c3 d5
4.♘f3 ♗e7 5.♗f4 O-O 6.e3
a6 7.c5 ♘bd7 8.♗d3 ♖e8
9.b4 c6 10.h3 b6 11.♗h2
bxc5 12.bxc5 e5 13.♘xe5
♘xe5 14.♗xe5 ♗xc5 15.O-O
♗d6 16.f4 ♕e7 17.♕c2 g6
18.♘a4 ♗b7 19.♖ab1 ♖a7
20.♖b3 ♘d7 21.♖xb7 ♖xb7
22.♕xc6 ♗xe5 23.♕xb7 ♗g7

24.♔h2 ♖b8 25.♕xd5 ♕xe3
26.♗c4 ♕xd4 27.♖xd4 ♗xd4
28.♖d1 ♘c5 29.♖xd4 ♘xa4
30.♗xa6 ♘c5 31.♗c4 ♘e6
32.♖e4 ♖b4 33.♔g3 ♔g7
34.♗d5 ♖b6 35.♔f3 ♖d6
36.♗xe6 fxe6 37.a4 ♖c6
38.a5 h5 39.♖a4 ♖a6
40.♔e4 h4 41.♔d4 ♔f6
42.♔c5 g5 43.fxg5+ ♔xg5
44.♔b5 ♖a8 45.a6 ♔f5
46.♖xh4 e5 47.♖a4 1-0

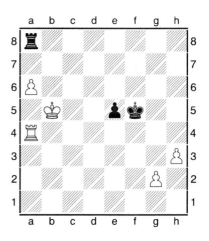

[Site "Munich"]
[Date "1941"]
[White "Alexander Alekhine"]
[Black "H Rohacek"]
[Result "1-0"]
[ECO "C83"]

1.e4 e5 2.♘f3 ♘c6 3.♗b5 a6
4.♗a4 ♘f6 5.O-O ♘xe4 6.d4
b5 7.♗b3 d5 8.dxe5 ♗e6
9.c3 ♗e7 10.a4 ♖b8 11.axb5
axb5 12.♘d4 ♘xe5 13.f3

♘c5 14.♗c2 ♗d7 15.b4 ♘b7 16.♕e2 ♘c4 17.♖e1 ♚f8 18.♗f4 ♘bd6 19.♘d2 g5 20.♘xc4 gxf4 21.♘e5 ♗f6 22.♘dc6 ♗xc6 23.♘xc6 ♕c8 24.♘xb8 ♕xb8 25.♕d2 ♕b6+ 26.♚h1 ♕c6 27.♗b3 ♗xc3 28.♕c1 d4 29.♕xf4 d3 30.♖ec1 d2 31.♖c2 ♕a6 32.♖d1 ♗g7 33.♖xc7 1-0

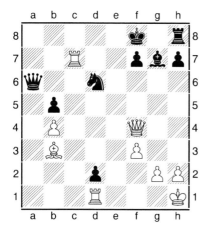

[Site "Munich"]
[Date "1941"]
[White "Peter Leepin"]
[Black "Alexander Alekhine"]
[Result "0-1"]
[ECO "A22"]

1.c4 {Notes by Alekhine} 1...e5 2.♘c3 ♘f6 3.g3 d5 4.cxd5 ♘xd5 5.♗g2 ♘b6 6.a4 {This move is not recommendable at this stage of the game, since white obtains no advantage and at the same time gives up to Black the square b4.} 6...a5 7.d3 ♗b4 {the first consequence of white's sixth move; otherwise the bishop would modestly have had to satisfy itself with the square e7.} 8.♘f3 ♘c6 9.O-O O-O 10.♗e3 ♗g4 11.♖c1 f5 {! A precisely calculated pawn sacrifice, the acceptance of which leads to rapid destruction foreseen by black here on the eleventh move.} 12.♘g5 {Apparently effective in view of the threats 13 ♘e6 and 13 ♕b3+.} 12...f4 {!} 13.♗xb6 ♕xg5 14.♗xc7 ♕h5 {Moe efficacious than 14...♘d4, to which White would have been able to respond with 15 f3. But now this move is impossible in view of 15...♗c5+ with an immediate win.} 15.♗xc6 {This eliminates one enemy but there still remains sufficient reserves. 15 ♗f3 would also have lost quickly after 15...♗xf3, followed by ...♖f6.} 15...bxc6 16.♖c2 {If 16 ♖e1 then 16...fxg3 17 hxg3 ♖xf2! 18 ♚xf2 ♗c5+.} 16...♗xc3 {The most exact. In the continuation from the plausible 16...f3 white would have been able to stop the direct mating threats with 17 h4! ♗xc3 18 ♖xc3 fxe2 19 ♕b3+, followed by 20 ♖e1 etc.} 17.♖xc3 ♗xe2 18.♕b3+ ♔h8 19.♖e1 ♕h3 {! This reveals the idea behind the exchange on the sixteenth move. For the only plausible move, 20 f3, I had prepared mate in eight moves: 20...fxg3! 21 ♖xe2 ♖xf3 22 ♖c1 ♖af8 23 ♕d1 (or 23 ♖g2 gxh2+ and mate in two) ♖f2! 24 ♖xf2 gxf2+ 25 ♔h1 f1 (♕) + etc.} 20.♗xe5 {After this move Black has the agreeable choice between mate with 20...f3 or with 20...♗f3.} 20...f3 {!} 0-1

[ECO "A22"]

1.c4 e5 2.♘c3 ♘f6 3.g3 d5 4.cxd5 ♘xd5 5.♗g2 ♘b6 6.a4 a5 7.d3 ♗b4 8.♘f3 ♘c6 9.O-O O-O 10.♗e3 ♗g4 11.♖c1 f5 12.♘g5 f4 13.♗xb6 ♕xg5 14.♗xc7 ♕h5 15.♗xc6 bxc6 16.♖c2 ♗xc3 17.♖xc3 ♗e2 18.♕b3+ ♔h8 19.♖e1 ♕h3 20.♗xe5 f3 0-1

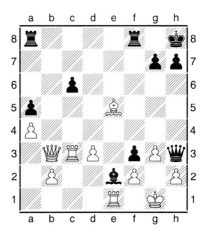

[Site "Munich"]
[Date "1941"]
[Round "09"]
[White "Georg Kieninger"]
[Black "Alexander Alekhine"]
[Result "0-1"]
[ECO "C64"]

1.e4 e5 2.♘f3 ♘c6 3.♗b5 ♗c5 4.c3 ♕f6 5.O-O ♘ge7 6.d3 h6 7.♘bd2 O-O 8.♘c4 ♘g6 9.d4 exd4 10.♗xc6 dxc6 11.♘xd4 ♖e8 12.♘b3

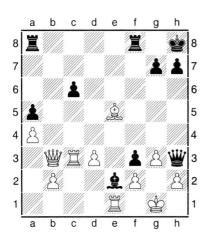

[Site "Munich"]
[Date "1941"]
[White "Peter Leepin"]
[Black "Alexander Alekhine"]
[Result "0-1"]

♗f8 13.♕c2 ♕e6 14.♘cd2 ♘h4 15.f3 c5 16.♖d1 ♘xg2 17.♔xg2 ♕h3+ 18.♔g1 ♗d6 19.♘f1 ♕xf3 20.♖d3 ♕xe4 21.♖d2 ♕h4 22.♖g2 ♗h3 23.♕f2 ♕e4 24.♗d2 ♕xg2+ 25.♕xg2 ♗xg2 26.♔xg2 ♖e2+ 27.♔f3 ♖ae8 28.♖d1 b6 29.♘c1 ♖2e6 30.b3 c4 31.bxc4 ♖f6+ 32.♔g2 ♖e4 33.♘e3 ♗c5 34.♖e1 ♗xe3 35.♖xe3 ♖g4+ 36.♖g3 ♖xc4 37.♖f3 ♖d6 38.♗f4 ♖d1 39.♘e2 ♖a1 40.♔g3 c5 41.♖e3 ♖xa2 42.h4 b5 43.h5 b4 0-1

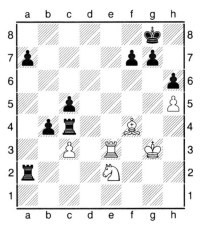

[Site "Salzburg"]
[Date "1942"]
[White "Paul Keres"]
[Black "Alexander Alekhine"]
[Result "0-1"]
[ECO "C34"]

1.e4 e5 2.f4 exf4 3.♘f3 ♘f6 4.e5 ♘h5 5.♕e2 ♗e7 6.d4 O-O 7.g4 fxg3 8.♘c3 d5

9.♗d2 ♘c6 10.O-O-O ♗g4 11.♗e3 f6 12.h3 ♗e6 13.♘g5 fxg5 14.♕xh5 g6 15.♕e2 g4 16.hxg4 ♗g5 17.♔b1 ♗xe3 18.♕xe3 ♗xg4 19.♕h6 ♖f7 20.♗g2 ♘e7 21.♖df1 ♖g7 22.♕f4 ♗e6 23.♘e2 ♘f5 24.♗h3 ♕d7 25.♖fg1 ♖f8 26.♕d2 ♘xd4 27.♕xd4 ♗xh3 28.♖xg3 ♗f5 29.♕xa7 b6 30.♕a3 c5 31.♕b3 ♗e4 32.♖d1 ♕f5 33.♘c3 c4 34.♕a4 ♕xe5 35.♖e3 ♗xc2+ 36.♕xc2 ♕xe3 37.♘xd5 ♕c5 38.♕c3 h5 39.a3 ♖f5 40.♘f6+ ♖xf6 41.♕xf6 ♕f5+ 42.♕xf5 gxf5 43.♔c2 ♔h7 44.♔c3 ♖g4 45.♖d7+ ♔g6 46.♖d6+ ♔g5 47.♖xb6 h4 48.♖b8 h3 49.♖g8+ ♔f4 50.♖h8 ♔g3 51.♖h5 h2 0-1

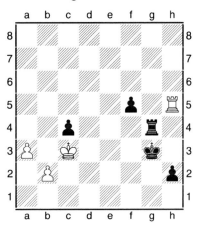

[Site "Salzburg"]
[Date "1942"]
[White "Efim Bogoljubov"]
[Black "Alexander Alekhine"]
[Result "0-1"]

[ECO "A45"]
1.d4 ♘f6 2.♗g5 d5 3.c3 ♘e4
4.♗h4 ♛d6 5.♘d2 ♗f5
6.♘gf3 ♘d7 7.♛b3 O-O-O
8.♘xe4 ♗xe4 9.♗g3 ♛c6
10.♘d2 ♗g6 11.e3 e6 12.c4
♛b6 13.c5 ♛a5 14.a3 e5
15.♛d1 c6 16.dxe5 ♛xc5
17.♖c1 ♛b6 18.♗e2 ♘c5
19.b4 ♘d3+ 20.♗xd3 ♗xd3
21.♘f3 ♗c4 22.♘d4 a5
23.♛g4+ ♖d7 24.♖xc4 dxc4
25.O-O c5 26.bxa5 ♛g6
27.a6 ♛xa6 28.♘e2 ♛e6
29.♛e4 f5 30.♛c2 g5 31.f4
g4 32.e4 ♖f7 33.exf5 ♖xf5
34.♗h4 ♗h6 35.♛e4 ♖hf8
36.g3 ♛d7 37.♖c1 ♖e8
38.♔g2 ♖exe5 39.fxe5 ♗xc1
40.♘xc1 ♛e6 41.h3 gxh3+
42.♔h2 ♖f2+ 43.♔g1 ♖g2+
44.♔h1 ♛d7 45.♛f3 ♛d4
46.♛f8+ ♔c7 47.♛e7+ ♔b6
48.♛d6+ ♛xd6 49.exd6 ♔c6
50.♗e7 ♖c2 51.♗g5 ♔xd6
52.a4 h5 0-1

[Site "Salzburg"]
[Date "1942"]
[White "Alexander Alekhine"]
[Black "Paul Keres"]
[Result "1-0"]
[ECO "C86"]

1.e4 e5 2.♘f3 ♘c6 3.♗b5 a6
4.♗a4 ♘f6 5.O-O ♗e7
6.♛e2 b5 7.♗b3 d6 8.c3 O-
O 9.♖d1 ♘a5 10.♗c2 c5
11.d4 ♛c7 12.♗g5 ♗g4
13.dxe5 dxe5 14.♘bd2 ♖fd8
15.♘f1 ♘h5 16.h3 ♗e6
17.♘e3 f6 18.♘h2 g6
19.♗h6 ♗f8 20.♗xf8 ♔xf8
21.g3 ♖xd1+ 22.♗xd1 ♖d8
23.a4 ♘c4 24.axb5 axb5
25.♘d5 ♛b7 26.b3 ♘d6
27.c4 bxc4 28.bxc4 ♗xd5
29.exd5 ♘g7 30.♘g4 ♛e7
31.♗c2 ♘ge8 32.h4 e4
33.♘e3 ♛e5 34.♖a7 ♔g8
35.♘g4 ♛d4 36.♗xe4 f5
37.♘h6+ ♔h8 38.♗c2 ♛f6
39.♛e6 ♛xe6 40.dxe6 ♖c8
41.♘f7+ ♘xf7 42.exf7 ♘d6
43.♗d3 ♔g7 44.f8♛+ ♔xf8
45.♖xh7 ♔g8 46.♖d7 ♘e8
47.h5 gxh5 48.♗xf5 ♖a8
49.♗e6+ ♔h8 50.♖d5 ♘f6
51.♖xc5 ♔g7 52.♗f5 ♖a3
53.♖c7+ ♔h6 54.♖f7 ♖a6
55.f4 h4 56.g4 1-0

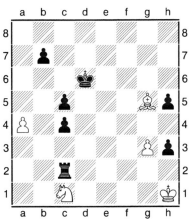

129

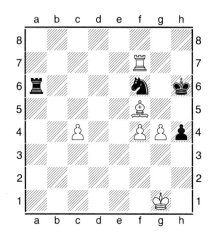

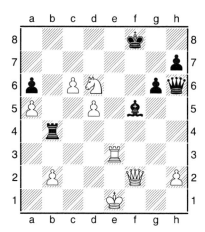

[Site "Salzburg"]
[Date "1942"]
[Round "07"]
[White "Alexander Alekhine"]
[Black "Paul Felix Schmidt"]
[Result "1-0"]
[ECO "C86"]

1.e4 e5 2.♘f3 ♘c6 3.♗b5 a6
4.♗a4 ♘f6 5.O-O ♗e7
6.♕e2 b5 7.♗b3 d6 8.a4 ♗g4
9.c3 O-O 10.♖d1 b4 11.a5
d5 12.exd5 e4 13.dxc6 ♗d6
14.d4 ♖e8 15.♗e3 exf3
16.gxf3 ♗h5 17.♘d2 ♘e4
18.♗xf7+ ♔xf7 19.♕c4+ ♔f8
20.fxe4 ♕h4 21.e5 ♗xd1
22.exd6 ♕g4+ 23.♔f1 cxd6
24.d5 ♕h3+ 25.♔e1 ♗c2
26.cxb4 ♖xe3+ 27.fxe3
♕xe3+ 28.♕e2 ♕h6 29.♖a3
♗f5 30.♖e3 g6 31.♕f2 ♖b8
32.♘c4 ♖xb4 33.♘xd6 1-0

[Site "Munich"]
[Date "1942"]
[Round "09"]
[White "Klaus Junge"]
[Black "Alexander Alekhine"]
[Result "0-1"]
[ECO "E02"]

1.d4 ♘f6 2.c4 e6 3.g3 d5
4.♗g2 dxc4 5.♕a4+ ♗d7
6.♕xc4 ♗c6 7.♘f3 ♘bd7
8.♘c3 ♘b6 9.♕d3 ♗b4
10.O-O O-O 11.♗g5 h6
12.♗xf6 ♕xf6 13.e4 ♖fd8
14.♖ad1 ♗e8 15.a3 ♗f8
16.♕e3 ♖ac8 17.♗h3 ♖b8
18.♖fe1 ♘a4 19.e5 ♕e7
20.♘xa4 ♗xa4 21.♖c1 b6
22.♗f1 c5 23.b3 ♗c6 24.dxc5
bxc5 25.♗c4 ♕b7 26.♖c3
♖d7 27.♖ec1 ♖bd8 28.♘e1
♖d4 29.f3 ♗e7 30.♖d3 ♕b6
31.♖cd1 ♕a5 32.♘c2 ♗g5
33.♕e2 ♖xd3 34.♖xd3 ♗c1
35.♕d1 ♖xd3 36.♕xd3 ♗b2

37.f4 ♗xa3 38.♘xa3 ♕e1+
39.♔f1 ♕e3+ 40.♔f2 ♕c1+
41.♔f1 ♕xa3 42.f5 ♗d5
43.♗xd5 exd5 44.e6 ♕xb3
45.♕e1 ♔f8 46.exf7 ♕b8
47.♔g2 d4 48.♕e6 ♕d8
49.♕c4 ♕d6 50.♕a4 ♕d5+
51.♔g1 ♕xf7 0-1

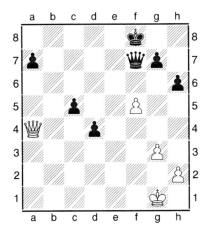

[Site "Munich"]
[Date "1942"]
[White "Alexander Alekhine"]
[Black "Paul Keres"]
[Result "1-0"]
[ECO "E17"]

1.d4 {Notes by Alekhine}
1...♘f6 2.♘f3 b6 3.c4 ♗b7
4.g3 e6 5.♗g2 ♗e7 6.O-O
O-O 7.b3 {Avoiding the
inevitable simplification that
would occur after 7 ♘c3
♘e4!} 7...d5
{Recommendable too is
7...c5 since 8 d5 would be

answered by 8...♘xd5!,
followed by 9...♗f6.} 8.♘e5
c6 {8...c5 is of course more
enterprising.} 9.♗b2 ♘bd7
10.♘d2 c5 11.e3 {Sustaining
the central tension and at the
same time gaining a certain
advantage in space.}
11...♖c8 12.♖c1 ♖c7 13.♕e2
♕a8 {? The rook at c7 is not
secure, and this move helps
white to undertake a
favorable mobilization. Much
better was 13...♕b8,
followed by 14...♖fc8.}
14.cxd5 ♘xd5 15.e4 ♘5f6
16.b4 {! Taking the greatest
possible advantage of the
deficient position of the
Black rook at c7.} 16...♖fc8
17.dxc5 bxc5 18.b5 a6 {?
Also after 18...♘xe5 19
♗xe5 ♖d7 20 ♘b3 Black's
game would be inferior but
allowing the opening of the
a-file is practically suicidal.}
19.a4 axb5 20.axb5 ♕a2
{Keres must have
overlooked the rejoinder. In
any case his position is
already hopeless.} 21.♘ec4
{!} 21...♕a8 22.♗xf6 {!
Winning the exchange
anyway.} 22...gxf6 {If
22...♗xf6 23 b6 or 22...♘xf6
23 ♘b6 etc.} 23.b6 ♖c6
24.e5 ♖xb6 25.♘xb6 ♘xb6
26.♗xb7 ♕xb7 27.exf6 ♗xf6

131

28.♘e4 ♗e7 29.♕g4+ ♔h8 30.♕f4 {! Threatening not only 31 ♕xf7 but also 31 ♘xc5!} 30...♗f8 31.♘xc5 ♕c7 {After 32...♖xc5 White would recover the piece either at d4 or at e5.} 32.♘xe6 ♕xf4 33.♘xf4 1-0

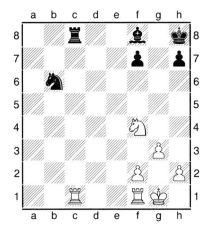

[Site "Munich"]
[Date "1942"]
[White "Alexander Alekhine"]
[Black "Gedeon Barcza"]
[Result "1-0"]
[ECO "C78"]

1.e4 {Notes by Alekhine} 1...e5 2.♘f3 ♘c6 3.♗b5 a6 4.♗a4 ♘f6 5.O-O ♗e7 6.♘c3 b5 7.♗b3 d6 8.♘d5 {!? With this interesting move I defeated Bogoljubov in the Munich tournament last year. The correct continuation for Black is 8...♘a5 when White

has at his disposal no particularly advantageous line.} 8...♗g4 9.c3 O-O {If Black had played ...♘xe4 either now or on his previous move the reply d4! would have had a demolishing affect.} 10.h3 {! Forcing the Bishop to declare its plans at this stage is very precise. After 10...♗h5 White would play 11 d3 without the loss of time.} 10...♗e6 11.d4 ♔h8 {! Preparing against 12 ♘xe7 which would now be refuted by means of 12...♗xb3 13 ♘xc6 ♗xd1 14 ♘xd8 ♗xf3 etc.} 12.♖e1 ♘d7 {And not 12...♘a5 because of the reply 13 ♘xe7 ♘xb3 14 ♘c6 ♕d7 15 axb3, followed by d5.} 13.♗c2 f6 14.a4 ♘a7 {If 14...♖b8 then 15 axb5 axb5 16 ♖a6 with a good game.} 15.axb5 axb5 16.♗e3 {Again threatening 17 ♘xe7, winning a piece.} 16...c5 17.dxc5 dxc5 18.♖a6 {! With the threat 19 ♕e1} 18...♗xd5 19.exd5 ♕c8 20.♕a1 ♕b7 21.b4 {! It will no longer now be possible to avoid 22 d6 etc.} 21...♖fb8 22.d6 ♗d8 23.bxc5 ♖c8 24.♖a2 e4 {Veritable desperation. If 24...♘xc5 there follows 25 ♗xc5 ♖xc5 26 ♗e4 etc.} 25.♗xe4 ♕xe4 26.♗d4 ♕g6

27.♖xa7 ♖xa7 28.♕xa7 ♘e5
29.♗xe5 1-0

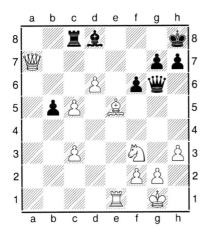

[Event "Prague CZE"]
[Site "It"]
[Date "1942"]
[White "Alexander Alekhine"]
[Black "K Richter"]
[Result "1-0"]
[ECO "♗13"]

1.e4 d5 2.exd5 ♘f6 3.c4 c6
4.d4 cxd5 5.♘c3 ♘c6 6.♗g5
e6 7.♘f3 ♗e7 8.♗d3 O-O
9.O-O dxc4 10.♗xc4 b6
11.a3 ♗b7 12.♕d3 ♘d5
13.♗xd5 ♗xg5 14.♗e4 f5
15.♘xg5 ♕xg5 16.♗f3 ♔h8
17.♖fe1 ♖ad8 18.♕f1 ♖xd4
19.♕b5 ♖d6 20.♘e4 ♕g6
21.♘xd6 ♘d4 22.♗xb7 ♘xb5
23.♘xb5 ♕f6 24.♘c3 e5
25.♖ad1 e4 26.♖d7 h5 27.h3
h4 28.♖ed1 ♔h7 29.♗a6 ♖f7
30.♖7d6 ♕g5 31.♖6d5 ♕f4

32.♘e2 ♕g5 33.♘d4 ♖f6
34.♗e2 ♔h6 35.♘c2 ♖f7
36.♘e3 g6 37.♗c4 ♕f4
38.♖d6 ♖c7 39.b3 ♔h7
40.a4 ♕e5 41.♖e6 ♕c3
42.♘d5 ♕c2 43.♖f1 ♔g7
44.f3 exf3 45.♖xf3 ♔h6
46.♘e3 1-0

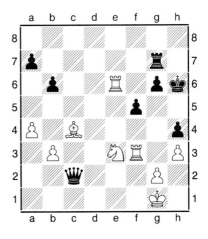

[Site "Munich"]
[Date "1942"]
[White "Alexander Alekhine"]
[Black "Braslav Rabar"]
[Result "1-0"]
[ECO "E02"]

1.d4 {Notes by Alekhine}
1...♘f6 2.c4 e6 3.g3 d5
4.♗g2 dxc4 5.♕a4+ ♗d7
6.♕xc4 ♗c6 7.♘f3 ♗d5
{Black loses too many tempi
with these bishop moves.
Better is 7...♘bd7 and if 8
♘c3 then 8...♘b6 9 ♕d3
♗b4, as it was played in the

133

game Junge–Alekhine in the same tournament.} 8.♕d3 c5 9.♘c3 ♗c6 {If 9...cxd4 there would follow 10 ♘xd5 ♕xd5 11 O–O with the strong threat of 12 ♘xd4.} 10.O–O ♘bd7 11.♖d1 cxd4 {If 11...♗e7 then 12 e4 and White with the threat of 13 d5, would practically force the exchange at d4, which would guarantee him the advantage of the bishop pair.} 12.♘xd4 ♗xg2 13.♔xg2 ♗e7 14.♕f3 {The queen now exerts strong pressure on the enemy queen's side.} 14...♕b6 {this move will be refuted by energetic combinative play. but 14...♕b8 15 ♘b3 with the threat of 16 ♗f4 would be equally unsatisfactory.} 15.♗e3 {! The consequences of this move are not very difficult to calculate, but it is interesting to prove that from this moment onwards Black already lacks any satisfactory defense. Against 15 ♕xb2 White replies 16 ♘cb5 and if 15...♘e5 there would follow 16 ♘db5!} 15...O–O 16.♘f5 ♗c5 {This apparent salvation will be refuted by a well–concealed combination. ♘or would the alternative 16...♕d8 17

♘xe7+ ♕xe7 18 ♕xb7 ♖fb8 19 ♕c7 ♖xb2 20 ♗d4 have saved the game.} 17.♘a4 ♕a5 18.♘xc5 ♘xc5 19.♘xg7 {! This wins at least a pawn and leads to a simply won ending. The only reply – excluding the text – would be 19...♘ce4, against which White would first have forced the black queen to abandon the fifth rank and would then have occupied the long diagonal with the bishop, with decisive effect: 20 b4! ♕e5 21 ♗f4 ♕b5 (or 21...♕c3 22 ♘h5!!) 22 a4! ♕xb4 23 ♗e5 etc.} 19...♔xg7 20.♗d4 {the strength of this move lies mainly in the fact that after 20...♘d7 White simply plays 21 ♗c3, with the unavoidable threat of 22 ♖xd7.} 20...♘ce4 21.♕xe4 ♕f5 {The endgame that follows is without any technical difficulties.} 22.♕xf5 exf5 23.♖ac1 ♖fe8 24.♖c7 ♖xe2 25.♖xb7 ♔g6 26.♗xf6 ♔xf6 27.♖d6+ {If 27...♔g7 there follows 28 ♖dd7 ♖f8 29 ♔f3 ♖c2 30 ♖dc7 ♖d2 31 ♔e3.} 1–0

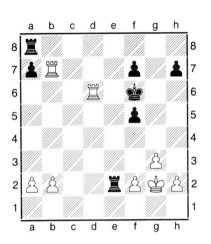

[Site "Crakow"]
[Date "1942"]
[White "Alexander Alekhine"]
[Black "Klaus Junge"]
[Result "1-0"]
[ECO "C86"]

1.e4 {Annotation by Alexander Alekhine.} 1...e5 2.♘f3 ♘c6 3.♗b5 a6 4.♗a4 ♘f6 5.O-O ♗e7 6.♕e2 b5 7.♗b3 O-O 8.c3 {In connection with the following move this is a safe method of preparing to counter the aggressive plan of black which was indicated by his seventh move.} 8...d5 9.d3 dxe4 {The opening of the queen's file is to White's advantage. But 9...d4 10. cxd4 ♘xd4 11. ♘xd4 ♕xd4 12. ♘c3 followed by 13. ♗e3 would also have involved some difficulty for Black.}

10.dxe4 ♗g4 11.h3 ♗h5 12.♗g5 {Preventing 12...♘a5 which would be refuted by 13. g4 ♗g6 14. ♘xe5 simply winning a pawn.} 12...♘e8 13.♗xe7 ♗xf3 {If immediately 13...♘xe7 then 14. g4 etc.} 14.♕xf3 ♘xe7 15.♖d1 ♘d6 16.♘d2 c6 {A better defensive idea would have been 16...♔h8 in order to be able to answer 17.♗c2 with 17...c6 and 17.♘f1 with 17...f5.} 17.♘f1 ♕c7 18.a4 {The opening of the a-file in the Ruy Lopez is almost without exception favorable to White.} 18...♖ad8 19.♘g3 ♘ec8 20.axb5 axb5 21.♘f5 {In order to maintain, after the possible exchange, a new weapon of attack in the form of the pawn at f5.} 21...♘b6 22.♕e3 ♘xf5 {after 22...♘bc4 White would acquire a decisive positional advantage by means of 23.♗xc4 bxc4 24.♕c5!} 23.exf5 c5 {It is already the end. To 23...♘d5 White would have replied 24.♕f3 after which Black's position could not be held.} 24.f6 gxf6 25.♕h6 f5 26.♗xf7+ {An elegant finish. Whether or not he captures the bishop Black loses material.} 26...♕xf7 27.♖xd8 ♘a4

28.b3 {If 28...♘xc3 there follows 29.♖aa8.} 1-0

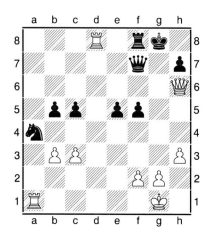

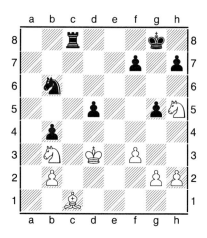

[Site "Prague"]
[Date "1943"]
[White "Alexander Alekhine"]
[Black "Jiri Podgorny"]
[Result "1-0"]
[ECO "B22"]

1.e4 c5 2.c3 d5 3.exd5 ♕xd5 4.d4 ♘c6 5.♘f3 ♗g4 6.♗e2 cxd4 7.cxd4 e6 8.♘c3 ♗b4 9.O-O ♕a5 10.a3 ♘f6 11.d5 exd5 12.axb4 ♕xa1 13.♘d2 ♗xe2 14.♕xe2+ ♘e7 15.♖e1 O-O 16.♘b3 ♕a6 17.♕xa6 bxa6 18.♖xe7 ♖ab8 19.b5 axb5 20.♖xa7 b4 21.♘e2 ♖fc8 22.f3 ♖a8 23.♖xa8 ♖xa8 24.♔f2 ♘d7 25.♘f4 ♘b6 26.♔e3 ♖c8 27.♔d3 g5 28.♘h5 1-0

[Site "Praha"]
[Date "1943"]
[Round "05"]
[White "Alexander Alekhine"]
[Black "Ruzena Sucha"]
[Result "1-0"]
[ECO "C00"]

1.e4 e6 2.♕e2 ♗e7 3.g3 d5 4.♗g2 ♘f6 5.d3 ♘c6 6.e5 ♘d7 7.♘f3 O-O 8.O-O f6 9.d4 fxe5 10.dxe5 ♖f7 11.b3 ♘f8 12.♗b2 ♘g6 13.♘bd2 ♕f8 14.c4 dxc4 15.♘xc4 ♗d7 16.h4 ♖d8 17.♘g5 ♗xg5 18.hxg5 ♕c5 19.♖ac1 ♕e7 20.f4 ♘f8 21.♗a3 ♕e8 22.♖fd1 g6 23.♕e3 a6 24.♘d2 ♗c8 25.♘e4 ♘d7 26.♖d2 ♘e7 27.♖xc7 ♘d5 28.♖xd5 exd5 29.♘d6 ♕e7 30.♗xd5 1-0

136

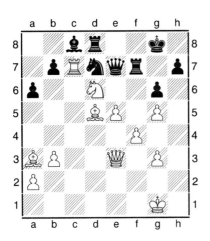

[Site "Praha"]
[Date "1943"]
[Round "14"]
[White "Jaromir Florian"]
[Black "Alexander Alekhine"]
[Result "0−1"]
[ECO "C41"]

1.e4 e5 2.♘f3 d6 3.d4 ♘d7
4.c4 g6 5.♗g5 f6 6.♗e3 ♘h6
7.h3 ♘f7 8.♘c3 ♗g7 9.♕d2
♘f8 10.O-O-O b6 11.c5
♘e6 12.dxe5 fxe5 13.♗b5+
♗d7 14.♕d5 O-O 15.c6 ♗c8
16.h4 h6 17.♗c4 ♘c5
18.♕d2 ♗e6 19.♗d5 ♗xd5
20.exd5 e4 21.♗xc5 bxc5
22.♘xe4 ♖b8 23.♘c3 ♘e5
24.♘xe5 ♗xe5 25.♕c2 ♕f6
26.h5 g5 27.♖he1 ♕xf2
28.♕g6+ ♗g7 29.♖e2 ♕f4+
30.♖dd2 ♖xb2 31.♕e4 ♖b4
32.♕xf4 ♖fxf4 33.♖d3 ♖bc4
34.♔c2 ♖fd4 35.♖f3 ♗e5
36.♖xe5 dxe5 37.♖d3 e4

38.♖e3 ♖xd5 39.♖xe4 ♖xe4
40.♘xe4 ♖e5 41.♘c3 ♖e6
42.♘d5 ♔f7 43.♘xc7 ♖xc6
0−1

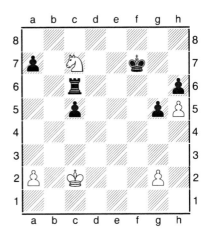

[Site "Praha"]
[Date "1943"]
[Round "18"]
[White "Alexander Alekhine"]
[Black "Ludek Pachman"]
[Result "1−0"]
[ECO "E33"]

1.d4 ♘f6 2.c4 e6 3.♘c3 ♗b4
4.♕c2 ♘c6 5.♘f3 d6 6.♗d2
O-O 7.a3 ♗xc3 8.♗xc3 ♖e8
9.♖d1 ♕e7 10.g3 e5 11.d5
♘b8 12.♗g2 ♘bd7 13.O-O
♘f8 14.♘h4 ♘h5 15.♘f5
♗xf5 16.♕xf5 g6 17.♕c2 f5
18.e3 e4 19.f3 exf3 20.♗xf3
♘f6 21.♗d4 ♘8d7 22.b4
♘e4 23.g4 fxg4 24.♗xg4
♕g5 25.♕g2 ♘f8 26.♖f4 h5

137

27.h4 ♕h6 28.♗h3 1−0

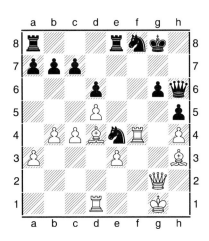

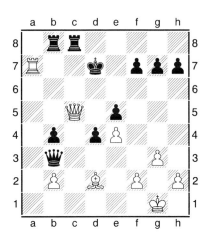

[Site "Prague"]
[Date "1942"]
[Round "11"]
[White "Alexander Alekhine"]
[Black "Klaus Junge"]
[Result "1−0"]
[ECO "D30"]

1.d4 d5 2.c4 e6 3.♘f3 ♘f6
4.g3 dxc4 5.♕a4+ ♘bd7
6.♗g2 a6 7.♕xc4 b5 8.♕c6
♖b8 9.O−O ♗b7 10.♕c2 c5
11.a4 ♗xf3 12.♗xf3 cxd4
13.axb5 axb5 14.♖d1 ♕b6
15.♘d2 e5 16.♘b3 ♘c5
17.♘xc5 ♗xc5 18.♖a6 ♕xa6
19.♕xc5 ♕e6 20.♗c6+ ♘d7
21.♗xd7+ ♔xd7 22.♕a7+
♔c6 23.♗d2 ♖hc8 24.e4
♕b3 25.♖a1 b4 26.♖a6+
♔b5 27.♖a5+ ♔c6 28.♕c5+
♔d7 29.♖a7+ 1−0

[Site "Warsaw"]
[Date "1943"]
[White "Alexander Alekhine"]
[Black "Efim Bogoljubov"]
[Result "1−0"]
[ECO "D30"]

1.d4 {Notes by Alekhine}
1...d5 2.c4 e6 3.♘f3 ♘f6
4.g3 dxc4 5.♕a4+ ♕d7 {The
exchange of Queens that
Black will force with this
maneuver gives him very
few advantages, because it
does not solve the chief
problem, which is the
development of the queen's
bishop.} 6.♕xc4 ♕c6 7.♘bd2
♕xc4 8.♘xc4 ♗b4+ 9.♗d2
♗xd2+ 10.♘cxd2 {Preferable
to 10 ♘fxd2 which, after
10...♘c6 11 ♘f3 ♘b4! would
have offered Black some
changes. Despite the
simplification Black still faces

a difficult problem: if he is compelled to play ...c6 what future will be left for the bishop? Boglojubov takes a radical measure; with the aim of protecting the points he prepares to castle long. In the continuation we shall see the weak side of this strategy.} 10...♞c6 11.♗g2 ♗d7 12.O-O O-O-O 13.♖ac1 ♖he8 14.♞c4 {It goes without saying that White will not allow ...e5.} 14...♖e7 15.a3 ♗e8 16.♖fd1 ♞d5 17.b4 ♞b6 18.b5 {! An important move which forces the knight to withdraw and permits the blocking of the queen's side. For if 18...♞xc4 then 19 bxc6 ♞xa3 20 cxb7+ ♔xb7 21 ♞e5+ ♔c8 22 ♞c6 ♗xc6 23 ♗xc6 ♖d6 24 ♖c3 followed by 25 ♖a1 and wins.} 18...♞b8 19.♞xb6+ axb6 20.a4 f6 21.♗h3 {Threatening to advance the d-pawn.} 21...♗d7 {♞ow it seems that Black is at last going to free himself by 22...e5.} 22.♞d2 {!! Decisive, because if 22...e5 there follows 23 ♞c4 with the threat of 24 ♞xb6 mate. What follows now is practically all forced.} 22...♖f8 23.♗g2 {! 23 ♞c4

would allow Black to play 23...♔d8, followed by 24...♗c8.} 23...c6 24.♞c4 ♔c7 25.e4 cxb5 {desperation, since there is no defense against the advance of the d-pawn.} 26.axb5 ♗xb5 27.d5 {! More accurate than 27 ♞a3+ ♗c6 28 d5, after which Black would not have been under any obligation to exchange pawns.} 27...exd5 28.♞a3+ ♗c6 29.exd5 ♖d7 30.♞b5+ ♔d8 31.dxc6 bxc6 32.♞d4 {! This wins at least a pawn. An instructive game from the strategic point of view.} 1-0

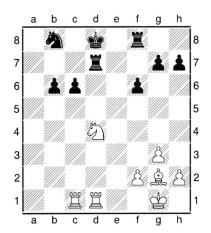

[Site "Prague"]
[Date "1943"]
[White "Friedrich Samisch"]
[Black "Alexander Alekhine"]
[Result "0-1"]
[ECO "C79"]

139

1.e4 {Notes by Alekhine}
1...e5 2.♘f3 ♘c6 3.♗b5 a6
4.♗a4 ♘f6 5.O−O d6 6.♖e1
{Better would have been
♗xc6+ followed by d4.}
6...b5 7.♗b3 ♘a5 {The
exchange of the White king's
bishop gives Black the
present of the best prospects
of obtaining equality.} 8.d4
♘xb3 9.axb3 ♘d7 {More
common and perhaps better
is 9...♗b7. The text move in
any case, provides White
with a problem which is not
very easy to resolve.}
10.dxe5 {And−after forty−five
minutes reflection!−Samisch,
dismayed, decides upon a
liquidation which hands over
to Black a very peaceful
game. Schmidt in his game
against Keres at Salzburg
1943 played the proper
maneuver: 10 ♗d2! followed
by ♗a5. Black had to make
considerable efforts to
achieve a drawn game.}
10...♘xe5 {♘ot 10...dxe5
because of 11 ♕d5.}
11.♘xe5 dxe5 12.♕xd8+
♔xd8 {The two Bishops
promise Black a few remote
prospects but the
exploitation of this
advantage is not an easy
matter.} 13.♗e3 ♗b7 14.♘d2

{♘c3 would be simpler.}
14...♗d6 15.f3 ♔e7 16.♗f2
♔e6 17.♘f1 g6 {It is evident
that Black must attempt to
open up the game in order to
leave the field free for his
bishops.} 18.c3 a5 {In order
to prevent 19 b4, followed by
♘d2−b3−c5.} 19.♖a2 {This
move has no effect. But it is
already difficult to indicate a
good defensive plan for
White.} 19...♖a6 20.♘e3 f5
21.exf5+ gxf5 22.♘c2 ♔f7 {!
This prevents 23 ♘d4+. In
this position f7 is the best
square for the king.} 23.b4
{White, after strenuous
efforts, will succeed in
exchanging one bishop but
in the meantime Black will
have secured other
advantages.} 23...a4 24.♗c5
♖g8 25.♔f2 ♖c6 {! After this
move White must make a
decision: yield to his
opponent the command of
the queen's file or opt for a
new restriction on the activity
of his pieces after 26 ♗e3 f4
etc. In this latter case Black
would also conserve
excellent winning chances.}
26.♗xd6 ♖xd6 27.♖e2 {?
Losing immediately. In any
case even if he had played
27 g3 (definitely not 27 ♖xe5
♖d2+ 28 ♖e2 ♖xg2+! winning

140

a piece) which was the best move, he would not have saved the game. For instance 27...♗d5 28 ♖aa1 ♗c4 29 ♖ad1 ♖gd8 30 ♖xd6 ♖xd6 and the entry of the rook to the seventh rank will be decisive.} 27...♗d5 {This wins the exchange after 28 ♖a1 ♗c4, and all further fight is impossible.} 0-1

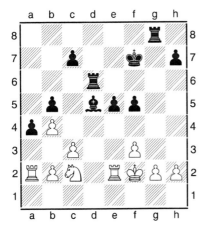

[Site "Prague"]
[Date "1943"]
[White "Alexander Alekhine"]
[Black "Milan Bartosek"]
[Result "1-0"]
[ECO "C07"]

1.e4 {Notes by Alekhine} 1...e6 2.d4 d5 3.♘d2 c5 4.♘gf3 ♘c6 5.♗b5 {White's inclination is to maintain the tension in the center for as long as possible. Black's next move although fairly plausible, is nonetheless a mistake which is perhaps decisive. Relatively better would be 5...cxd4 whereupon White can castle since the defense of the pawn at d4 would only create difficulties for Black.} 5...♗d7 6.exd5 exd5 7.O-O ♘xd4 {It is quite clear that Black will not manage to castle on the king's side. Thought he exchanges arising from the text move one perceives that he is trying to prepare to castle long, which furnishes him -although only comparatively so- with the best chance of resistance.} 8.♘xd4 cxd4 9.♕e2# ♗e7 10.♘f3 ♗xb5 11.♕xb5+ ♕d7 12.♕e2 O-O-O {If 12...♘f6 then, naturally, 13 ♖e1 and Black cannot castle.} 13.♗f4 {! Virtually forcing the exchange of bishops and at the same time eliminating a very useful defensive piece.} 13...♗d6 14.♗xd6 ♕xd6 15.♘xd4 ♘f6 {The problem of creating an attack is not very easy to resolve. ♘either 16 ♘f5 ♕f4! nor 16 ♘b5 ♕b6 would have any result. On the other hand Black is going to occupy the e-file with his

141

rooks, which will procure a counter-attacking advantage. White's next move is the only one likely to give him a lasting initiative.} 16.♕f3 {! This threatens 17 ♘f5 and at the same time 17 ♘b5.} 16...♕b6 17.♖fd1 ♖he8 {It is clear that the capture of the b-pawn, either now or on the following moves, would have deadly consequences for Black.} 18.a4 ♖e4 19.a5 ♕c5 {For example, if 19...♕xb2 then 20 c3!} 20.c3 ♖de8 21.h3 {! Making use of a moments respite to open up an escape square for the king. This move will be found in analogous positions in many of my games.} 21...♕c7 22.a6 b6 23.c4 {! 23 ♘b5 ♕c5 24 ♘xa7+? ♔b8 would be premature but the move played is very effective because against 23...dxc4 White responds with 24 ♘b5 winning the exchange.} 23...♕c5 24.♘f5 {Threatening to win by 25 ♘xg7.} 24...♕b4 25.cxd5 ♖f4 26.♕d3 ♖e5 27.♖ac1+ ♔d7 {If 27...♔b8 then 28 d6 etc.} 28.♘e3 ♘e4 29.♘g4 {!} 29...♖e8 30.g3 {This wins at least the exchange since the rook cannot retreat because

of 31 ♖c4. But 30 ♖c4 played immediately would constitute an error owing to 30...♘xf2!} 30...♘c5 {This move allows an even more rapid finish.} 31.♖xc5 ♖e1+ 32.♖xe1 ♕xe1+ 33.♔g2 ♖xg4 34.♕f5+ {followed by mate in a few moves.} 1-0

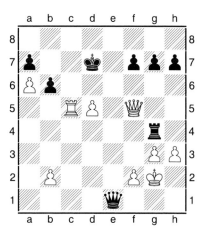

[Site "Salzburg"]
[Date "1943"]
[White "Alexander Alekhine"]
[Black "Paul Felix Schmidt"]
[Result "1-0"]
[ECO "C78"]
1.e4 e5 2.♘f3 ♘c6 3.♗b5 a6 4.♗a4 ♘f6 5.O-O ♗e7 6.♘c3 b5 7.♗b3 d6 8.♘d5 ♗e6 9.♖e1 ♘a5 10.♘xe7 ♕xe7 11.d4 ♘xb3 12.axb3 ♘d7 13.h3 f6 14.♘h4 exd4 15.♘f5 ♕f7 16.♕g4 ♘e5 17.♕d1 ♗xf5 18.exf5 O-O

142

19.♕xd4 ♖fe8 20.♗e3 ♘c6
21.♕c3 ♕d7 22.b4 ♖e4
23.♗d2 ♖c4 24.♕f3 d5 25.b3
♖e4 26.♖xe4 dxe4 27.♕xe4
♖e8 28.♕d3 ♕xd3 29.cxd3
♖e2 30.♖d1 ♘d4 31.♔f1 ♖e5
32.g4 ♘xb3 33.♗f4 ♖e7
34.♖b1 ♘d4 35.♖c1 c6
36.♖a1 ♖a7 37.♗e3 ♖d7
38.♖xa6 h5 39.gxh5 ♘xf5
40.♔e2 ♘d4+ 41.♔d2 ♔h7
42.♖a8 g6 43.hxg6+ ♔xg6
44.♖g8+ ♔f5 45.♖h8 ♘f3+
46.♔c3 ♘e5 47.♗d4 c5
48.♗xc5 ♖xd3+ 49.♔c2 ♖a3
50.h4 ♘d3 51.♔d2 ♖b3
52.♔c2 ♖a3 53.♖b8 ♘xf2
54.♖xb5 ♘e4 55.♗d4+ ♔g4
56.♖d5 ♖h3 57.b5 ♖xh4
58.b6 ♖h7 59.♔d3 ♖e7
60.♖a5 ♘d6 61.♖a7 ♖e8
62.♖d7 ♘f5 63.♗c5 ♘g3
64.b7 ♘e4 65.♗a7 1-0

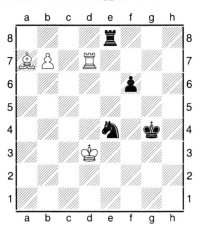

[Site "Salzburg"]
[Date "1943"]
[White "Jan Foltys"]

[Black "Alexander Alekhine"]
[Result "1/2-1/2"]
[ECO "E32"]

1.d4 ♘f6 2.c4 e6 3.♘c3 ♗b4
4.♕c2 O-O 5.♘f3 c5 6.dxc5
♘a6 7.♗d2 ♗xc5 8.e3 b6
9.♗e2 ♗b7 10.O-O ♘b4
11.♕b1 a5 12.♖d1 ♕b8
13.a3 ♘c6 14.♘g5 ♘e5
15.♘ce4 ♘xe4 16.♘xe4 ♗e7
17.♗c3 f5 18.♘g3 d6
19.♘h5 ♖f7 20.♕c2 ♕c7
21.♘f4 ♕c6 22.♗f1 ♖f6
23.♕e2 ♖h6 24.♖ac1 a4
25.f3 ♖c8 26.♘d3 ♘xc4
27.♘b4 ♕e8 28.♗xg7 ♔xg7
29.♖xc4 d5 30.♖xc8 ♕xc8
31.♖d2 ♕c7 32.f4 ♗c5
33.♔h1 e5 34.♘xd5 ♕d8
35.♘f6 ♕xf6 36.♖d7+ ♔g6
37.♖xb7 exf4 38.♕f3 ♗xe3
39.h3 ♕xb2 40.♕d5 ♕b3
41.♕d7 ♕g8 42.♗d3 ♔g5
43.♕xf5+ ♔h4 44.♖xh7 ♖xh7
45.♕xh7+ ♕xh7 46.♗xh7
♗c5 1/2-1/2

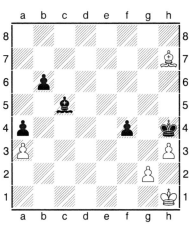

[Event "Gijon it"] [Site "ESP"] [Event "Madrid"]
[Date "1944"] [Round "06"] [Site "Madrid"]
[White "Antonio Medina [Date "1945"]
Garcia"] [White "Alexander Alekhine"]
[Black "Alexander Alekhine"] [Black "Francisco Jose
[Result "0–1"] Perez"]
[ECO "C53"] [Result "1–0"]
1.e4 e5 2.♘f3 ♘c6 3.♗c4 [ECO "C71"]
♗c5 4.c3 ♗b6 5.d4 ♕e7 6.d5 1.e4 e5 2.♘f3 ♘c6 3.♗b5 a6
♘d8 7.d6 cxd6 8.♘a3 ♘f6 4.♗a4 d6 5.c4 ♗d7 6.♘c3 g6
9.♕d3 a6 10.♗g5 h6 11.♗xf6 7.d4 ♗g7 8.♗g5 f6 9.♗e3
♕xf6 12.♖d1 ♗c7 13.♗d5 ♘ge7 10.O–O O–O 11.d5
♘e6 14.g3 ♖b8 15.♘c4 O–O ♘b8 12.c5 h6 13.♘d2 f5
16.♔e2 b5 17.♘e3 b4 18.c4 14.exf5 gxf5 15.f3 ♗xa4
b3 19.a3 ♘c5 20.♕d2 ♗b7 16.♕xa4 dxc5 17.♕b3 ♖f7
21.♗xb7 ♖xb7 22.♘d5 ♕e6 18.♕xb7 ♘d7 19.♘c4 ♖f6
23.♕e3 ♗d8 24.♘d2 f5 25.f3 20.♕b3 ♖b8 21.♕a3 f4
♗g5 26.exf5 ♕xf5 27.♘e4 22.♗xc5 ♘f5 23.♘e4 ♖g6
♘e6 28.♘xg5 ♕c2+ 29.♖d2 24.♗a7 ♖b5 25.d6 ♕a8
♕xc4+ 30.♕d3 ♕xd3+ 26.♗f2 cxd6 27.♖ad1 ♘f6
31.♖xd3 hxg5 32.♖c1 ♘d4+ 28.♘exd6 ♗f8 29.♕d3 e4
33.♔f2 ♖b5 34.♘c7 ♖c5 30.♘xe4 ♘d5 31.a4 ♘b4
35.♖xc5 dxc5 36.♘xa6 d6 32.♕d2 ♖b7 33.♕xf4 ♖f7
37.♔g2 ♖c8 38.a4 ♖a8 34.♘e5 ♘d5 35.♕d2 1–0
39.♘c7 ♖xa4 40.♘e8 ♖a6
0–1

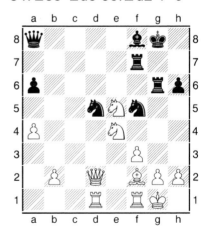

144

[Site "Almeria"]
[Date "1945"]
[White "Alexander Alekhine"]
[Black "Lopez Julio"]
[Result "1−0"]
[ECO "C10"]

1.e4 e6 2.d4 d5 3.♘d2 dxe4
4.♘xe4 ♘d7 5.♘f3 ♘gf6
6.♗d3 ♗e7 7.O−O O−O 8.c3
b6 9.♕e2 ♗b7 10.♖d1 ♖e8
11.♘e5 h6 12.♗f4 ♘d5
13.♗g3 ♕c8 14.♕h5 ♖f8
15.♘g4 f5 16.♘xh6+ gxh6
17.♕g6+ ♔h8 18.♕xh6+
♔g8 19.♕xe6+ ♔h8
20.♕h6+ ♔g8 21.♕g6+ ♔h8
22.♗e5+ ♘xe5 23.dxe5 ♕e8
24.♕h6+ ♔g8 25.♘g5 ♗xg5
26.♕xg5+ ♔h8 27.♗xf5 ♕f7
28.♕h6+ ♔g8 29.♗e6 ♘e7
30.♖d3 ♘f5 1−0

[Site "Almeria"]
[Date "1945"]
[White "F. Martinez Moreno"]
[Black "Alexander Alekhine"]
[Result "0−1"]
[ECO "A47"]

1.d4 ♘f6 2.♘f3 b6 3.c4 ♗b7
4.♘bd2 e6 5.g3 c5 6.e3
cxd4 7.exd4 ♘c6 8.♘b3 d5
9.cxd5 ♕xd5 10.♗g2 ♗b4+
11.♗d2 ♕e4+ 12.♕e2 ♗xd2+
13.♔xd2 O−O 14.♘h4
♕xe2+ 15.♔xe2 ♖ad8
16.♖ad1 ♗a6+ 17.♔e3 ♘b4
18.f4 ♘c2+ 19.♔f2 ♘g4+
20.♔f3 ♘ce3 21.♖dg1 ♖c8
22.h3 ♗b7+ 23.♔e2 ♖c2+
24.♔e1 ♘f2 25.♘d2 ♗xg2
26.♖xg2 ♘xh1 0−1

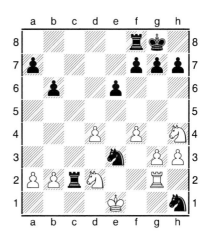

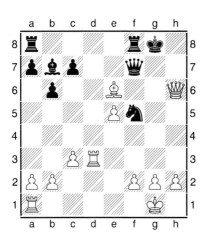

[Site "Melilla"]
[Date "1945"]
[White "Alexander Alekhine"]
[Black "Juan Manuel Fuentes"]
[Result "1-0"]
[ECO "C51"]

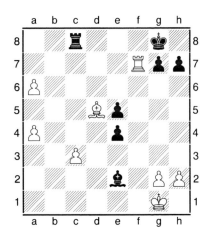

1.e4 e5 2.♘f3 ♘c6 3.♗c4
♗c5 4.b4 ♗b6 5.a4 a6 6.♘c3
♘f6 7.♘d5 ♘xd5 8.exd5
♘d4 9.O-O d6 10.♘xd4
♗xd4 11.c3 ♗a7 12.d4 ♕h4
13.♗d3 O-O 14.dxe5 dxe5
15.♕e2 ♖e8 16.♗e3 ♗g4
17.f3 ♗xe3+ 18.♕xe3 ♗h5
19.♕e4 ♕xe4 20.fxe4 a5
21.♖ab1 c6 22.bxa5 cxd5
23.♖xb7 dxe4 24.♗c4 ♖f8
25.a6 ♖ac8 26.♗d5 ♗e2
27.♖fxf7 ♖xf7 28.♖xf7 1-0

146

CPSIA information can be obtained at www.ICGtesting.com
Printed in the USA
LVOW040902021211

257437LV00001B/28/P